STO

ALLEN COUNTY PUBLIC LIBRARY

ACPL ITEM
3 1833 00420 039

DISCARDED

W9-CTM-122

12-21-60

MUSIC
AT THE COURT OF
FREDERICK THE GREAT

FREDERICK THE GREAT AS A YOUNG MAN

From a painting by Pesne
Courtesy The Bettmann Archive

MUSIC

AT THE COURT OF
FREDERICK THE GREAT

❖❖❖❖❖❖❖❖❖❖❖❖❖❖❖❖❖❖❖❖❖❖❖❖❖❖

ERNEST EUGENE HELM

❖❖❖❖❖❖❖❖❖❖❖❖❖❖❖❖❖❖❖❖❖❖❖❖❖❖

NORMAN

UNIVERSITY OF OKLAHOMA PRESS

LIBRARY OF CONGRESS CATALOG CARD NUMBER: 60–14105

COPYRIGHT 1960 BY THE UNIVERSITY OF OKLAHOMA PRESS,
PUBLISHING DIVISION OF THE UNIVERSITY.
COMPOSED AND PRINTED AT NORMAN, OKLAHOMA, U.S.A.,
BY THE UNIVERSITY OF OKLAHOMA PRESS.
FIRST EDITION.

TO SALLIE

WHO MAKES EVEN BOOK-WRITING

A MATTER OF COURSE

1141965

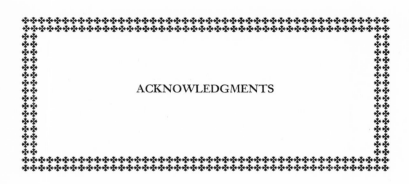

ACKNOWLEDGMENTS

My warm appreciation goes to Professor George Morey of North Texas State College, Denton, for his help and valuable suggestions in the writing of this book. His encouragement has made the task a pleasant experience. I am also grateful to the library staff of North Texas State College for the solution of many complex bibliographical problems and to the staff of the Nationalbibliothek in Vienna for making their rarest sources available. Finally, an adequate acknowledgment of my wife's help would involve writing a catalog, so I must be satisfied with saying that as guide and critic she has been indispensable.

Ernest Eugene Helm

Iowa City, Iowa
October 15, 1960

CONTENTS

ILLUSTRATIONS AND MUSICAL FIGURES

MUSICAL FIGURES

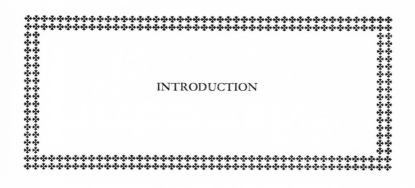

INTRODUCTION

It is unfortunate that the fame of great historical figures is founded so often on their political and military achievements. The prosecution of war, the acquirement of real estate, and the substitution of one form of government for another have traditionally been the most favored subjects of recorded history. In this respect Frederick II of Prussia is no disappointment to historians; he obligingly provides abundant evidence of his ability to change national boundaries. But once Frederick as conqueror has been disposed of, there remains, insistently, a figure whose greatness is the result of more unusual qualifications: Frederick the statesman and reformer, the man of letters and philosopher, the musician and patron of music.[1]

---

[1] Some well-known works on Frederick as statesman and reformer: L. Paul-Dubois, *Frédéric le Grand, d'après sa correspondance politique*

For, during his seventy-four years (1712–86), this indefatigable monarch was able to accomplish significant things in each of these fields.

Frederick the musician was a versatile composer and a skillful flutist, but his musical importance lies almost solely in his patronage; because he was no ordinary patron. The main structure of Berlin's musical life during the middle of the eighteenth century was organized and regulated according to the workings of one brain: Frederick's. Although he built an opera house, paid performers, and provided opportunity for composers to compose, these things could have been done by almost anyone having the necessary means. Frederick was uniquely important as a patron because he specified what should be composed or composed it himself; he told his librettists what to write or wrote it himself; he selected performers, scenery, and costumes personally; his taste as an experienced and proficient musician, and as a broadly educated, articulate product of eighteenth-

---

(1903); H. Pigge, *Die Staatstheorie Friedrichs des Grossen* (1904); G. Künstel, *Politisches Testament Friedrichs des Grossen von 1752* (1911); and Arnold Berney, *Friedrich der Grosse, Entwicklungsgeschichte eines Staatsmannes* (1934). Among those dealing with him as man of letters and philosopher are *Voltaire et Frédéric* by Le Brisoys Desnoiresterres (1870); *Die Erziehung Friedrichs des Grossen* by Ernst Bratuschek (1885); and *Friedrich der Grosse als Philosoph* by Eduard Zeller (1886).

Although a few works deal in part with Frederick's musical patronage, no objective and systematic evaluation of this patronage exists. A discussion of Frederick's patronage of the opera, together with a perfunctory treatment of his evening palace concerts, is contained in Georg Thouret's *Friedrich der Grosse als Musikfreund und Musiker* (1898). Thouret does not deal with the King's influence on composers of symphonies, keyboard music, chamber music, songs, and sacred music. He does not mention the leadership of Frederick's Berlin in musical theory, criticism, scholarship, and aesthetics. Perhaps the main fault of this work is that it is completely in the tradition of an exalted Frederick: to Thouret, the King was a hero in every sense of the word, in music as in all other matters. Today Frederick's musical patronage is regarded less worshipfully, even in Germany; from a distance of two centuries it is apparent that while he was an immensely powerful musical force, he was as much a villain as a hero.

century enlightenment, pervaded the musical activities of every Berliner.

Obviously, this musical dictatorship was both good and bad. At the same time that it provided an unprecedented marshaling of musical forces and a great blossoming of musical activity, it also promoted artistic narrowness. Nevertheless, it is undeniable that the patronage of Frederick the Great forms a solid segment of music history, and that statements such as the following are not mere patriotic effusions:

> ... Frederick's unswerving artistic policy is the very basis of his musical importance, because music—as all else in Prussia —stood under the imperious influence of royal personality; it is commonplace to speak of a "Frederician" period in music. . . . In the reign of Frederick the Great lies the foundation of Berlin's musical place in Germany and in the world.[2]

The dimensions of the King's patronage are partly indicated in the names of some of the composers, theorists, and writers on music over whom he reigned aesthetically. The following men were actually in his service: K. H. Graun, J. G. Graun, C. P. E. Bach, J. J. Quantz, Franz Benda, K. F. C. Fasch, J. P. Kirnberger, and F. W. Marpurg. Also in Frederick's employ were many of the leading singers of Europe and most of the librettists of Berlin. On the periphery of the royal circle of influence were J. A. Hasse, the great Saxon composer, and Gottfried Silbermann, one of the greatest and earliest makers of pianofortes.[3] The Berlin Opera itself was virtually created by Frederick in 1742 with the construction of a magnificent opera

[2] Berta Witt, *"Der königliche Musikus," Allgemeine Musikzeitung,* Vol. LXIII (August 21, 1936), 34.

[3] It was on one of Silbermann's pianofortes in Frederick's palace that J. S. Bach improvised on the "royal theme" (by Frederick himself) which was to become the basis of the *Musical Offering.* See p. 234.

house, becoming, under his artistic dictatorship, one of the most famous in Europe. Charles Burney, writing in 1789, gives his own estimate of Frederick's musical activities:

> From the year 1742, when the late King of Prussia fixed the musical establishments of his opera and court, so many eminent musicians were engaged in his service, that Berlin seems to have given the law to the rest of Germany, not merely from the great number of excellent composers and performers within its precincts, but theoretical and critical writers.[4]

Frederick's great importance as a patron of music was, then, the result of a rare combination of attributes and circumstances: his musical understanding as a composer and performer, his wealth and power as a monarch, and his desire to govern personally the artistic realm which was his property.

[4] Charles Burney, *A General History of Music from the Earliest Ages to the Present Period*, with critical and historical notes by Frank Mercer, II, 948.

MUSIC

AT THE COURT OF

FREDERICK THE GREAT

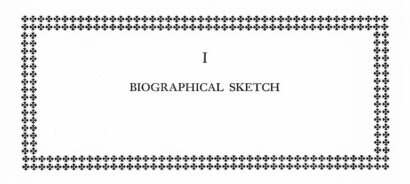

I

BIOGRAPHICAL SKETCH

THE PRINCE

FREDERICK II, CROWN PRINCE OF PRUSSIA, was born in 1712, grandson of the first Prussian king, Frederick I (1657–1713) and son of Frederick William I (1688–1740). The Crown Prince's father and grandfather had accomplished more than any of the other Hohenzollerns before them toward transforming this once-obscure electorate into the Prussia which until 1918 was a universal prototype of the militaristic state.

Frederick I had done his share of kingdom-building without sacrificing the intellectual and cultural life of his court and his subjects; but Frederick William I, the "barracks king," would have none of any activity which did not increase Prussia's military power. He did not read, he despised all forms of art, he was no supporter of cultural institutions, and he considered writers, musicians, and poets to be social parasites. His chief

3

joys were hunting, drinking, and drilling his battalions; his prized possession was a regiment of abnormally tall soldiers, collected from all parts of Europe and known as the "Potsdam Giants." Young Frederick could not have had a more unsuitable father.

Those who knew Frederick as a child could hardly have expected that he would become the greatest of all the Prussian conquerers. He was quiet and delicate, completely the opposite of his father, and showing considerably more musical and literary than military abilities. Nevertheless, the King determined from the first to make his son a great general. His instructions to Frederick's governors state that the Prince was to be "a good Christian, accomplished horseman, man of honor, stoical, courteous, pious without bigotry, a good judge of works of culture, with all the manners, graces, ease, and self-control which come of frequenting good company." But they also specify that he must deny himself "operas, comedies, and other follies of the laity." They prohibit his study of Latin; limit his study of history to a detailed knowledge of European politics for the century and a half preceding his father's reign; and require that he know French and German, the rights of nations, agriculture, and the mathematics of war. Piety (Calvinism) was to be instilled in the Prince, along with the strict discipline and unvarying daily routine of a soldier. To insure his son's rapid development, Frederick William also included the instruction that the Prince was never to be left alone.[1] At the age of four Frederick began to learn the fifty-four movements of Prussian drill. His father forced him to learn to fire a pistol when very young in order to accustom him to the sounds of battle. His toys were miniature cannons, lead soldiers, guns, drums, tents, flags.

Fortunately for Frederick, the King did not at first actively oppose his son's cultural development. Until he was seven years

[1] Pierre Gaxotte, *Frederick the Great,* trans. by R. A. Bell, 7–11.

old the Prince had a well-educated French governess, according to the custom in royal households. His tutor, Monsieur Jacques Egide Duhan de Jandun, was a musician and a man of real culture; more than any other person, he was responsible for the breadth of Frederick's interests. Duhan found it possible to disobey many of the King's instructions without being severely punished. He taught Frederick Latin in secret and introduced him to mythology with such books as Fénelon's *Les Aventures de Télémaque.* The Queen Mother, Sophie Dorothea, daughter of the King of England, joined successfully with Duhan in trying to mitigate the King's severity—partly because of her affection for her son and partly because she enjoyed thwarting any of her husband's plans. She had at least a superficial liking for music, and during Frederick's childhood held small impromptu concerts among the social groups of the castle. She encouraged the Prince and his sisters, Anna Amalia and Wilhelmina, to study music as soon as it became apparent that each of them was musically talented.[2]

Frederick William's opposition to music study had not yet become virulent by his son's seventh year, for at the age of seven the Prince began taking lessons in clavier, thorough bass, and four-part composition from the cathedral organist, Gottlieb Heyne, actually at the King's suggestion.[3] The previous Christmas one of the gifts from father to son had been a Psalm book with melodies by Marot.[4] Frederick began an informal study of the flute with one of the palace staff, probably Duhan, at about the same time as his first lessons with Heyne. A daybook in which the Prince's expenses for the month of September, 1719,

[2] Heinz Becker, *"Friedrich II," Die Musik in Geschichte und Gegenwart,* Vol. IV.

[3] *Ibid.*

[4] Georg Thouret, *Friedrich der Grosse als Musikfreund und Musiker,* 10.

were listed by his tutors contains the entry, "for mending the flute, four *Groschen*."[5]

Frederick's character was thus solidly formed by the time the King awakened to the fact that his son was taking inordinate advantage of musical and literary opportunities, despising everything military, and, in fact, everything German. Frederick's manners and dress were French until he became king in 1740; his favorite language was French from his childhood until his death, and all his important writings are in that language, which he always knew better than the language of his own country. It is true that familiarity with the manners, customs, and speech of France was considered a necessary attribute of any educated eighteenth-century European; but Frederick adopted them wholesale, showing only open contempt for German habits and life. His rough Prussian father could not endure having a French son. The conflict between father and son was aggravated by the King's uncontrollable, drunken rages and the Prince's unmilitary, even foppish ways. The answer which Frederick William gave to one of Frederick's many attempts at reconciliation shows both the narrowness of the father and the affectations of the son:

> He who does not love his father is self-willed and wicked. Love of a father means doing his will, not only when he is present but even when he is out of sight. Secondly, he knows very well that I cannot stand an effeminate boy, who has no manly tastes, who is shamefaced, who cannot ride a horse or shoot, and who crowns all by not washing himself; who curls his hair like a madman and does not have it cut. And I have reproached him a thousand times for all this but to no purpose. Moreover, he is proud and vain. Apart from a very few, he speaks to no one. He is not popular. He is not affable. He grimaces like a madman and only does my will when constrained and forced to do it. He does nothing from

[5] Thomas Carlyle, *History of Frederick II of Prussia*, I, 383–84.

6

filial love; his only pleasure is to follow his own inclinations; he is good for nothing. That is my answer.[6]

Frederick William called the Prince a "flutist and poet," a name which he considered suitably contemptuous. His whole life was that of a soldier; to his son a military uniform was a "shroud," and gentility was the only worthwhile goal.

Accordingly, the King increased the severity of the restrictions placed on Frederick; now his instructions were no longer to be freely interpreted. At the age of thirteen Frederick was appointed captain in a royal regiment at Potsdam. He was required to follow his father everywhere; when not with Frederick William he was kept under constant surveillance. An ambassador to Berlin at about that time found the Prince in ill health, looking prematurely aged because of the strenuous schedule he had to follow. But in spite of all the King's efforts, Frederick showed little military aptitude. On one occasion soon after his appointment he fell from his horse in front of the generals, wounding himself with the pommel of his sword.[7] His father's dislike for him was expressed often and violently, usually in the form of incredible kinds of corporal punishment. A Saxon diplomat reported that Frederick's father "thwarts his inclinations and desires. . . . He has only to know what will please his son in order to refuse it him."[8]

The Prince's reaction to this degrading treatment shows that the innate strength for which he was so well known as a king was already part of his character as a boy. Instead of breaking, he learned the art of passive resistance; instead of dissolving into tears, he learned to control himself, to keep himself inwardly remote from the humiliating circumstances of his life. He did not give up his pursuit of literature and music, nor did he ever

[6] Gaxotte, *Frederick the Great*, 32–33.
[7] *Ibid.*, 21.
[8] *Ibid.*

intend to do so. Under the pretension of going hunting, he and his servant Fredersdorff often went into the remotest, thickest forests they could find and played flute duets.[9] He had long been accustomed to reading secretly borrowed, forbidden novels. Of *Pierre de Provence,* a tale of knightly and romantic adventures, he relates:

> I was not allowed to read it, and I used to hide it. I slept between my governor, General Finck, and my valet. When they were fast asleep I used to step over the valet's bed and go into another room where there was a lamp in the chimney corner. I used to crouch there and read. But one night the marshal's cough woke him up. He did not hear me breathing, groped for me in vain, called out. I ran in quickly. I said that I had had a call of nature. I hid my book, and kept off it after that.[10]

The fact that Frederick would one day be king undoubtedly made it easier for him to get the assistance of secret confederates, among whom were a banker, a town councillor and his ever-faithful tutor, Duhan. These three helped him indulge his passion for reading: at the age of fifteen he owed the banker 7,000 thalers (about $14,000); in the town councillor's house he had hidden away a library which consisted of exactly 3,775 volumes in 1730, chosen mostly by Duhan and embracing almost all human knowledge.[11]

Early in 1728 Frederick William went to Dresden to visit the brilliant court of Augustus II the Strong, Elector of Saxony and King of Poland. He took the sixteen-year-old prince with him. If he had known that his son was to gain there a series of

[9] François J. Fétis, "*Frédéric II,*" *Biographie Universelle des Musiciens,* Vol. III.

[10] Gaxotte, *Frederick the Great,* 16.

[11] *Ibid.,* 23–24.

musical impressions which would never be forgotten, he would certainly have left him at home. Besides taking part in a round of fetes, ballets, and masked balls—and having his first intimate contact with the opposite sex, in the person of one of Augustus' beautiful mistresses—Frederick saw his first opera, a magnificent production of Hasse's *Cleofide*. Here he heard the playing of Johann Joachim Quantz (1697–1773), who was to be his flute teacher and court composer for thirty-two years. During this visit Frederick played the flute in an orchestra of professionals for the first time. A letter signed "Frederick the Philosopher" and dated January 26, 1728, which he sent to Wilhelmina from Dresden, mentions the flutist Buffardin, the violinist Pisendel, and the lute player Weiss, in addition to Quantz.[12]

During August of the same year, Augustus returned the visit to Berlin, bringing his musicians with him. Much to Frederick's delight, Frederick William soon left Berlin on a series of military maneuvers, taking Augustus and leaving the musicians. Intoxicated with the novelty of being surrounded by music at home, Frederick and Wilhelmina took part in a concert every day at Monbijou, the Queen's residence. Frederick affectionately called his flute "Principessa"; Wilhelmina's lute was named "Principe." It was during this time that the Prince, with his mother's co-operation, offered Quantz a position as his teacher; but since the great flutist was already obligated to Augustus, Frederick had to be satisfied at first with occasional long visits by Quantz, usually twice a year.[13] Naturally, the King objected to the lessons; but the Queen, from long practice a master of intrigue, secretly provided both the means and the authority for them.[14]

[12] Margaret Goldsmith, *Frederick the Great*, 43–45.

[13] J. J. Quantz, "*Herrn Johann Joachim Quantzens Lebenslauf, von ihm selbst entworfen,*" *Historisch-Kritische Beyträge sur Aufnahme der Musik*, ed. by F. W. Marpurg, I, 246.

[14] Becker, "*Friedrich II,*" *Die Musik in Geschichte.*

One of C. F. Nicolai's many anecdotes about Frederick, which was reportedly told him by Quantz and which we have no reason to doubt, illustrates the tragicomic machinations of a prince determined to pursue his own interests: One day in the summer of 1730, after Frederick had spent the morning carrying out his soldierly duties, he took off his hated uniform, donned French dress and began a musical afternoon with Quantz. In a front room his friend and fellow-conspirator, Lieutenant Katte, stood guard. Quantz and Frederick had hardly started when Katte rushed in, whispering, "The King is coming!" Katte quickly packed the flutes, cases, music, and stands into Quantz's arms and ushered him into a small side room which was always so hot in summer that it was called the "oven." In the meantime Frederick changed back into Prussian dress, but did not have time to exchange his French hair-bag for the Prussian queue. The King came in, looked through all the books he could find, searched the room (but not the "oven") and stayed for about an hour—while Quantz roasted.[15]

Frederick was never, even in early childhood, an ardent Christian. He was so poorly prepared for his confirmation that the court chaplain had to double his lessons in order to avoid having the King's son fail the test.[16] It is not difficult to understand this lack of enthusiasm for religion, which was later to develop into full-fledged denunciation. Frederick was naturally repelled by his father's brand of Calvinism, and as a perceptive youth he shared in the antireligious spirit of the times. By a series of inevitable steps he was to come more and more under the influence of eighteenth-century enlightenment, to the point of view of Voltaire, Bayle, Wolff, Diderot. The very beginnings of this trend in Frederick's religious beliefs were detected and denounced by the King, and by 1730 Frederick William's anx-

[15] Thouret, *Friedrich der Grosse*, 15.
[16] Gaxotte, *Frederick the Great*, 21.

iety for his son's soul had reached fever pitch. In addition to the usual punishments, the Prince was forbidden secular books, gambling, dancing, and—once again—music.[17]

During Frederick's seventeenth and eighteenth years the problem of marriage compounded the difficulties between father and son, finally leading to a terrible climax. The English monarchy desired a double union between Wilhelmina and the Prince of Wales, and Frederick and the Princess Amelia, daughter of George II. This would have been a logical procedure for both royal houses, since a close political relationship already existed between them. Sophie Dorothea was the sister of George II. Frederick, although never really wanting marriage, was amenable to the union, even carrying on a secret correspondence with the English court and asserting that he would marry no one but Amelia. However, after a short period of negotiation Frederick William refused to allow the ceremony. The only discoverable reason for his refusal was his dislike of his son, which reached a peak during the years 1729 and 1730. Carlyle quotes the following letter from Frederick to his mother (Potsdam, December, 1729):

> I am in the uttermost despair. What I had always apprehended has come on me. The King has entirely forgotten that I am his son. This morning I came into his room as usual; at the first sight of me he sprang forward, seized me by the collar, and struck me with a shower of cruel blows with his rattan. I tried in vain to screen myself, he was in so terrible a rage, almost out of himself; it was only weariness that made him give up.[18]

The capacity for withstanding punishment which had sustained the Prince for so many years had finally reached its limit.

[17] *Ibid.*, 85.
[18] Carlyle, *History of Frederick II*, II, 148.

After the King refused to allow his marriage, Frederick made plans during the winter of 1729–30 to escape from Prussia to France, intending to go from there to England and the protective custody of George II, his uncle, although the English king had by no means promised him protection. Two of his friends, Lieutenant Katte and Lieutenant Kieth, were called upon to aid him in what was literally a life-and-death venture. Katte was a young man of musical and literary talent, probably the closest friend of Frederick's lifetime. The escape attempt was made on August 4, 1730, while Frederick was part of the King's entourage on a tour of south Germany. It failed at the very beginning; Frederick had been found out ahead of time by Colonel von Rochow, his overseer.

Kieth escaped to England. When the King received word of the capture of Frederick and Katte, he had them put into solitary confinement at Wesel, a small city in the duchy of Cleves. Frederick William then continued the tour as if nothing had happened, finally reaching Wesel on August 12, 1730. Frederick, considered a deserter from the army, was questioned intensively throughout his imprisonment, first at Wesel, later at Cüstrin. It is probable that public opinion and lack of a sufficiently serious charge were the only reasons preventing the King from executing his son. The Prince's confinement within the walls of the prison at Cüstrin, about forty miles northwest of Berlin, lasted until November 20. During that time the King seized his library and exiled the librarian and Duhan to Memel. Frederick William found out about an innocent flirtation of Frederick's with Dorothea Elizabeth Ritter, the sixteen-year-old daughter of a town rector. Although both were completely innocent, he had her whipped and put into the prison at Spandau to do hard labor "forever." On November 5 Frederick was forced to stand at his cell window and watch as Katte, his closest and most devoted friend, was beheaded.

The Prince's confinement did not end with his release from the prison itself. His father's instructions to Pastor Müller (the minister whose duty it was to bring Frederick back to the "true religion") explain another part of the sentence imposed upon the prisoner:

> The whole town shall be his prison; he will not be able to leave it. I shall give him duties from morning until night in the Chambers of War, of Domains and of Government. He will work at economic affairs, receive accounts, read the laws, make extracts. But before any of this happens, I shall require him to take an oath to obey my will strictly in all things, and to act as befits a faithful servant, subject, and son. If he rebels again he will lose his right to the throne and to the electorate, and even, in certain circumstances, his life.[19]

During the first part of his stay at Cüstrin Frederick was not allowed to speak to anyone privately. The three men who watched over him were required to work in relays so as never to leave him alone, by day or night. He lived a Spartan life, full of humdrum activities, empty of music and literature. In prison he had persuaded his jailers to procure a flute for him and to permit his playing (sometimes Fredersdorff had visited to accompany him) but the first months of imprisonment within the town of Cüstrin did not allow the pursuit of any muse whatever.

One would hardly expect that the shattering events through which Frederick had lived could result in growth of any kind, yet the experiences of his eighteenth year brought about a sobering of his character, rather than its destruction. He had never been openly rebellious; he had always reacted to his father's pronouncements with at least external solicitude. Now his solici-

[19] Carl Hinrichs, *Der Kronprinzenprozess, Friedrich und Katte,* 162.

tude was doubled. He managed to develop a real interest in the collection of taxes, the promotion of the farms and factories of Cüstrin, the reclamation of land, and the making of war. He began gradually to grow in the King's favor, but he could not change his character entirely. When he made bold enough to request readmission to the army, Frederick William replied with a flat refusal, accompanied by eloquent and bitter sarcasm:

> Every time there is a hunt or a trip or some such occasion which you should attend, you manage to avoid it in order to read a French book or a collection of *bons mots* or a comedy, or you plead fatigue, or you spend your time playing the flute. What good would it do if I should truly satisfy your heart's desire, if I should bring a *maître de flûte* from Paris, with a dozen flutes and a stack of music books, plus a mob of comedians and a big orchestra, plus two dozen loud-mouthed French actors and dancers, giving them a fine theater in which to display their talents? All this would please you more than a company of Grenadiers, since, according to your judgment, the Grenadiers are only "trash"; but a *petit-maître*, a trifling Frenchman, a *bon mot*, a musician, a comedian—these are noble, these are kingly, these are *digne d'un prince*.[20]

Nevertheless Frederick's life became gradually more bearable at Cüstrin. By November of 1731 he was able to obtain a conditional pardon from the King, enabling him to attend Wilhelmina's unwilling marriage to the Margrave of Bayreuth, and while in Berlin he was readmitted to the army and promised a regiment.

The Prince's own marriage was still a problem which his father was determined to settle as soon as possible, and which Frederick wished fervently to avoid:

[20] Thouret, *Friedrich der Grosse*, 13.

As long as I am left a bachelor, I will thank God that I am one, and if I marry I shall certainly make a very bad husband, for I feel neither constant nor enough attached to the fair sex . . . the very thought of my wife is a thing so disagreeable to me that I cannot think of it without a feeling of distaste.[21]

After some prospecting among the vassal states of Austria, Frederick William agreed upon a suitable bride for his son: Princess Elizabeth Christina of Brunswick. By every sort of deception possible, Frederick sought to delay or prevent the marriage, but marriage was the price of freedom. The formal ceremony of betrothal took place on March 10, 1732. By early summer the Prince, finally at liberty, had left Cüstrin and was in command of a regiment at Ruppin. However, he continued to make excuses delaying the marriage, promising the King's chamberlains in secret that it would bring the Princess a life of misery and isolation, since he wanted nothing whatever to do with her. He succeeded in delaying the ceremony fifteen months; the marriage was celebrated June 12, 1733. From that time until the end of Frederick's life his wife received from him only a cold acknowledgment of her existence. She never saw his favorite home, Sans Souci, which was built in Potsdam in 1747; and she lived in such complete separation from him that she gave a party in her own residence, Schönhausen, while he was dying, not having been told that he was ill.

Once married—nominally, at least—and in better favor with the King, Frederick began the happiest phase of his life: the period from 1733 to 1740, during which he was at last able to lead an independent and princely existence. The year 1732 marks the beginning of his real patronage of music. From the start of his residence at Ruppin he maintained a small group of instru-

[21] Gaxotte, *Frederick the Great*, 97–98.

mental musicians, which by 1736 had grown into an orchestra of considerable importance, having in its membership the main segment of the first Berlin School and the foundation of the coming Berlin Opera Orchestra. Even during the most terrible part of the conflict with his father, Frederick had not neglected his own development as a musician, and in Ruppin his lessons in flute and composition with Quantz continued, although Quantz was unable to join his service until 1741. When Karl Heinrich Graun came to Ruppin as *Kapellmeister* in 1735, one of his duties was to give Frederick instruction in composition.[22]

In 1736 Frederick moved into his mansion at Rheinsberg (about ten miles north of Ruppin), bringing with him a full retinue of musicians, men of letters, and intellectuals. The term "Philosopher of Rheinsberg," which is used to describe the Frederick of these years, is certainly not a misnomer. The voices of the leading thinkers of mid-eighteenth-century Europe were heard there: Maupertius, Gravesande, Fontenelle, Rollin, Hénault, Algarotti. On the walls the Prince hung paintings by Watteau and Lancret; he memorized whole scenes of French plays, especially those of Racine; he read and reread Voltaire's *Charles II* and Wolff's *Metaphysics*. Frederick began his famous correspondence with Voltaire on August 8, 1736; a real friendship and identity of interest existed between the two from the very beginning (although they discovered later, at Sans Souci, that the friendship which had flourished by correspondence did not fare as well under the hazards of personal contact). In elegant French they discussed literature and philosophy, the degeneracy of the church and the supremacy of reason, and rules of grammar and rhetoric. Under Voltaire's tutelage Frederick improved his poetry, broadened his intellectual horizons, and finally repudiated Christianity (although he continued to believe in the existence of a Supreme Being and became a Free-

[22] Becker, *"Friedrich II," Die Musik in Geschichte.*

mason in 1738). Under Frederick's patronage Voltaire succeeded in gaining support for his ideas and the ideas of his fellow-philosophers; here at last was a true philosopher-king, a monarch who was able to recognize and foster the efforts of great men.

Carlyle's description of Rheinsberg, while very sketchy (especially concerning music), gives a good picture of the general atmosphere there:

Except the old Ruppin duties, which imply continual journeyings thither, distance only a morning's ride; except these, and occasional commissions from Papa, Friedrich is left master of his time and pursuits in the new Mansion. . . . Friedrich's taste is for Literatures, Philosophies: a young Prince bent seriously to cultivate his mind . . . and he does seriously read, study and reflect a good deal; his main recreations, seemingly, are Music, and the converse of well-informed, friendly men. In music we find him particularly rich. Daily, at a fixed hour of the afternoon, there is concert held . . . and if the Artists entertained here for that function were enumerated (high names, not yet forgotten in the Musical world), it would still more astonish readers. I count them to the number of twenty or nineteen; and mention only that "the two Brothers Graun" and the "two Brothers Benda" were of the lot; suppressing four other fiddlers of eminence,[23] and a pianist who is known to everybody.[24]

The Prince has a fine sensibility to Music: does himself, with thrilling adagios on the flute, join in these harmonious acts, and, no doubt, if rightly vigilant against the Nonsenses, gets profit, now and henceforth, from this part of his resources.[25]

[23] Joseph Blume, Georg Czarth, Johann Kaspar Grundke, and Ehms (see p. 88).

[24] Christoph Schraffrath (see p. 88). Carlyle should, of course, have said "cembalist."

[25] Carlyle, *History of Frederick II*, III, 29.

Frederick's activities are further illustrated in a letter from the Princess Elizabeth to her mother (considering Frederick's treatment of the Princess, it also illustrates her forced sense of duty to him):

> Those who seek for art, true and clear philosophy, and wit should come here: they will find everything in a state of perfection, as our master is in control of it all. I have never seen anyone work as hard as he does: from six in the morning until one o'clock he works at reading, philosophy and all the other noble studies. Dinner lasts from half-past one until three o'clock. After that we drink coffee until four and then he gets down to work again till seven in the evening. Next music begins and lasts till nine o'clock. Then he writes, comes to play cards, and we generally sup at half-past ten or eleven. . . . I can truthfully say that he is the greatest prince of our time.[26]

The Prince felt that he was building within himself the qualities of fairness and justice: "I want men in our society to be accorded honor in proportion to the honor they have earned."[27] He believed, as might be expected, that man had only an earthly life, and that his only reward would be the reward of earthly accomplishment: "The point is not that a man should trail the indolent and useless thread of his days to the age of a Methuselah, but that the more he meditates, the more he performs fine and useful actions, the more he lives."[28]

But Rheinsberg was no monastery. A First Table was constantly maintained; parties, balls, banquets, and fetes of various kinds were very common; much wine was consumed; Frederick got further and further into debt. Nor did the Prince desire only

[26] Gaxotte, *Frederick the Great,* 131–32.
[27] Thouret, *Friedrich der Grosse,* 17.
[28] Gaxotte, *Frederick the Great,* 148.

an idyllic life of isolation. He had already acquitted himself well as a soldier during the winter of 1733–34, taking part willingly in a battle against the French for Poland and keeping notebooks of maneuvers. He was well-informed in worldly affairs, especially European politics. While at Rheinsberg he produced his *Considérations sur l'état présent du corps politique de l'Europe* and his *Anti-Machiavel*. The *Considérations* discuss the increasing military might of Austria and France and show the need for a third power (meaning, no doubt, Prussia) for keeping in check any possible aggression. The *Anti-Machiavel,* written at the suggestion of Voltaire and issued by him, is a rather naïve refutation of Machiavellian ideals in favor of the enlightened view that "the prince is not the absolute master, but only the first servant of the people."[29] However, these noble words of an idealistic prince should not cause us to ignore other words written by him at Rheinsberg: "War chastens lechery and pomp; it teaches sobriety and fasting; it uproots all that is effeminate."[30] Nor should we even go so far as to think of Frederick as completely "enlightened," as this excerpt from a letter to the King shows:

Everything is more or less in order in the regiment, except that a plot has been discovered at Nauen. The ringleader belonged to Major Quadt's company. . . . As soon as the second battalion is back here, I will have a court-martial held, and as the rogue's case is a serious one I think he will be condemned to death. This example will not be without its uses, and I hope that in the future it will serve to restrain other traitors.[31]

Finally, it should be mentioned that Frederick had two ma-

[29] J. Sime, "Frederick II," *Encyclopaedia Britannica*, Vol. IX.
[30] Gaxotte, *Frederick the Great*, 109.
[31] *Ibid.,* 140.

terial reasons for becoming, at Rheinsberg, both "enlightened" and a despot: He wanted to deprive the monarchy of its religious background, of the dangerous concept of "divine right"; and he realized that only a despotic rule could be successful over the vast miscellany of territories, peoples, and cultures which made up his kingdom.

THE KING

One can well imagine the impatience with which the Prince waited for the throne. His ideals and plans had solidified during his life at Ruppin and Rheinsberg; he felt himself eminently able to rule, properly prepared in every way; but the throne remained occupied by another. After the campaign of 1733–34 the King had fallen ill but had unexpectedly recovered. There can be no doubt that Frederick was disappointed to have his father remain alive. One of his poems, written at about that time, expressed his discouragement:

> The throne is for me but an image illusory,
> But a cheating phantom of frivolous glory.[32]

Frederick William managed to continue his increasingly alcoholic existence until May 31, 1740. The twenty-eight-year-old Frederick gave his father a funeral of due magnificence; but it is hardly likely that among the myriad plans occupying the new king's mind there was much room for thoughts of mourning. He had waited a long time, and had planned the first part of his reign with such thoroughness that he did not need to hesitate.

The beginning of the reign was like a fairy tale. Frederick

[32] *Ibid.* (translated by Gaxotte).

was intoxicated with the pleasure of being King. . . . He was indefatigable, rose at dawn, worked without a single break, accepted volumes of poetry, sent off hundreds of letters, held reviews, founded a journal, chose ambassadors, created the Order of Merit, appointed a marshal, rushed from Berlin to Rheinsberg and from Potsdam to Charlottenburg, and complained that the days were twenty-four hours too short.

One after another appeared twenty edicts of a sort to make a philosopher swoon with delight: the abolition of torture, the opening of State granaries to prevent a rise in the price of bread, the suppression of Church dispensations for marriages between distant relatives, the suppression of the compulsory building which was ruining so many Berliners, prohibition of ragging in the army, mitigation of the penalties inflicted on women convicted of "having caused the fruit of their wombs to perish," institution of a Department of Commerce and Manufactures in the heart of the Central Office, permission given for countryfolk to make their own beer for home consumption, and a solemn declaration that everyone in the States of the King of Prussia was free to choose his own way to salvation.[33]

The philosopher Wolff, who had been expelled from the University of Halle by Frederick William, was returned to his professorial chair; Duhan was brought back from Memel; Kieth returned from England; the Academy of Letters, which had been made a laughing stock by Frederick William, was restored. Hardly two months after his accession, the new king sent Karl Heinrich Graun on a trip to the major cities of Italy in search of singers. He commissioned the architect Knobelsdorf to begin work at once on the new opera house. The Berlin Opera was born on the day of Frederick William's death.

Unfortunately, many of Frederick's actions as king were not so admirable. His first opportunity for military conquest came

[33] *Ibid.*, 176–77.

soon after his accession, and he took full advantage of it; the conqueror developed along with the artist. Although a discussion of the war-making of an historic patron of music might seem incongruous, it is necessary in this case; because the meteoric rise of Prussia under Frederick proves that the strongest side of this king's personality, in spite of all his artistic tendencies, was his ruthless genius as a conqueror.

On October 20, 1740, the Emperor Charles of Austria died, leaving only his daughter, Maria Theresa, to inherit a vast assortment of Hapsburg dominions. Among these dominions were the three Silesian duchies on which Prussia had an ancient claim. Before he died Charles had persuaded the other European powers to accept a "pragmatic sanction," or universal promise to honor Maria Theresa's right to the possession of all his lands; but soon after his death Austria's neighbors ignored their promise, and Maria Theresa found her kingdom attacked from all sides by France, Bavaria, and especially Prussia. Frederick had at first pretended friendship but he soon asserted his claim to Silesia by marching an army of thirty thousand men into the district, occupying the important city of Breslau without going through the formality of declaring war. Although Maria Theresa was able to repulse her other enemies, she was forced to grant Silesia to Frederick in order to induce him to retire from the war.

This War of the Austrian Succession was only the beginning of Frederick's conquests. In 1744 the Prince of East Friesland died without heirs; the Prussian king took that territory. During the same year Maria Theresa determined to recover Silesia. Upon hearing of her intention, Frederick reacted boldly, capturing the imagination of his people: he formed a union with Bavaria and concluded a secret treaty with France, then suddenly invaded Bohemia, taking Prague. Even though he was forced to retreat, he won a series of victories during 1745, and the Peace of Dresden (December 25, 1745) once again gave him title to Silesia.

By this time, at the age of thirty-three, Frederick was being watched by the entire civilized world. The skillful rule, the amazing energy, the vast intellectual breadth of this enlightened despot caused his popularity among his people to become legendary even while he created new legends. After the Peace of Dresden the King devoted himself solely, for a time, to the internal development of Prussia. He promoted industry and elementary education, drew up a new code of laws, furthered the draining of swamps and the extension of the canal system, and built up his army to an even greater strength; although he maintained serfdom, he did a great deal to lighten the peasant's burden; he established colonies, populating them with immigrants; he was good-natured toward his people, calling himself *"l'avocat du pauvre"* and freely giving audience to anyone with a genuine grievance.

Amid all these activities he found time to direct the now-brilliant Berlin Opera in every small detail, to compose, to play flute concertos at his private concerts, to write poetry, prose, and opera libretti, and to entertain and be entertained by his intellectuals. Lessing composed odes in his honor; Johann Glein, the Halberstadt poet, wrote of Frederick as a being almost divine. In 1752 Voltaire was welcomed royally to Sans Souci, where he spent one or two hours each day with the King, continuing in person the interchange of verse and ideas which had begun by correspondence many years before. While visiting Frederick he finished his *Siècle de Louis XIV* and wrote articles for a philosophical dictionary. But his vain, capricious manner was irritating to Frederick, who, in turn, singled him out as the subject of cruel jokes; and these two great men whose initial attraction had been so strong eventually found themselves alienated from one another.

Maria Theresa had not lightly given up Silesia, and her continuing determination to recover it led to the Seven Years' War (1756–63), a conflict which spread over the whole face of Europe and involved every civilized nation. Maria Theresa's ambassador at Paris was successful in persuading France to aid Austria in an attack on Prussia, in spite of two centuries of French hostility toward the Hapsburgs; and Russia, Sweden, and Saxony also entered into the alliance against Frederick. Thus Prussia was completely surrounded by enemies and apparently doomed, but it was during the Seven Years' War that Frederick earned the title, "the Great." Taking the offensive himself, he moved into Saxony, then Bohemia. In 1757 he defeated both his French and German enemies in the famous battle of Rossbach, after which England joined Frederick's side against the French, and the Swedes and Russians left the field. Nevertheless, as the war progressed it appeared that Prussia would, after all, be erased from the map of Europe. At this point Frederick had an amazing stroke of good fortune: A new Russian Czar, Peter III, ascended the throne. He was a great admirer of the famous King of Prussia, and one of his first acts was to conclude peace. At this news Maria Theresa agreed to give up her struggle for repossession of Silesia. The Peace of Hubertushof (February 15, 1763) restored national boundaries to their prewar positions.

Although the Seven Years' War was no more than the successful defense of stolen property, Prussia emerged from it a world power, the archrival of Austria for the leadership of central Europe; and Austria, the Hapsburg empire, began the decline which was to end in 1918 with its collapse. Needless to say, Frederick's popularity with the North Germans reached truly heroic proportions. The battles of the war were told and retold as heroic deeds, becoming colorful and romantic epics in the hands of poets and painters. Seldom has a king been so revered by his subjects; even today the descendants of those subjects speak of *"Vater Fritz"* with reverence.

This reverence would be deeper had Frederick not taken part in the partition of Poland in 1770, after joining with Catherine of Russia in every possible effort to continue the anarchist government which made Poland such a vulnerable country. By taking possession of the Polish territory between Brandenburg and Prussia, Frederick made his kingdom geographically continuous for the first time. Later attempts by the Polish government to make itself more efficient were consistently thwarted by Prussia and Russia, paving the way for even more territorial thievery by Catherine and Frederick's successor, Frederick William II. Frederick's standards of political morality were not abnormally low: Austria, Prussia's old enemy, took part in this same partition of defenseless Poland.

Frederick's last major act of aggression—or last great conquest, depending on one's point of view—took place from 1777 to 1779: the War of the Bavarian Succession. Maximilian Joseph, Elector of Bavaria, died without heirs. The resulting competition between Prussia and Austria for the territory of Bavaria ended on May 13, 1779, with the Treaty of Teschen; Austria (now under the rule of Joseph II) received the circle of Burgau, Prussia received the Franconian principalities. Until he died Frederick was jealous of Austria's power. In 1785 he formed a league of princes, the *Fürstenbund*, for the defense of Germany against what he, of all people, considered aggressive movements by Joseph II.

In summing up Frederick's positive accomplishments, his panegyrists—Carlyle, for example—give us an unspotted picture of a heroic and noble reformer; while those, such as Macaulay, who consider Frederick only the merciless father of Prussianism, tend to discount for various reasons every advance made by

25

him. Books about Frederick which appeared during or immediately after the first World War, such as Norwood Young's *The Life of Frederick the Great* and Heinrich Gotthard von Treitschke's *The Confessions of Frederick the Great*, are often so consistently and bitterly derogatory as to be almost worthless as judgments of the Prussian king's actions. The middle position between these extremes is appropriately stated by a musicologist, Paul Henry Lang, in a general discussion of enlightened absolutism:

> . . . new economic culture was the bulwark of enlightened absolutism, for the rulers wanted their subjects to be industrious and well-to-do, knowing that this was the best way to keep the state treasury filled. The methods used in attaining this aim were often arbitrary and even brutal, but on the whole the policy promoted cultural progress, for the new benevolent despotism was very active in all fields of culture. It organized life minutely in all its aspects, regulating and administering it by a vast police force. Such regulation of private life is repugnant to the modern man, but it wrought sheer wonders in eighteenth-century society. . . . All this was not done for humanitarian reasons alone . . . but the recognition and remedying of deeds and problems was a capital achievement.
>
> The same creative spirit that characterized political life enlivened arts and letters. Not since the Italian Renaissance had these enjoyed such universal love and support. The enlightened absolutism was indefatigable in its creative fervor; palaces, castles, theaters, schools, academies and universities rose everywhere, and artists and musicians were busy delivering the many works commissioned by their employers. This intense artistic activity was, of course, a logical means of glorifying ruler and state, for the poet's and artist's achievements enhanced the reputation of the state and the dignity of the ruler. The universities, neglected in the pre-

vious century, received ample support and showed immense activity in academic studies. Scientific and artistic academies, created in every residential city, were responsible for the unprecedented productivity in arts and letters. Many of these institutions, such as the Bavarian Academy and the Prussian Academy, have remained bodies of the highest cultural importance to our day.

Brilliant as all this cultural life was, it represented only a fancy of the king. The idea of human dignity never entered Frederick's mind, and once a passing interest was satisfied the greatest scholar or artist of the century became a mere court attendant. We must not lose sight of the fact that enlightened absolutism wanted enlightenment but not liberty.[34]

If this concept of enlightened absolutism is kept in mind, it is perhaps easier to understand the motives behind the military exploits of a man whose nature was thoroughly artistic. Frederick the Great was first of all a soldier and statesman, and only secondly an artist and promoter of art; but his great contributions to humanity as a progressive monarch and as a force in German cultural life are, when seen from the perspective of the twentieth century, more deserving of mention in history than all of his conquests, no matter how spectacular.

[34] *Music in Western Civilization,* 569–70.

II·

FREDERICK AS MUSICIAN

"NEVER CRITICIZE the composition of a Royal Highness
—you do not know who may have written it."[1] This
statement by Johannes Brahms, showing his distrust
of the musical pretensions of royalty, is not without justification.
The kings and princes of music history, while often supplying
livelihood for creators of music, have seldom been more than
amateur musicians themselves. Frederick the Great, however,
was an exception to this rule. He was more than a dilettante,
even more than a good performer. The surprising breadth and
depth of his musical abilities made him an unusual patron, one
whose dictates were based on personal creative experience. A
look at three aspects of his own life as a musician—his perform-

[1] A. W. Thayer, *The Life of Ludwig van Beethoven,* trans. by H. E. Krehbiel, III, 20.

ance, his compositions, and his musical taste—will help us understand his reign over the musical life of Berlin.

The opinions of six of Frederick's contemporaries, when considered together, present a very favorable picture of his flute playing. They are given by Franz Benda, chamber-musician to the King for forty years; Karl Friedrich Fasch, court cembalist for thirty years; J. F. Reichardt, *Kapellmeister* from 1755 until Frederick's death; Elizabeth Mara, leading soprano at the Berlin Opera from 1771 to 1780; Charles Burney, the distinguished musical historian, who visited the Prussian court in 1772 and heard Frederick's private concerts there; and Baron J. F. von Bielfeld, whose report of his visits to Rheinsberg contains the earliest of all these descriptions.

Benda: He is known throughout the world for his singular ability with this instrument.[2]

Fasch [Karl Friedrich Zelter, telling of Fasch's remarks]: Fasch, who served the King for thirty years and outlived him by twelve years, said to me on several occasions that he had heard only three virtuosi who could perform a truly noble and moving adagio. The first was his friend Emanuel Bach at the clavier; the second, Franz Benda on the violin; and the third, the King on the flute.[3]

Reichardt: The King's virtuosity was most evident in his playing of adagios. He had modeled his style on that of the greatest singers and instrumentalists of his time, especially

[2] Franz Benda, *"Auto-Biographie von Franz Benda,"* ed. by C. Freiherr von Ledebur, *Neue Berliner Musikzeitung,* Vol. X (August 6–27, 1856), 269.

[3] Joseph K. F. Müller-Blatteau, *"Karl Friedrich Zelters Rede auf Friedrich den Grossen,"* *Deutsche Musikkultur,* Vol. I (August–September, 1936), 171.

Franz Benda. Without doubt he had a strong feeling for everything he played. His melting nuances—particularly his accents and little melodic ornaments—bespoke a delicate, sensitive musical nature. His adagio was a gentle flow, a pure, subdued, often stirring, song: the surest evidence that his beautiful playing came from his soul.[4]

... he played adagios with so much inner feeling, with such noble, moving simplicity and truth, that his audience seldom listened without tears.[5]

Mara: Contrary to what many say, he does not play like a king at all, but is an excellent performer. He has a strong, full tone and a great deal of technique.[6]

Bielfeld: The evening is devoted to music. The Prince holds concert in his salon; attendance is by invitation only . . . . The Prince usually plays the flute. He handles the instrument with complete authority; his embouchure, as well as his fingering and articulation, are peerless. I have often had the honor of standing behind him during his performances, and have been especially impressed by his adagios.[7]

Burney: The concert began by a German flute concerto, in which His majesty executed the solo parts with great precision; his *embouchure* was clear and even, his finger brilliant, and his taste pure and simple. I was much pleased, and even surprised with the neatness of his execution in the *allegros*, as well as by his expression and feeling in the *adagios;* in short, his performance surpassed, in many particulars, any thing

[4] Gustav Lenzewski, *Die Hohenzollern in der Musikgeschichte des 18. Jahrhunderts,* 29–30.

[5] J. F. Reichardt, *"Musikalische Anekdoten von Friedrich dem Grossen," Musikalisches Kunstmagazin,* Vol. II (1791), 40.

[6] Frederick the Great, *Friedrichs des Grossens Musik Werke,* ed. by Philipp Spitta, I, ix.

[7] Richard Münnich, *"Friedrich der Grosse und die Musik," Zeitschrift für Musik,* Vol. CIII (August, 1936), 914.

I had ever heard among *Dilettanti,* or even professors. His majesty played three long and difficult concertos successively, and all with equal perfection.[8]

Some other descriptions of Frederick's performance are not complimentary. The often-acrimonious Reichardt, in one of his many self-contradictions, makes these remarks about the scales practiced by the King: "His perseverance with these boring exercises is worthy of notice, but even more noteworthy is the fact that all this dull work does little to help him cope with difficult passages or perform an allegro with the fire and flash which his lively personality demands."[9] And Burney, at another concert, noted that

> The cadences which His Majesty made were good, but very long and studied. It is easy to discover that these concertos were composed at a time when he did not so frequently require an opportunity of breathing as at present; for in some of the divisions, which were very long and difficult, as well as in the closes, he was obliged to take his breath, contrary to rule, before the passages were finished.[10]

One more fault of Frederick's flute playing was unevenness, or capriciousness, of tempo. Fétis, in describing C. P. E. Bach's task of accompanying the King, says that it "was not without difficulty, because of the irregularity of beat in the monarch's performance."[11]

The total weight of all these descriptions, favorable and unfavorable, seems to indicate that Frederick's competence as a performer set him above the rank of dilettante. When objective evidence is added to these opinions, the conclusion is reached

[8] Charles Burney, *The Present State of Music in Germany*, II, 152–53.
[9] Reichardt, *"Musikalische Anekdoten,"* *Musikalisches Kunstmagazin*, Vol. II (1791), 40.
[10] Burney, *The Present State of Music*, II, 154–55.
[11] Fétis, *"Frédéric II,"* *Biographie Universelle des Musiciens*, Vol. III.

that this royal flutist must have played quite respectably, even according to the most musicianly standards. He began his study of the flute at about the age of seven and commenced his lessons with Quantz at sixteen. His interest in the flute was not casual, but vital; he usually practiced four or five times daily during the early part of his reign, and three or four times during each day of his later years. Reichardt, Frederick's *Kapellmeister*, gives this schedule of a typical day's practice: immediately after rising in the morning, before or after the morning meeting of the cabinet, after lunch, and, of course, at the evening concert.[12]

> The flute served him as a means of relaxing the tensions of his reign, of freeing himself . . . during the mornings before cabinet meetings, when Frederick paced up and down in his room, improvising freely on the flute and pondering on various matters, there often came to him . . . the most fortuitous answers to many of the day's problems. Even on the battlefield and in winter quarters, his flute played an important role.[13]

Reichardt also describes the manner of Frederick's morning practice:

> The morning exercises are accomplished by reading through a long chart containing various kinds of scale passages. First he plays the natural scale of d–e–f♯–g–a–b–c♯–d, and so forth; then d–f♯, e–g, f♯–a, g–b, a–c♯, b–d, c♯–e, etc., then d–e–f♯–d, e–f♯–g–e, f♯–g–a–f♯, and so forth, through all octaves; then all the exercises are played in descending motion; then all of the foregoing is repeated one half-step higher, etc. Every day the same routine is followed.[14]

[12] "*Musikalische Anekdoten,*" *Musikalisches Kunstmagazin,* Vol. II (1791), 40.
[13] Thouret, *Friedrich der Grosse,* 133–34.

These exercises, which today seem quite ordinary, must have been something of a novelty then in order to merit such attention. They were part of a book of studies for the flute, composed by both Quantz and Frederick. It is obvious that these studies were important to the King, because he possessed four copies, three of which were designated for specific locations: the Stadtschloss, Sans Souci, and Charlottenburg. Apparently they were used everywhere Frederick played. Burney mentions seeing a copy of some "Solfeggi" for flute on one of the tortoise-shell music stands in the Neue Palais.[15] An exercise from one of these books[16] (Fig. 1) was scribbled by the King on the blank side of an étude by Quantz.

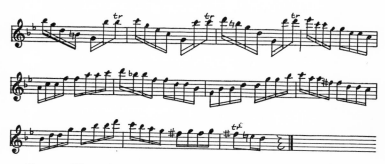

Fig. 1.—Flute étude by Frederick, from a book of flute exercises by himself and Quantz.

Frederick was extremely nervous when playing. He always learned new pieces thoroughly, in private, before practicing them with his orchestra, and he was careful to be warmed up before each performance. Burney gives us an interesting account of the moments before a concert:

[14] Erwin Schwarz-Reiflingen, "*Friedrich der Grosse als Flötist*," *Allgemeine Musikzeitung*, Vol. LXVI (1939), 478–79.
[15] *The Present State of Music*, II, 146.
[16] Cited in Thouret, *Friedrich der Grosse*, 132.

I was carried to one of the interior apartments of the palace, in which the gentlemen of the king's band were waiting for his commands. This apartment was contiguous to the concert-room, where I could distinctly hear his majesty practicing *Solfeggi* on the flute, and exercising himself in difficult passages previous to his calling in the band.[17]

At Rheinsberg the King often played six concertos and one sonata, without an intermission (though as he grew older, shortness of breath became a problem, as Burney relates, and he was forced to "limit" himself to about three pieces at a time).[18] In spite of his slight build, he was barrel-chested; he had all the breath capacity necessary for a flutist, at least until the last ten or fifteen years of his life.[19] His death mask, and the one portrait of him painted from life, show that he had the mouth and lip formation needed for good embouchure.

Frederick's own flute works bear witness to his ability as a performer, since they contain many demanding passages. An excerpt (Fig. 2) from the second movement of his Sonata No. VI (Spitta edition),[20] not at all unusual, certainly demands good breath control, as well as an adequate technique.

One cannot fail to be impressed with the King's talent for playing the flute when it is realized that his instruments were made almost a century before the first Boehm flutes and were extremely primitive by today's standards. The ascendancy of the flute and its literature dates from the early eighteenth century, and, as we shall see in a later chapter, Quantz played an

---

[17] *The Present State of Music*, II, 150–51.

[18] Reichardt, *"Musikalische Anekdoten,"* *Musikalisches Kunstmagazin*, Vol. II (1791), 40.

[19] Schwarz-Reiflingen, *"Friedrich der Grosse als Flötist,"* Allgemeine *Musikzeitung*, Vol. LXVI (1939), 479.

[20] Frederick the Great, *Friedrichs des Grossens Musik Werke*, ed. by Spitta, Vol. I.

FIG. 2.—Frederick II, Sonata No. VI, second movement, measures 121–43.

1141965

important role in improving the instrument and providing music for it. But the fact remains that the crudity of the instruments which were available to Frederick is a real tribute to his aptitude and perseverance. In a pamphlet published in 1932,[21] Georg Müller, a well-known German flutist of the time, describes some of the flutes then existing which were used by the King. They were found in the Hohenzollern Museum, in Monbijou Castle, at Sans Souci, in the Berlin municipal collection of musical instruments, and in the Heimat-Museum of Potsdam. Two of the instruments were made of ivory, each having one key (E flat); one was of amber with two golden keys (E flat and D sharp);[22] four were of ebony, each with two silver keys; and one was of boxwood, having a single key.

[21] *Friedrich der Grosse, seine Flöten und sein Flötenspiele.*
[22] See the section on Quantz in chapter IV.

35

Müller was able to rejuvenate three of the ebony instruments and the one made of boxwood. Since they were all badly dried out, he treated them with a monthly bath of oil and water for eight months, causing each of the ebony flutes to absorb fifteen to seventeen grams of moisture. During these eight months he practiced daily the embouchure and tonguing (to the best of his knowledge) of the eighteenth-century flutist, accustoming himself to the small blow holes of these instruments. The results of this admirable bit of research were disappointing. Müller was able to extract only a thin, dull tone from the flutes; no tone would speak without being forcibly articulated. The D and G scales were difficult to play in tune; the tones F sharp, G sharp, and B were especially faulty in intonation. For every single tone a different embouchure was required. Of the influence of temperature changes, the discouraged Müller makes this comment: "I must say that the downright peevish sensitivity of the ebony flutes to any change in temperature is almost unbelievable."[23] In brief, he was amazed that Frederick or anyone could produce enjoyable music from these instruments, concluding that they must have required "early, thorough training and long study."[24]

The elegant rococo music rooms of Frederick's palaces and mansions were not the only settings for his playing. His flute went with him to the battlefields, to Silesia, Saxony, Bohemia, and Moravia;[25] in his tent or in winter quarters he made music as usual. Often he sent to Berlin for an accompanist. During the winter of 1760–61 he was joined by Fasch, who accompanied him on a portable clavier (*Reiseclavier*). This curious little instrument, made in Paris by Marius, broke down into three pieces for easy carrying, and was part of Frederick's equipment for

[23] *Friedrich der Grosse, seine Flöten und sein Flötenspiele,* 11.
[24] *Ibid.,* 12.
[25] Thouret, *Friedrich der Grosse,* 134.

every campaign.[26] In the last campaign of the Seven Years' War, the King sent for a quartet of musicians. The carriage delivering them had hardly stopped rolling before they were ordered to prepare for a concert. Frederick, thus accompanied, played a piece and exclaimed, enchanted, "That tastes like sugar!"[27] Surely it must have been important for this king to make music.

The decline of Frederick's performing ability was evident as early as the winter of 1760–61, when he sent for Fasch. Fasch reports that he found

> an old man, considerably changed and given an appearance of deep melancholy by five years of battles, worry, sorrow and hard work. He had completely lost his former lively aspect; he was aged far beyond his years. And his playing was sour.[28]

By the end of the Seven Years' War Frederick had become *"der alte Fritz";* he had lost a front tooth, and his fingers had become stiff.[29] In winter quarters during 1778–79 his flute served him for the last time. He was short of breath, more of his teeth were missing, and gout had so stiffened his fingers that they were unusable for flute playing. Early in 1779, as he packed his flute before returning to Potsdam, he remarked to Franz Benda, "My dear Benda, I have lost my best friend."[30]

The following poem, written by Frederick in winter quarters at Breslau on December 28, 1761, is quite touching in spite of its technical deficiencies; for one can well imagine that "Monsieur Vacarmini" is the Frederick who is losing his performing ability:

[26] *Ibid.,* 137.
[27] *Ibid.,* 136.
[28] *Ibid.,* 135.
[29] *Ibid.,* 136.
[30] Reichardt, *"Musikalische Anekdoten," Musikalisches Kunstmagazin,* Vol. II (1791), 40.

Conte du violon

Certain Monsieur Vacarmini,
Elève harmonieux de Monsieur Tartini,
Voyageoit pour se faire entendre
Par les trois quarts de l'univers.
Un beau jour produisant en Flandre
Lui, son violon, et ses airs,
Il se trouvoit en compagnie
Où le monde, ébahi de tant d'accords divers
D'une exécution hardie,
Stupide admirateur de ses talens divins,
Redoubloit d'applaudir et de battre des mains.
Les concerts achevés, un étourdi l'aborde,
Lui dit: daignez à moi, comme à mes citadins,
Accorder une grâce . . . ah! tout je vous accorde;
Ordonnez, dit l'artiste, elle est à votre choix . . .
De votre violon détachez une corde,
Et puisqu'il vous en reste trois,
Voyez, si vous pourrez suppléer par vos doigts
Au défaut de la chanterelle.
Cette invention est nouvelle,
Dit l'autre, et pourtant je verrai
Comment je vous contenterai.
Sur trois cordes il joue, étend les doigts, démanche,
Et produit des accords doux et mélodieux.
Son auditeur plus curieux
Veut encore qu'on lui retranche
Une corde; il en resta deux.
Le joueur, comme on peut le croire,
S'en acquitta moins bien; cependant avec gloire.
Sur cela le jeune insensé
Voulut qu'il n'en gardât plus qu'une.
Le pauvre artiste, à bout poussé,
Lui joue à force d'art une chanson commune.
Alors l'importun sans façon

Détache la corde dernière:
Encore un air! mon bon garçon,
Ça, ça, je t'en fais la prière.
Mais l'instrument muet ne rendit plus de son.
Par le conte, s'il peut vous plaire,
Apprenez, chers concitoyens,
Que malgré tout le savoir-faire
L'art reste court sans les moyens.

À Breslau le 28 Décembre 1761[31]

Although Frederick's moderate keyboard facility provided some consolation for him during his later years (Reichardt attests to his ability at the clavier),[32] the decline of his performing ability was accompanied by a decline of interest in all music. Curiously enough, then, music in Berlin stagnated as the King lost his ability to perform adagios.

COMPOSITIONS: MUSIC AND LIBRETTI

Music

The first consequential list of Frederick's musical compositions, made by C. F. Nicolai (1733–1811),[33] is riddled with errors. The latest (1923) scholarly statement of what Frederick did and did not compose, given by H. J. Moser,[34] is accompanied by its author's admission that a truly reliable and exact list cannot yet be made. Between these two attempts lie those of Kothe (1869), Spitta (1889), Thouret (1898), and Mennicke (1906); though each is scholarly, each shows the difficulty or impossibility of determining the King's compositions exactly.

This veil of obscurity was hung by Frederick himself. His

[31] Thouret, *Friedrich der Grosse*, 135–36.
[32] Wilhelm Kothe, *Friedrich der Grosse als Musiker, sowie als Freund und Förderer der Musikalischen Kunst*, 2–3.
[33] Thouret, *Friedrich der Grosse*, 162–63.
[34] *Geschichte der Deutschen Musik*, Vol. II, Bk. 1, 269–72.

music was heard only within palace walls or, rarely, at the Opera House, and he did not consider his compositions worthy of publication. They remained scattered about his music rooms after his death, mementos of his consumption of music rather than his creation of it. During the King's lifetime one work had been published, without his knowledge or permission, by Balthasar Schmid of Nuremburg;[35] but this was an isolated incident. After Frederick's death, J. F. Reichardt undertook the publication of his former patron's music, but left the task uncompleted. Of this attempt Spitta says, "We should not regret its never having been finished, for Reichardt openly spoke of these compositions as mere curiosities. It would have been impossible for him to make a reliable evaluation of them."[36] Some fifty years after the King's death (*c.*1835), the Crown Prince—later Frederick William IV—ordered that the palaces in and around Potsdam be searched for manuscripts by Frederick the Great. There was no immediate musical result of this expedition: the flute compositions were gathered up and bundled together, but not edited, since they had only a "historical interest."[37]

In 1840, on the hundredth anniversary of Frederick's accession, a performance was given of the same *sinfonie* which Schmid had unlawfully published many years before. It was "edited" for the occasion by S. W. Dehn, who omitted both the middle and last movements, struck out the flute part in the first movement, and gave the piece an erroneous title.[38] The slight reawakening of interest in Frederick's music caused by this occasion did, however, result in the publication of the marches a few years later (edited by W. Wieprecht).

[35] A *sinfonie*, composed in 1743 and used in 1747 as the overture to a *Serenata* (*Schäferspiel*). Cf. Philipp Spitta, "*Vorwort*," *Friedrichs des Grossens Musik Werke*, i.

[36] "*Vorwort*," *Friedrichs des Grossens Musik Werke*, ii.

[37] *Ibid.*

[38] *Ibid.*, ii–iii. Dehn gave the title of *il Rè Pastore* to this *Serenata*, saying that the text was from a libretto of the same name by Villati; but

The year 1886, a century after the King's death, saw the beginning of a long period of intense interest in every facet of his personality. One product of this interest was Spitta's edition of twenty-five of the flute works, published by Breitkopf and Härtel and financed by Kaiser Wilhelm I. Since that time there has been a deluge of editions, mostly from Germany.[39]

Thus Frederick's compositions were not given serious attention until the last few years of the nineteenth century, and it is easy to understand the difficulty of making an exact and reliable catalogue of them. The following list, now generally agreed upon, must be divided into three categories: (1) compositions definitely by Frederick, (2) compositions probably by him, and (3) compositions once considered his work, but no longer considered so.

(1) Compositions definitely by Frederick:
 121 sonatas for flute and cembalo
 4 concertos for flute and string orchestra
 4 books of *Solfeggi* for flute
 March in E-flat Major
 March, composed in Mollwitz, 1741
 March, composed in 1756
 Sinfonie (Italian overture) in D Major, composed in
   1743 and used as overture to a *Serenata* in 1747
 2 arias in the above *Serenata*
 3 arias in K. H. Graun's opera, *Demofoonte*, 1746

Spitta shows that the only libretto with this title came from the pen of Metastasio and was first used in 1751, four years after the performance of the *Serenata*. Moreover, Franz Gehring's article on Frederick in *Grove's Dictionary* says that the only title given on the score of this work, a copy of which is in the Berlin State Library, is *Serenata fatta per l'arrivo de la Regina Madre à Charlottenburg*. Unfortunately, Dehn's error was perpetuated many years.

[39] An excellent list of these editions is contained in Becker, "*Friedrich II*," *Die Musik in Geschichte und Gegenwart*.

An aria in K. H. Graun's opera, *Il Guidizio di Paride*, 1752

An aria in the pastorale, *Il trionfo della fedeltà*, 1753 (a *pasticcio*, in collaboration with Graun and Quantz)

Elaboration of an aria from Hasse's *Cleofide*

3 secular cantatas (lost)

(2) Compositions probably by Frederick:
Sinfonie (Italian overture) in G Major
Air des Houlans ou marche du Roi de Prusse
An aria in K. H. Graun's opera *Galatea ed Acide*, 1749

(3) Compositions once considered his work, but no longer considered so:
Another *Sinfonie* (Italian overture) in G Major
Sinfonie (Italian overture) in A Major
Several little dance pieces for clavier
Hohenfriedberger Marsch
An aria in K. H. Graun's opera, *Coriolano*, 1749

Affixing an exact date to some of Frederick's works is even more of a problem than listing their titles. From the above list it can be seen that the stage works, two marches, and one *sinfonie* are already supplied with dates (taken either from records of performances or from notations on the manuscripts). Determining the time of composition for the others is somewhat more of a problem; nevertheless, it is a problem worth investigating because of the close relationship between the King's composing career and his activities as a patron.

The richest original sources of information concerning the approximate dates of these compositions are the letters written by Frederick to his sister Wilhelmina, the Margravine of Bayreuth. Wilhelmina, too, was a talented performer—on lute and flute—as well as an amateur composer. Since the Prince was very fond of his sister and regarded her musical opinions very highly, his letters to her contain several references to his own compositions.

On August 24, 1735, he wrote to her: "I have advanced far enough in composition to be able to write a symphony. When it is finished, I shall take the liberty of sending it to you."[40] Early in 1736 Quantz, visiting the court of Bayreuth, delivered a concerto by his royal pupil to Wilhelmina. The concerto is mentioned in a letter of January 12:

> I use the occasion of Quantz's departure to assure you, my dear sister, of my perfect friendship. I have given him a concerto for you (of my own composition), since it seems that you wish to have one. I hope that I shall be able to send something better, and that it will be more pleasing to you."[41]

One of the lost cantatas was written very early in the Prince's life as a composer. He mentions it to Wilhelmina in a letter of February 3, 1737:

> I am finally fulfilling my promise to send you the cantata, *Vergil*, which you have requested. I have made it only for you, my dear sister, and I hope that it will not leave your hands or come into the possession of anyone else.[42]

(Perhaps it was Wilhelmina's careful obedience to Frederick's request which prevented this cantata from ever being found.) The same letter also shows us that Frederick was laboriously occupied at that time in writing a concerto, which he obviously considered to be similarly unworthy of mention:

[40] Frederick the Great, *Oeuvres de Frédéric le Grand,* ed. by Johann D. E. Preuss, Vol. XXVII, Bk. 1, 34.
[41] *Ibid.,* 37.
[42] *Ibid.,* 46.

It is only because of the dryness of my imagination that you have not yet received the concerto I am working on. I have given it my best efforts, but I have not yet been able to find a harmony good enough to be offered to you, and I wait for my good genie to inspire me with one.[43]

Within a month (March 2, 1737) Wilhelmina was sent the promised concerto, together with an unexpected gift: "At last, here is the promised concerto, plus an 'unpromised' solo [sonata] which I take the liberty of sending you. . . ."[44] The frequency of Frederick's mention of compositions during this period shows that the last few years at Rheinsberg were among his most productive as a composer. By 1738 Bielfeld, the visitor to Rheinsberg, was able to write that the Prince "had composed a number of sonatas himself."[45]

Concerning the age of the flute works, Philipp Spitta has given interesting proof that they were virtually finished by the time the Seven Years' War began. Before his proof can be properly understood, however, the manuscripts with which he worked must be discussed.

There exist only six original flute manuscripts, all sonatas, in Frederick's hand. The main sources of the King's sonatas and concertos are therefore not these originals, but are the manuscripts written by copyists and collected under single covers for Frederick's daily use at concerts. There are two identical books containing the sonatas and two others, also identical, containing the concertos. The reason for this duplication is apparent in the inscriptions on the covers: "*pour Potsdam*" and "*pour le nouveau Palais*" on the sonatas; "*pour Charlottenburg*" and "*pour Potsdam*" on the concertos. The sonatas are numbered, but they are mixed in with sonatas composed by Quantz, and a separate ac-

[43] *Ibid.*
[44] *Ibid.*, 48.
[45] Münnich, *"Friedrich der Grosse," Zeitschrift für Musik,* Vol. CIII (August, 1936), 914.

companying list (fortunately extant) designates the composer of each number. That is, numbers 88 through 105 are by Quantz, 106 through 141 are by the King, 142 is by Quantz, and so on. Although this system of numbering is confusing at first glance, in practice it had a logical reason: Frederick performed only his own and Quantz's flute compositions. Therefore by "mixing" them beforehand and playing them in rotation—as both Nicolai[46] and Burney[47] tell us he did—he was assured of giving equal attention to both of his favorite flute composers and of not favoring some works more than others. The numbering is truly chronological; this is indicated by Frederick's own notation, on Sonata 122, that this sonata is indeed the one hundred twenty-second composed for his collection.

Spitta's interesting deductions concerning the age of the sonatas[48] can now be understood:

(1) The sonata books contain the same pieces.

(2) The sonata book "*pour le nouveau Palais*" is significantly younger, by twenty or thirty years, than its mate "*pour Potsdam*," as is shown by the condition of the paper and the characteristics of the writing.

(3) The sonatas "*pour Potsdam*" were all copied (judging from the handwriting) at the same time, with the exception of four pieces which were copied contemporaneously with the sonatas "*pour le nouveau Palais*."

(4) But these four pieces were placed at the beginning and in the middle of the numerical series, not at the end. Furthermore, Frederick's very first contribution to the collection, number 106, was among these four. The obvious conclusion is that these four were replaced, due to excessive wear, rather than added as new compositions. This conclusion is sup-

---

[46] Spitta, "*Vorwort*," *Friedrichs des Grossens Musik Werke*, vii.
[47] Burney, *The Present State of Music*, II, 151.
[48] Spitta, "*Vorwort*," *Friedrichs des Grossens Musik Werke*, v–vi.

ported by the fact that the covers of this collection were replaced for the same reason. Consequently all the pieces in the collection *"pour Potsdam"*—every sonata composed by Frederick—can be said to have been put into this collection at approximately the same time.

(5) The *nouveau Palais* was built in 1769. Even if the collection of sonatas for use at this palace had not been assembled until, say, some five years later, this would still place the probable date of the older collection *"pour Potsdam"* before 1756, the first year of the Seven Years' War.

The deductions of Spitta concerning the age of the concertos[49] are simpler: Both collections of concertos are twenty to thirty years older than the sonatas *"pour le nouveau Palais,"* yet one of these collections of concertos was used in the *nouveau Palais* without change or addition; therefore the concertos also date from before 1756.

Additional evidence supports these conclusions regarding the dates of the flute works. One of the six sonatas in original manuscript was number 262 in the collections. In the same folio with this composition was found the march composed (according to its own superscription) in 1756. Since number 264 was Frederick's last sonata, Spitta concludes that the King's production of flute works was drawing to a close at about that time.[50] Another bit of information on this subject is given by Henri de Catt, the King's reader. He states in his memoirs of the years 1758–60 that one day during the first campaigns of the war Frederick told him that he had composed one hundred and twenty flute solos.[51] This is almost exactly the number of flute works attributed to him today.

[49] *Ibid.*
[50] *Ibid.*, viii–ix.
[51] Henri de Catt, *Frederick the Great, the Memoirs of his Reader, Henri de Catt,* trans. by F. S. Flint, II, 96.

The compositions which are specifically dated also fall within the period ending in 1756. Every fact connected with Frederick's production of original music shows, then, that this production had ceased by that date. It would be quite surprising if all of this evidence did not prove that the Seven Years' War brought the King's composing career to an end; for his interest in his artistic provinces gradually declined as it became more and more necessary to devote his energies to the task of saving Prussia. The decline was permanent; the rigors of the war ended both his desire to create music and his activities in making Berlin a center of musical culture.

In the foreword to his edition of the flute works, Spitta gives his primary reason for devoting time to the compositions of Frederick the Great: "It is and remains certain that his music gives the listener a profound insight into the inner life of a unique person. This fact is sufficient reason for publishing his compositions."[52] This is not just a recommendation of the historical value of Frederick's flute works; it is also a confession of their mediocrity. None of the King's contemporaries could sincerely consider his compositions great art, and no scholar has ever ventured to admire them for more than a moderate amount of musical worth.

Yet, Frederick's compositions show an understanding and a facility which is far above that of an amateur. Admiration for him on this basis was expressed by such men as Quantz, Fasch, Nicolai, Büsching, Zelter, and Rellstab.[53] It does not seem unreasonable to take their opinions at face value, considering the thoroughness of Frederick's training and the prolificacy of his compositions. His lessons in composition began when he was only eight years old (with Heyne) and continued throughout his composing career; and it is obvious that he possessed not only

[52] Spitta, *"Vorwort," Friedrichs des Grossens Musik Werke*, xiii.
[53] Thouret, *Friedrich der Grosse*, 138.

musical talent, but also great intelligence. The total weight of these evidences of his musical creativity brings one to the conclusion that his compositions, though not masterworks, must be worthy of study.

The first basis for criticism of the King's music is not the music itself, but the manner in which it was composed: Frederick "sketched" most of his works. Usually his sketching consisted of writing just melody and bass. Sometimes the melody was written and verbal directions were supplied for the composer who happened to be doing the "filling in." Only occasionally was every note composed by Frederick himself.

His detractors have made much of this apparent lack. Reichardt, who felt that Frederick should be considered no more than an amateur composer, describes the *"Königliche"* (inferring "amateurish") method of composition with relish:

> The King also composed, and his composing was certainly a kingly art. He wrote out the upper voice in notes and indicated with words what the bass or the other accompanying voices should do. Here the bass was to proceed in eighth-notes, here was a passage for violin alone, here all parts should be in unison, and so on. This musical sign language was usually transformed into music by Herr Agricola.[54]

This statement, written in 1791, is a misrepresentation of Frederick's ability as a composer, but it has been considered accurate for many years, being repeated almost verbatim in such sources as the musical dictionaries of Fétis and Scholes. Reichardt would like the reader to believe that the King invariably wrote only the melody. He states that Agricola, who was far from being a great composer, was Frederick's main assistant, forgetting the more important contributions of Quantz, Graun, and Benda. His pri-

[54] *"Musikalische Anekdoten," Musikalisches Kunstmagazin,* Vol. II (1791), 40.

mary misrepresentation, however, is his inference that the King needed assistance because of a lack of skill, whereas the real cause was insufficient time.

In order to save time, Schütz, Hasse, Graun, Heinichen, Handel and Beethoven—among others—often left the filling-in or the orchestration of their work to assistants; and even today, "sketching" is a fairly common practice. Frederick's own procedure is partially illustrated by a note in his own handwriting, written on his march in E flat, the melody and bass of which he had composed himself: "To Concertmaster Benda. No middle voices, please, except for a trumpet part—and have the music copied out. Frederick."[55]

Frederick's lessons in composition with Heyne had consisted of four-part settings of Psalm tunes and chorale melodies; strict counterpoint, using church modes (he writes of having been "plagued" by the "plagal modes");[56] and instruction in thorough bass.[57] In Ruppin and Rheinsberg he studied composition with K. H. Graun and did well enough to finish a *sinfonie* by 1735, which Graun corrected.[58] A later *sinfonie,* written in 1743 for strings, flutes, oboes, and horns,[59] was composed entirely by Frederick. He showed it to Quantz, who could find nothing to correct except a copying error in the bass part.[60] The six original flute manuscripts that are extant bear witness to the King's understanding of composition: all of the corrections— some of which consist of major changes, even alterations of entire movements—are in the handwriting of the composer. Quantz stated positively that Frederick had composed both melody and

---

[55] Thouret, *Friedrich der Grosse*, 176.
[56] Spitta, "*Vorwort,*" *Friedrichs des Grossens Musik Werke*, x.
[57] *Ibid.*
[58] *Ibid.*
[59] See notes 35 and 38 of this chapter.
[60] Spitta, "*Vorwort,*" *Friedrichs des Grossens Musik Werke*, x.

49

bass to every one of his sonatas;[61] this is certainly borne out by the extant manuscripts.

It is illogical to infer, in the face of all this evidence, that Frederick's "sign language" was used only because of a lack of ability on his part. When one considers what a typical day must have been like in the life of this busy monarch, it is surprising to find that he had time to compose at all. It is interesting to consider, too, what his compositions might have been like had he been able to compose at his leisure. Perhaps, in such a case, this statement by Nicolai would not be flattery: "Everyone who has seen the solos written by the King must agree that, on the whole, the harmonies of this 'dilettante' are better ordered than those of many of today's *Professori di Musica*."[62]

Even though Frederick composed only the melody and the bass (usually unfigured) for most of his flute pieces,[63] they comprise the most substantial portion of his compositions, in quality as well as in number. This is to be expected, since he had a thorough understanding of the flute and composed for it over a period of some twenty years. In the form and style of all his compositions for flute he is completely the submissive pupil of Quantz, who, in turn, takes as his models the sonatas of Tartini and the solo concertos of Vivaldi.

The King's sonatas follow their model (Tartini, through Quantz) precisely, with hardly a deviation. They are clearly homophonic.[64] The plan of their movements is almost always the same: slow–fast–very fast. Of the twenty-five sonatas edited by Spitta, twenty-four follow such schemes as adagio–allegro–presto, "cantabile"–allegro–presto, "amorevole"–allegro assai–presto, "grave ed affetuoso"–allegro ma non molto–tempo giusto,

---

[61] *Ibid.,* x–xi.

[62] *Ibid.,* xi.

[63] In the Spitta edition, which is the source for every one of Frederick's flute works mentioned here, the bass is realized by Paul Graf Waldersee.

[64] There is one exception: the last movement of Sonata II, which is

etc.[65] The exception, Sonata III, consists of four movements which merely make the speeding-up process more gradual: lento–allegretto–allegro assai–vivace assai. First movements are usually through-composed or in three-part (A B Á) form, beginning and ending in the tonic key and modulating during the middle of the movement to closely-related keys. Second and third movements are most often in simple binary form, with each section repeated and with key schemes according to a much-used plan (Fig. 3).

> Section A (repeated): begins in a major key, ends in the dominant of that key (or, begins in a minor key, ends in the relative major of that key)
> Section B (repeated): begins in the same key as the end of section A, ends in the same key as the beginning of section A.
> or, represented schematically:

A	B
I ————— V	V ————— I
or	
i ————— rel.	rel. ————— i
Major	Major

Fig. 3.—Usual formal plan for second and third movements of Frederick's sonatas.

Although the form of these sonatas is hardly unique, Frederick was quite able to use this form as an expressive musical vehicle. The slow movements afforded the most interesting glimpse into the personality of their composer. They are in-

fugal. Spitta surmises ("*Vorwort*," *Friedrichs des Grossens Musik Werke,* viii) that this sonata was probably written in 1747, the year of J. S. Bach's visit to Potsdam, and was influenced by Bach.

[65] Frederick often labeled the movements of his sonatas with adjectives indicating mood as well as tempo, in accordance with a rule stated by Quantz in the *Versuch,* 299, Schering edition.

variably suffused with feeling; they depict the sentimental Frederick who, in De Catt's memoirs, weeps when remembering his childhood, or when reading a scene from Racine, or when moved by the loyalty of his soldiers. It is easy to understand how, when he played one of these adagios, "his audience seldom listened without tears"; for the pathos they expressed was not yet worn out. The opening adagio of Sonata XIII (Spitta edition) (Fig. 4) is an average example.

F IG . 4.–Frederick II, Sonata No. XIII, first movement, measures 1–7.

In a few first movements Frederick gives himself a wider latitude of expression by resorting to instrumental recitative. Although this was something of an innovation at the time, the idea was not originally Frederick's; he had already seen an instrumental recitative in a clavier sonata by C. P. E. Bach.[66] Nevertheless, he uses it effectively, as in the opening movement of Sonata II (Fig. 5).

[66] Spitta, "*Vorwort*," *Friedrichs des Grossens Musik Werke*, xii–xiii. See the section on C. P. E. Bach in chapter IV.

Fig. 5.—Frederick II, Sonata No. II, first movement, measures
1–12.

One more example of a first movement might be pointed out
as being perhaps more elegant and less sentimental: that of
Sonata XVI (Fig. 6). It is a *Siciliano* (like the opening movements of Sonatas III and XXV); its simple, pastoral nature precludes any attempt at profundity.

Fig. 6.—Frederick II, Sonata No. XVI, first movement,
measures 1–4.

Although the faster movements often contain meaningless
passagework and hackneyed ideas, they do not permit too much
indulgence in tender emotions, and would probably be more
congenially accepted by modern listeners. The closing allegro

of Sonata XVII (Fig. 7), is a good example of this more straightforward aspect of the sonatas.

In most formal respects, the four flute concertos composed
by the King look very much like the concertos of Vivaldi. The
music of Vivaldi exerted a profound influence on Quantz, and
the majority of the rules for concerto composition which are
contained in Quantz's *Versuch* are obviously based on his study
of Vivaldi's solo concertos.[67] Therefore Frederick's concertos
are indirect imitations of those composed by the great Italian
master. They are homophonic throughout. In each of them, the
key is vigorously announced and emphasized in the opening
orchestral tutti. Throughout the first and last movement (always fast) there is the driving, mechanical rhythm typical of
the late Baroque concerto. In the slow movements the solo part
is given great expressive latitude, in the Vivaldi manner. Several
motives are present in every movement, although Frederick
always favors one or two of these. No such thing as theme development exists in any of the King's compositions. Key relationships are quite conservative: The beginning and end of every
movement in Concertos I and II is in G Major; in Concerto III
(in C Major) there is a modest excursion to the relative minor as
the basic key of the second movement; and the second movement of Concerto IV (in D Major) goes unusually far in having

[67] See the section on Quantz in chapter IV.

F<small>IG</small>. 7—Frederick II, Sonata No. XVII, last movement, measures 1–27.

its beginning and ending in the dominant key. The modulations within the body of each movement are equally conservative. Solo and tutti passages alternate in prescribed order in every movement. In obedience to Quantz's rules, Frederick's *ritornelli* are not always scored for the orchestra but are occasionally given to the solo flute for additional interest.

It is interesting to compare the solo concertos of Vivaldi with those of Frederick. For Vivaldi, the concerto form was a pattern to be richly decked in musical ideas, to be changed or even ignored if necessary. For Frederick—and Quantz—it was an edict handed down from a greater master, to be obeyed because it guaranteed not only an easy path to follow, but also easy originality. Where Vivaldi is impulsive, Frederick is careful; where the construction of a Vivaldi allegro is determined by the breathless pace of irresistible musical invention, an allegro by Frederick is studied, painstaking and "correct." Vivaldi's concertos often defy systematization of the terms "solo," "tutti," and even "solo concerto"; Frederick's can be diagrammed very conveniently. In short, the concertos—like the sonatas—suffer from schematism.

Some of the best writing of the four concertos is contained in Concerto III (Spitta edition). It begins with a bustling orchestral tutti (Fig. 8).

Fig. 8.—Frederick II, Concerto No. III, first movement, measures 1–8.

This opening tutti is followed eventually with the first entrance of the solo flute (Fig. 9).

Fig. 9.—Frederick II, Concerto No. III, first movement, measures 21–24.

After another tutti announcement of the opening theme, a new motive, which is to be the basis of a long sequence, is brought in by the flute (Fig. 10). This figure, the theme of the opening tutti, and the first solo theme are the three main ideas of the first movement.

Fig. 10.—Frederick II, Concerto No. III, first movement, measure 51.

The second movement (Fig. 11) is quite short in comparison with the other two, and consists of nothing more than free *affetuoso* wanderings of the flute against an orchestral accompaniment which is similar throughout to these opening measures.

Fig. 11.—Frederick II, Concerto No. III, second movement, measures 1–2.

The opening tutti of the final allegro (Fig. 12) is characterized by the use of Lombardic rhythm (), a fairly com-

59

FIG. 12.—Frederick II, Concerto No. III, last movement, measures 1–9.

mon trait of eighteenth-century German composers. Half a dozen motives are contained in this movement, but the opening tutti theme and two themes heard in the solo are its main materials. The first of the two solo themes is shown in Fig. 13.

FIG. 13.—Frederick II, Concerto No. III, last movement, measures 48–52.

The second solo theme, if it can be called a theme, is only a sequential elaboration of a running pattern (Fig. 14).

Fɪɢ. 14.—Frederick II, Concerto No. III, last movement, measures 80–83.

In order of interest, Frederick's overture to the *Serenata* of 1747 does not rank far behind the flute works. This little *pasticcio* was first performed on the occasion of Sophie Dorothea's arrival in Charlottenburg on August 4 of that year. Schmid's publication of its overture was apparently not in vain, for the entire work was eventually publicized rather widely. *Grove's Dictionary* supplies us with an interesting list of its performances in England and America. It was staged four times, together with Handel's *Alexander's Feast*, at the little Haymarket Theatre in London during April of 1755. Three performances were given at the Great Room on Dean Street in Soho: on February 2, 1756, with Handel's *Acis and Galatea;* on March 16, 1756, again with Handel's *Alexander's Feast* (at Handel's request); and once more on February 16, 1760. On October 27, 1890, under the title "Moltke-Feier," it was performed at the Metropolitan Opera in New York.[68]

The first and last movements of this overture are orchestrated

[68] Franz Gehring and Alfred Loewenberg, "Frederick II," *Grove's Dictionary of Music and Musicians*, Vol. III.

for strings (only a quartet was used in the original performance), two oboes, and two horns; the slow movement is written for two flutes and two violins. The beginning of the first movement[69] is shown in Fig. 15.

Fig. 15.—Frederick II, Overture to the *Serenta* of 1747, first movement, measures 1–6 (piano reduction).

Frederick's marches have always been the best-known of all his compositions, since they are closely connected with his accomplishments as a great general and are a part of German tradition. The King had a strong interest in the value of military music. According to a popular anecdote, he once asked one of his officers, at the conclusion of a battle, to name the man who

[69] Cited in Thouret, *Friedrich der Grosse*, 159–61.

he thought had behaved most bravely. The officer's answer was, of course, "Your Majesty." Frederick said, "You are wrong. It was a fife player whom I saw in the front lines twenty times and who never stopped his tootling."[70]

It is easy to see that the intrinsic musical value of the marches is not the reason for their popularity. Their style is pedantic. They were meant to be performed in the traditional style of Prussian infantry music, with the melody played by an oboe, the bass played by a bassoon, and filling-in (optional) accomplished by a trumpet. The usual tempo for these marches was about half the speed of modern march tempo: seventy-two steps per minute.[71]

Of the marches attributed to Frederick, his authorship of the one in E flat is most solidly proved. This march has been used traditionally by the *Alexander-Regiment* in Berlin and the *Gardehusaren* in Potsdam.[72] It is quoted here (Fig. 16) in its en-

[70] Thouret, *Friedrich der Grosse*, 175–76.

[71] *Ibid.*, 176–77.

[72] An acquaintance of the author, whose home is in Prussia, recalls hearing her father whistle this march. As a boy he had been a student at the military academy in Potsdam.

FIG. 16.—Frederick II, March in E flat.

tirety,[73] as the King composed it (the trumpet part added by Fasch is lost).

Frederick was most guilty of "sketchiness" in the case of his opera arias. Since, in most of them, he composed only the melody, even Thouret, Frederick's chief musical apologist, must admit that the arias "can not be considered as fully representa-

[73] Cited in Thouret, *Friedrich der Grosse*, 178–79.

tive of the King's composing ability."[74] They do provide examples, however, of one of his best characteristics as a composer:
melodic inventiveness. The ability to create good melody is
peculiarly independent of formal training, and is usually indicative of a composer's talent, whether that talent be cultivated
or latent. Frederick's ability as a melodist might therefore be
taken as further evidence that his capacities in composition
were never fully realized. One of his arias in *Demofoonte*, "*Non
odi consiglio*" (Fig. 17), is a particularly good example.[75]

FIG. 17.—Frederick II, Aria "*Non odi consiglio*," from *Demofoonte*, measures 1–32 (melody only).

[74] *Friedrich der Grosse*, 143.
[75] Cited in Thouret, *Friedrich der Grosse*, 148–49.

Libretti

Frederick's libretti must be mentioned along with his musical compositions, for they show another aspect of his creative self and give further insight into his actions as a patron. Participation in the creation of opera texts gave the King expression for both his literary and musical talents. Since opera was such a natural artistic outlet for him, and since the most spectacular results of his patronage took place in the field of opera, it is probable that both the number and quality of his libretti would have been much greater if his reign had been less arduous.

The number of libretti actually produced by Frederick is almost as indefinite as the number of his musical compositions. This is caused by the fact that the amount of his participation in writing different libretti varied from merely nagging his librettists to being personally responsible for the entire production. His authorship of the libretti for Graun's *Sulla* (1753) and *Montezuma* (1755) is positively established. That is, he composed the complete texts for these operas in French prose, and had them translated into Italian verse by his court poet, Tagliazucchi.[76] For the operas *I fratelli nemici* (1756) and *Merope* (1756), both also composed by Graun, Frederick supplied less complete texts, which Tagliazucchi completed and translated into Italian verse. Only sketches of the plots were supplied for *Coriolano* (1749) by Graun and *Il tempio d'amore* (1755) by Agricola. From these sketches, Villati (another poet of his court) composed the text for *Coriolano* and Tagliazucchi the text for *Il tempio d'amore*. It is possible, but unproved, that Frederick had a hand in Villati's adaptation of *Ifigenia in Aulide*, by Racine; this libretto was set to music by Graun in 1748. The King's participation in Graun's opera *Fetonte* (1750) is dubious, though it

[76] The work of Frederick's librettists is discussed on pp. 152–53.

was once thought that he was responsible for at least part of its libretto (an adaptation by Villati of a Quinault libretto).

There are two complete libretti, then, which are unquestionably Frederick's, at least in their untranslated state: *Sulla* and *Montezuma*.[77] Of these two, *Montezuma* has had the widest following. It is an important work in the history of eighteenth-century German opera because it represents the best artistic efforts of both Graun and Frederick, and because it contains some attempt at reform. In this opera, for once, the King and his *Kapellmeister* are not reactionary; for a short time they are among the avant-garde. *Montezuma* is progressive in two respects: it substitutes the cavatina for the much-abused *da capo* aria, and it deals with a fairly modern subject instead of one from antiquity.

The cavatinas in *Montezuma* (Fig. 18) have a simple form and key scheme.

Section A: begins in the tonic key, ends in
   the dominant key
Section B: begins in the dominant key, ends
   in the tonic key
   Or, represented schematically:

$$
\begin{array}{cccc}
\text{A} & & \text{B} & \\
\text{I} & \text{V} & \text{V} & \text{I}
\end{array}
$$

FIG. 18.—Form and key scheme of cavatinas from *Montezuma*.

There are no repetitions and no opportunities for improvisation by the singer. The use of this form in the opera was brought about by close co-operation between Frederick and Graun—or perhaps it would be better to say that Graun did as he was told,

[77] Only the poetry for these is extant, not the original prose.

because Frederick takes most of the credit for the innovation. Following are extracts from letters which he wrote to Wilhelmina during his work on the libretto:

> March 10, 1754: I have been amusing myself by writing an opera, which I shall take the liberty of sending to you when it has been corrected.[78]

> April 16, 1754: I take the liberty of placing at your feet a Mexican who is not yet completely educated. I have taught him to speak French; now he must learn Italian. But before putting him to all this trouble, I beg you to tell me frankly how you feel about him, and whether you think he is worth the effort. Most of the arias are to be sung without repeats; there are to be only two arias for the Emperor and two for Eupaforice. I do not know what you will think of the whole ensemble, the succession of scenes, the dialogue, the idea which I am trying to express; but nothing is pressing me now, and I can easily change anything you might find to correct. It will be easy to judge the effect which this spectacle can produce. You have an admirable French troupe, and can have them go through it in your room; all that is necessary is to have each one read his part.[79]

> May 4, 1754: I am charmed to hear that you would be pleased with my opera. As for cavatinas, I have seen some by Hasse which are infinitely prettier than [*da capo*] arias, and which are quickly performed. Repeats are not worthwhile unless a singer really knows how to vary the music; but in any case I consider it an abuse to repeat the same thing four times.[80]

November 21, 1754: I have listened to the rehearsal of

[78] Frederick the Great, *Oeuvres de Frédéric le Grand*, ed. by Preuss, Vol. XXVII, Bk. 1, 241.
[79] *Ibid.*, 241–42.
[80] *Ibid.*, 243.

Montezuma and have put the performers through their paces according to the real meaning of the work. I believe this opera will please you. Graun has created a masterpiece; it is all in cavatinas.[81]

Frederick describes himself as perhaps more of a reformer than he actually was, and does an injustice to his composer by inferring that Hasse provided the model cavatinas. Graun had already used this form in *Artaserse* (1743), *Europa galante* (1748), and *Angelica e Medoro* (1749). Moreover, the *da capo* aria had begun to decline in Germany by the 1730's, so any mid-eighteenth-century idea of doing away with it could not be wholly original. Finally, the general cause of reform espoused by Gluck had its beginnings in Vienna in 1752, and Frederick could easily have borrowed some of his ideas of reform from there. But Frederick must be given credit for the idea of writing an entire opera in cavatinas. After *Montezuma*, Graun used the cavatina in all of his operas. Frederick's influence on him is well illustrated in Graun's *Semiramide*, which was begun at about the same time Frederick started his work on the libretto of *Montezuma:* the first act of *Semiramide* uses *da capo* arias exclusively, the second act contains two cavatinas, and the third act is made up entirely of cavatinas.

Although the plot of *Montezuma* is partially modeled after Voltaire's *Alzire*, it is honestly a credit to Frederick. The characters are well defined and quite unlike the stock figures of most *opera seria,* and there is a general "un-Italian" quality about the work. In addition, Frederick's heart is in the story, because it is eloquently anti-Christian: The conquering Cortez is a religious bigot who intends to make Christians of the Mexicans at any price. The nobility of their civilization and their happiness in it serve only to intensify his rage against them. In the

[81] *Ibid.,* 251–52.

name of Christianity, then, he destroys Mexico. Montezuma is a great king who prefers to die rather than accept beliefs which seem unnatural to him. Historical truth was not Frederick's primary concern. This is evident in his letter to Count Francesco Algarotti, written in October of 1753, just as he was getting into serious work on the libretto:

> If your operas [in Italy] are poor, you will find a new one here which will perhaps not surpass them. It is called *Montezuma*. I chose this subject, and I am adapting it at present. You know, of course, that I shall be on the side of Montezuma, that Cortez will be the tyrant, and that as a result a few telling remarks can be made, even in music, against the barbarousness of the Christian religion. But I forget that you are in a country of inquisition; I ask you to accept my apology, and I hope that you will soon return to an heretical country where even the opera serves to reform customs and destroy superstitions.[82]

Thouret, the eulogist, feels that the King's music is more valuable than his poetic writings, in spite of the fact that Frederick himself placed the higher value on his literary works.[83] Moser, a more disinterested scholar, asserts that the libretti are more valuable than the music because of their progressiveness.[84] If one considers Frederick's influence as a patron more important than his own artistic productions, the literary and musical sides of his creative life are viewed merely as background material; for it is certain that while his compositions of whatever kind are forgotten, the mark of his patronage is indelible.

[82] *Ibid.*, XVIII, 90.
[83] *Friedrich der Grosse*, 140–41.
[84] *Geschichte der Deutschen Musik*, II, 270.

MUSICAL TASTE

The personal taste of a great patron is often the most important single influence on the creations of his artists, sometimes more important than the tastes of the artists themselves. This was particularly true of Frederick; the whole foundation of Berlin's musical life during the mid-eighteenth century rested tenuously upon his royal whims. Compared to the crucial factor of Frederick's likes and dislikes, his abilities as a composer and performer are almost inconsequential (yet it is hardly likely, of course, that he would have taken such a personal and powerful interest in musical matters if he had not considered himself qualified, as a producing musician, to do so).

Frederick's musical preferences can be simply stated. His taste in opera was for the *opera seria* of Hasse and Graun, two of the most thoroughly Italianized German composers of the eighteenth century; and the only instrumental music for which he really cared was that which included a flute part and was composed either by himself or Quantz. He had no appreciable desire to hear sacred music, songs not connected with opera, or solo keyboard performance. Like most composers of his period, he thought of counterpoint as a worn-out, though venerable, tool of musical ages long dead, concurring with Voltaire (who knew almost nothing about music) in the opinion that all contrapuntal music fell under the heading of "plainchant."[85] His distaste for old music, though, did not guarantee that he would like new music. In spite of his preference for cavatinas over *da capo* arias and his casual interest in the aesthetics of opera, he was not really interested in the operas of reformers like Gluck; and he called the symphonies of Haydn "a shindy that flays the ears."[86] In fact, every development which progressed beyond the music

[85] Thouret, *Friedrich der Grosse*, 31–32.
[86] Gaxotte, *Frederick the Great*, 379.

of Graun, Hasse, or Quantz was, according to Frederick, a symptom of artistic decay.

The narrow musical path followed by the King did occasionally become wide enough to touch other composers. During the summers, while no *opera seria* were playing at the opera house, Frederick had an occasional *Schäferspiel* or *intermezzo* performed in one of the palace theaters. He was not totally unaware of the achievements of his cembalist, C. P. E. Bach; his chamber musicians, Franz Benda and J. G. Graun; and his last *Kapellmeister*, J. F. Reichardt. He allowed some performances of the music of Fasch, Agricola, Nichelmann and his other musical servants. However, the summer *intermezzi* and *Schäferspiele* never reached the level of full-scale *opera buffa;* the King never realized that C. P. E. Bach was revolutionizing keyboard technique and composing sonatas and symphonies which were to be models for other composers; he did not see in Franz Benda the founder of a great school of violin playing; the *Singspiele* and the *Lieder* of Reichardt escaped his notice completely.

The King's attitude toward music written before his time is shown in a rather pompous and patronizing letter to Prince William of Orange, October 19, 1737:

> Please give my highest regards to your good wife. She does me too much honor in wanting to know my thoughts on the operas of Handel. I am infinitely obligated for her attention, but I beg you to tell her that the beautiful days of Handel have passed; their genius is exhausted; their taste is foreign. Let me know if you have a singer and what kind of voice he has. I will send you some songs by my composer, which I hope will satisfy your wife's musical taste.[87]

Frederick's opposition to music written after the mid-eight-

[87] Carl H. Mennicke, *Hasse und die Brüder Graun als Symphoniker*, 469.

eenth century is expressed more strongly, in a letter to Maria
Anthony of Saxony (January, 1777):

> . . . the public here is amusing itself with Hasse's opera
> *Cleofide,* which has returned to the theaters. Thus the good
> things remain with us; if we have heard them in other times,
> we like always to hear them again. But new music, on the
> other hand, has degenerated to mere noise, bludgeoning our
> ears rather than caressing them. Noble song is lost to this
> generation. In order to find it again, we must return to Vinci,
> Hasse and Graun.[88]

The composers for the Berlin Opera during Frederick's
reign were exclusively German. The style in which they composed for the Opera was exclusively Italian, according to the
taste of the times. The dancers (and, incidentally, the actors of
the *Schauspiel*) were mostly French; the singers were almost all
Italian. In Frederick's opinion, "Only the French know how to
create comedy, only the Italians can sing, and only the Germans can compose."[89] On the latter point the Berlin Opera
diverged from general practice. Most of the musical centers of
Germany at that time were conquered by Italian composers as
well as performers; and it is to Frederick's credit that, in nationality at least, the composers of his "serious" music were all
Germans. Although he admitted to a liking for the operas of the
Neapolitan dramatic composer, Leonardo Vinci (whom both
Hasse and Graun imitated), he was opposed in principle to the
idea that Italians could compose as well as sing. He grudgingly
called opera composed by Italians "dumb stuff—pleasing to the
ears, though, when sung well."[90] He had a similar distrust for

---

[88] Frederick the Great, *Oeuvres de Frédéric le Grand,* ed. by Preuss,
XXIV, 292.
[89] Kothe, *Friedrich der Grosse als Musiker,* 17.
[90] R. Batka, *"Friedrich II als Musiker,"* Der *Kunstwart,* Vol. XXV
(January 24, 1912), 132.

French music, which he considered "childish,"[91] and he expressed his aversion to it by ordering Graun to stop composing French overtures.[92]

The petrifaction of Frederick's taste was a gradual process, but the process began very early in his life. In a letter to Wilhelmina dated March 2, 1747, he appears to be the fairest and most intelligent of patrons:

> . . . I must tell you that I have heard the arias of *Fêtes Galantes*, which are charming . . . a sculptor from Paris will soon be with us . . . I am still waiting for the arrival of a painter of no mean talent. I pass my life thus, dividing my time between the arts, having a taste for all and excluding none.[93]

Yet even by 1747 the aesthetic ideals which he would never forsake were already solidly formed. He distinguished between "useful" arts and arts "for pleasure." Philosophy, history, and languages came under the first heading; music and the theater under the second.[94] Although he felt that the Opera was culturally beneficial to his subjects, his own purpose in pursuing music was for the relaxation and entertainment it afforded. In order to keep his desire for entertainment from interfering with duties of state, Frederick set aside an inviolable period of time each day for attending to essentials.[95]

The King demanded that music have three attributes: singable and interesting melody, deep feeling, and correctness. These standards are typically *Berlinische;* Frederick was only voicing

[91] *Ibid.*
[92] See the section on Graun in chapter IV.
[93] Frederick the Great, *Oeuvres de Frédéric le Grand,* ed. by Preuss, Vol. XXVII, Bk. 1, 156.
[94] Becker, *"Friedrich II," Die Musik in Geschichte und Gegenwart,* Vol. IV.
[95] *Ibid.*

the most commonly held opinions of his fellow musicians. He felt that the Italians were unsurpassable in their ability to write singable melody, but were unable to match the Germans in portraying deep feeling because of too much emphasis on virtuosity.[96] In order to meet Frederick's requirement for "correctness," music needed to be correct in Teutonic fashion: That is, it had to be the product of a learned mind, containing intellectual as well as emotional interest. Two of his own statements illustrate his adherence to this maxim: "I am always pleased to see the creative activity of intellect expressed in music."[97] "When I hear beautiful music by a learned composer, it is as pleasing to me as hearing learned discourse at the dinner table."[98] In fairness to the King, this desire for learnedness in music should be cited as one musical standard which he did not import from Italy. However, he achieved this "learned" quality in an ironic fashion: by having his Italian music composed by Germans.

Frederick's disavowal of Christianity was, no doubt, the main reason for his dislike of sacred music; and his coolness toward polyphonic music, sacred or secular, was partly due to its association with the church. He probably never heard a cantata of J. S. Bach. If he had been able to listen to Bach's music as an unprejudiced musician, he could not have failed to find it at least agreeable. But the very essence of Protestant Christianity was contained in the sacred works of Bach; they expressed the apotheosis of a spirit which was anathema to Frederick. The King considered Bach's chorales, notably *"Nun ruhen alle Wälder,"* to be "dumb stuff."[99] Since he was much too musical to eschew this chorale on an artistic basis (Mozart once said

[96] Thouret, *Friedrich der Grosse*, 34.
[97] Batka, *"Friedrich II als Musiker,"* Der Kunstwart, Vol. XXV (January 24, 1912), 132.
[98] *Ibid.*
[99] Thouret, *Friedrich der Grosse*, 29.

that he wished he had composed it),[100] the natural conclusion is that he rejected it not as music, but as religion.[101]

As a performer and composer, Frederick was able to be specific about some of the technical standards of opera which he expected his musicians to follow: There should be a variety of keys and moods in successive arias; theater music should avoid the minor key except when portraying tragic or pathetic circumstances, because its basic purpose is to be cheerful and agreeable; in the recitative there should be many, varied, and skillful modulations; in each opera there should be at least one great recitative which is accompanied by full orchestra. Instrumental accompaniments should be clear and not overshadow the voice; in final sections there should be a good deal of unison writing in order that the close of the piece be strong.[102]

This list of standards resulted from the thinking of an intelligent musician. If Frederick had been able to let his musical ideals grow naturally, these well thought-out expressions of his taste would perhaps have developed in tempo with the times; but the strenuous duties of his reign and the Seven Years' War never permitted his musical fancy to roam past the boundaries imposed by the music of Quantz, Hasse and Graun. When the seven years of fearful battle for the existence of his country had ended, Frederick returned to Potsdam a quite different patron. He had lost his former enthusiasm for the opera, the theater, and the evening concerts. During the last years of his life the artistic institutions which he had fostered were no more than

---

[100] *Ibid.*

[101] Frederick forbade the playing of religious music on the tower carillons of the churches of Berlin and Potsdam, although he was very much interested in the carillons and similar instruments from a musical point of view. Cf. Ernst Simon, *"Friedrich der Grosse und die Mechanischen Musikinstrumente," Zeitschrift für Instrumentenbau,* Vol. XXXII (April 11, 1912), 743–46.

[102] Adolph Kohut, *"Johann Friedrich Reichardt," Neue Musikzeitung,* Vol. XXIV (November 27, 1903–January 8, 1904), 6.

an oppressive burden to him, maintained only because he had committed himself to their support during his youth.

Because Frederick's interest in all music declined along with his performing ability, Burney was at least partially justified in saying that this was "proof that his Majesty's chief pleasure in the art was derived from his own performance."[103] The King's taste was similarly frozen regarding other arts. He would have nothing to do with Goethe, whose poems were, in his opinion, "disgusting platitudes."[104] The French dancers who had given him such pleasure in earlier years eventually irritated him with their "twitching."[105] In constructing his Neue Palais and later buildings he remained faithful to the same rococo style which he had liked when he was twenty.

Many people of intelligence agreed at least partially with Frederick's musical opinions. For example, J. F. Reichardt expressed, for a while, the politically advantageous belief that the King was a bulwark protecting good music, "which by him alone was preserved in the state of its greatest blossoming. . . ."[106] (Reichardt changed his opinion not long thereafter.) Thouret hesitates to make any unfavorable statement about the King's musical taste. As he puts it, Frederick remained "true to old music."[107] He is quite fair, however, in pointing out that Frederick's adherence to the flute music composed by himself or Quantz was largely because there was so little other solo literature for the transverse flute at the time. Thouret also asks a provocative question: Why should the King not be allowed to follow his own preferences in musical matters?[108]

[103] A General History of Music, II, 962.
[104] Gaxotte, Frederick the Great, 379.
[105] Batka, "Friedrich II als Musiker," Der Kunstwart, Vol. XXV (January 24, 1912), 132.
[106] Witt, "Der königliche Musikus," Allgemeine Musikzeitung, Vol. LXIII (August 21, 1936), 511.
[107] Thouret, Friedrich der Grosse, 192.
[108] Ibid., 106. See the section on Quantz in chapter IV.

Perhaps the most devastating single opinion of Frederick's musical taste is given by Burney in his *Present State of Music in Germany*, a fascinating account of his visits to the various musical capitals of that country. Although Burney's summing up of music in Berlin is characteristically opinionated (especially concerning contrapuntal music, which he never hesitates to condemn), it shows remarkable perspicacity on the part of its author:

It was not at first my intention to detain my reader so long in Berlin, and its environs; but the musical performances in his Prussian majesty's dominions, have been so much celebrated during his reign, that they merited a particular investigation; it is now, however, time to sum up the evidence, and it would be the highest injustice to deny, that Berlin has long had, and still has, a great number of *individuals* among the musical professors, whose abilities are great and striking; but with respect to the *general* and *national* style of composition and performance, it seems at present, to be so much formed upon *one model*, that it precludes all invention and genius. Perhaps, it would be equally rational to suppose, that the blood of a Quantz or a Graun, if injected into the veins of another composer, would circulate better than his own, as to imagine, that *their* ideas and thoughts, when he has adopted them, will suit him better than those which he has received from nature.

Of all the musicians who have been in the service of Prussia, for more than thirty years, Carl P. E. Bach, and Francis [Franz] Benda, have, perhaps, been the only two, who dared to have a style of their own; the rest are imitators; even Quantz and Graun, who have been so much imitated, formed themselves upon the works of Vinci and Vivaldi. M. Quantz is an intelligent man, and talks well concerning music; but talking and composing are different things; when he wrote his book, more than twenty years ago, his opinions were enlarged and liberal, which is not the case at present; and Graun's compositions of thirty years ago, were elegant and simple, as he was among the first Germans to quit fugue and laboured contrivances; and to allow, that such a thing as melody existed, which harmony should support, not suffocate; but though the world is ever rolling on, most of the Berlin musicians, defeating its motion, have long contrived to stand still.

Upon the whole, my expectations from Berlin were not quite answered, as I did not find that the style of composition, or manner of execution, to which his Prussian majesty has attached himself, fulfilled my ideas of perfection. Here, as elsewhere, I speak according to my own feelings: however, it would be presumption in me to oppose my single judgment to that of so enlightened a prince; if, luckily, mine were not the opinion of the greatest part of Europe; for should it be allowed, that his Prussian majesty has fixed upon the Augustan age of music, it does not appear that he has placed his favour upon the best composers of that age. Vinci, Pergolese, Leo, Feo, Handel, and many others, who flourished in the best times of Graun and Quantz, I think superiour to them in taste and genius. Of his majesty's two favourites, the one is languid, and the other frequently common and insipid,—and yet, their names are *religion* at Berlin, and more sworn by, than those of Luther and Calvin.

There are, however, schisms in this city, as elsewhere; but heretics are obliged to keep their opinions to themselves, while those of the establishment may speak out: for though a universal toleration prevails here, as to different sects of Christians, yet, in music, whoever dares to profess any other tenets than those of Graun and Quantz, is sure to be persecuted.

Hence, the music of this country is more truly German than that of any other part of the empire; for though there are constantly Italian operas here, in carnival time, his Prussian majesty will suffer none to be performed but those of

Graun, Agricola, or Hasse, and of this last, and best, but very few. And, in the opera house, as in the field, his majesty is such a rigid disciplinarian, that if a mistake is made in a single movement or evolution, he immediately marks, and rebukes the offender; and if any of his Italian troops dare to deviate from strict discipline, by adding, altering, or diminishing a single passage in the parts they have to perform, an order is sent, *de par le Roi,* for them to adhere strictly to the notes written by the composer, at their peril. This, when compositions are good, and a singer is licentious, may be an excellent method; but certainly shuts out all taste and refinement. So that music is truly stationary in this country, his majesty allowing no more liberty in that, than he does in civil matters of government: not contented with being sole monarch of the lives, fortunes, and business of his subjects, he even prescribes rules to their most innocent pleasures.[109]

[109] Vol. II, 230–35.

III

OPERA AND INSTRUMENTAL MUSIC

UNDER FREDERICK'S PATRONAGE

F REDERICK'S MUSICAL PATRONAGE can be conveniently divided into three major periods: 1732 to 1740, when he fostered only instrumental music; 1740 to 1756, the years during which his Berlin Opera blossomed and flourished; and 1763 to 1786, the period during which all his musical establishments declined. (From 1756 to 1763 the Seven Years' War caused such a curtailment of royal musical life that these years represent a virtual interruption of patronage.) During the half-century of Frederick's support and direction of music in Berlin, his influence was exerted chiefly through two organizations: his court orchestra and his opera company. These two organizations merged when the *Hofkapelle* was used as the basis of the opera orchestra, but the court instrumentalists never lost their separate identity. In this section the orchestra and the opera will be discussed together, according to the chronology of the three periods outlined above. However, since Frederick's most striking single act of patronage was his creation of the Berlin Opera, it will first be necessary, in order that the importance of this achievement be fully understood, to describe the state of opera in Berlin during the years preceding his accession in 1740.

As early as the end of the sixteenth century, various forms of *Musikalisches Schauspiel* were being performed in the Berlin court. Although these were not true operas, they show that interest in dramatic-musical forms existed in Berlin from the earliest years of opera. The first record of hired singers is from 1616, during which year one Bernardo Pasquino Grassi from Mantua and a Giovanni Alberto Maglio from Florence were engaged as singers at Berlin.[1] The next evidence of "operatic" activity is not until 1696: a performance of a musical allegory entitled *Florens Frühlingsfest*. In this performance, the part of Cupid was sung and danced by none other than Frederick William (the "barracks king," father of Frederick the Great), as Crown Prince![2]

The first production in Berlin of what might be called real opera was that of *La festa del Hymeneo* on June 1, 1700. The music for this work was composed by Attilio Ariosti (court composer at Berlin from 1679 to 1703) and Carl Friedrich Rieck, chamber musician of the court. The text, in Italian, is by the Abbot Mauro. This performance was occasioned by the marriage of the Princess of Brandenburg, Louise Dorothea Sophie, with the Crown Prince of Hesse-Cassel. Writing in 1852, Louis

---

[1] Louis Schneider, *Geschichte der Oper und des Königlichen Opernhauses in Berlin*, 1.
[2] *Ibid.*, 3.

82

Schneider gives his opinion of this work, which was still in the Berlin *Königliche Bibliothek* at the time of his writing, and which he inspected: "This was an opera in the fullest sense of the term. Naturally, it was in the odd, imperfect form of its time; but not even the productions of the Hamburg or Dresden Operas could be considered more highly developed."[3] The "opera house" for this performance was a theater built over the King's stable. This theater, known as *"der Stallplatz,"* was last used as such in 1708. When Frederick William came to power he changed it, appropriately, into an army supply depot; and it was completely dismantled when Frederick II built his first palace theater.[4]

Schneider noted that the score of *La festa del Hymeneo* requires a dancing company of forty (directed by one Desnoyers) as well as enough machinery (built by Thomas Giusti) to make haloed angels fly—all of which must have required a sizable theater. The dancers consisted largely of court personnel, as in a masque; among them was the unwilling Crown Prince, Frederick William. Toward the end of the marriage celebration the entire court traveled to Oranienburg, where another, smaller, opera was given. This opera was in German (a contemporary report describes it as being in *"der eigenen Muttersprache"*), and was one of the very first in that language to be performed in Germany. Unfortunately, it was lost, and the names of its composer and librettist are not known.[5]

Frederick I did not spare expense in celebrating the marriage of his daughter: on June 6 one more opera was given, this time at Charlottenburg. This final flourish, entitled *der bestrafte Hochmuth des Schäfers Atis*, was the work of Ariosti and Mauro. There was dancing between the three acts and at the

3 *Ibid.,* 4.
4 *Ibid.,* 5.
5 *Ibid.,* 4–10.

end of this work, but the dancing was accomplished by professionals, and for once Prince Frederick William was spared.[6] Perhaps the unwilling boyhood performances by the father of Frederick the Great played a part in making him despise the arts so thoroughly. Once, at the command of his mother, he was scheduled to play the part of a juggler and clown in a court performance at Charlottenburg. After he had stepped upon the stage—before the whole court—he suddenly decided he had had enough, tore his costume to shreds, dashed out of the theater, and hid himself.[7]

In 1701 Berlin was a "tour stop" for a group of Hamburg artists, who performed three ballets by Reinhard Keiser and Nothnagel: *Endymion, Phaeton,* and *Orpheus.*[8] On July 12 of the same year another three-act work by Ariosti was given at the Charlottenburg palace: *La fede ne' tradimenti* (with a text by G. Gigli which had been composed in 1689). The music for this opera is lost.[9] In July, 1702 the birthday of Frederick I was commemorated with a one-act "*Schauspiel mit Gesang und untermischten Tänzen*," entitled *Polifemo.* The dialogue of this little work is in French and the songs are in Italian; the authors of the text are not known. The music was created jointly by Ariosti and the great Giovanni Battista Bononcini. (Bononcini was brought to Berlin for a short time, from 1703 to 1705, by Queen Sophie Charlotte.) Sophie Charlotte, for whom Charlottenburg is named, played the cembalo part for this musical production.[10]

It was during the first years of the eighteenth century that private investors began to promote public opera and drama per-

---

[6] *Ibid.,* 11–12.
[7] *Ibid.,* 12.
[8] *Ibid.,* 13–14.
[9] Alfred Loewenberg, *Annals of Opera,* 54.
[10] This work was broadcast from Berlin on August 6, 1937. Cf. Loewenberg, *Annals,* 54.

formances along the *Poststrasse*. (One of the most industrious entrepreneurs on this street of theaters was Herr Hessig, whose main occupation was as personal servant to Frederick I and who was later *Burgermeister* of Berlin.) The Protestant church objected strongly to worldly amusement, and since the public theaters did not enjoy the immunity of royalty they were the target of bitter attacks by the clergy. One of the tracts published by the church affords interesting information on what was considered objectionable, as well as the subject matter of the operas:

> . . . in our opera houses and on our stages, heathenism advances and Christendom retreats. . . . In this Satan's chapel built onto God's church, where Jehovah is mentioned in disgusting songs and Beelzebub offers every conceivable joy and gratification, (1) the singers and players derive a pagan theology from Greek and Latin fables and a philosophy from the Prodigal Son's way of living; (2) effeminate foreigners representing sirens sing lustful Ovidian Venus-songs; (3) the merrymakers with fiddles and fifes make licentious music, continuing in the dissoluteness of Adam; (4) Sylvester cavorts around with his Herodias sister and Harlequin does a wanton French dance. . . .[11]

As a result of this opposition by the clergy, the first attempts at giving opera performances for paid admission were a failure. Not until the more liberal reign of Frederick the Great were the promoters of opera for the Berlin public successful.

In early 1705 the Queen died; late in the same year the princess who had been married in 1700 died also. For almost two years there were no performances in Berlin; but in December, 1706, when Frederick William and Sophie Dorothea were married, the magnificence of the accompanying celebration made

[11] Schneider, *Geschichte der Oper*, 20–21.

up for the King's two years of abstinence from opera. The festivities lasted almost three weeks and closed with a "musical play and ballet" entitled *der Sieg der Schönheit über die Helden.* The poetry for this production was written by the court poet von Besser and the music was composed by Gottfried Finger, A. R. Stricker, and Jean Baptiste Volumier.[12] During the year 1707 three *Masqueraden-Schauspiele,* closer in form to masque than opera, were enjoyed by the society of the court: *die vier Welttheile, Frühjahr und Herbst,* and *das Frohlocken des Helicons und der Musen.* The poetry for all three of these was suplied by von Besser; the composer of their music is unknown.[13]

On August 20, 1708, the King remarried, and an opera was given for the occasion; but it was lost soon thereafter and little is known of it. In December of the same year Frederick I had one more opera, *Alexanders und Roxanens Heirath,* performed in Berlin. The libretto of this work was again by von Besser and the music was composed by Stricker.[14] No more operas were commissioned by Frederick I before he died in 1713.

Thus the opera "patronage" of Frederick I lasted only from 1696 to 1708, and the few productions which he fostered were usually for special occasions, being performed by visiting artists rather than a permanent company. When Frederick William came to power in 1713, all operatic activity within the city of Berlin ceased. The history of the great organization known as the Berlin Opera, then, does not begin until the reign of Frederick the Great.

FIRST PERIOD OF PATRONAGE, 1732–1740

From 1732 to 1736 at Ruppin, and from 1736 to 1740 at Rheinsberg, the Prince was a patron of instrumental music only. The few musicians with whom he began his clandestine

[12] *Ibid.,* 23–27.   [13] *Ibid.,* 28.   [14] *Ibid.,* 28–36.

soirées in 1732 were acquired hesitantly, and were kept carefully hidden during visits from Frederick William. As Frederick's favor with his father increased, though, so did the musicians at Ruppin; and by 1736, when the Prince and his bride
moved into Rheinsberg Castle, his group of instrumentalists had
become a full-fledged *Kapelle*. By this time Frederick had
abandoned any serious attempt at keeping his musical activities
secret from the King, and Frederick William had given up hope
of making his son forsake his "effeminate" pursuits.

However, the Ruppin-Rheinsberg orchestra never reached
the level of full legitimacy as long as the King was alive, and the
Prince dared not risk more fatherly disfavor by including operatic performances in his amusements. Even if the King had permitted Frederick to have opera artists in his court, it is unlikely
that Frederick's strained budget would have been adequate to
pay them; this kind of singer usually came from Italy and demanded a much higher salary than that ordinarily paid to a
native musician. Therefore the Master of Ruppin and Rheinsberg patronized only an orchestra, and vocal music was no more
than an incidental, exceptional pastime.

Information documenting the growth of Frederick's Ruppin
orchestra is fragmentary, but a few dates are definite which tell
when some of the more important members joined his service.
It is probable that Michael Gabriel Fredersdorff, the faithful
servant and flutist who had accompanied the Prince in secret for
many years, was the first musical servant at Ruppin. The "Brothers Benda" and the "Brothers Graun," as Carlyle terms them,
were also among the first: Johann Gottlieb Graun arrived in
1732, Franz Benda in 1733, Johann Benda in 1734, and Karl
Heinrich Graun (as *Kapellmeister*) in 1735. Hennert's *Beschreibung des Lustschlosses und Gartens . . . zu Rheinsberg* gives us a
list[15] of the seventeen musicians who moved with Frederick

[15] Cited in Mennicke, *Hasse und die Brüder Graun*, 468–69.

87

from Ruppin to Rheinsberg in 1736: Karl Heinrich Graun, *Kapellmeister* and tenor; Franz Benda, *Concertmeister* and tenor; Johann Gottlieb Graun, violinist; Johann Benda, violinist; Christoph Schaffrath, cembalist; Johann Gottlieb Janitsch, bass violist; Joseph Blume, Georg Czarth, Johann Kaspar Grundke, and Ehms (first name missing), violinists; Anton Hock, cellist; Reich, violist; Petrini, harpist; Michael Gabriel Fredersdorff, flutist; Ernst Gottlieb Baron, theorbist; J. I. Horzizky, hornist; and another (unnamed) hornist.

This orchestra was probably complete by 1734. Frederick finished his first *sinfonie* in that year, which perhaps indicates that his own musicians were then capable of playing it, and K. H. Graun's being named *Kapellmeister* soon after his arrival in 1735 shows that the orchestra must have been fairly well established at the time of his appointment. By modern standards, an orchestra of only seventeen members is dimunitive; but according to the standards of the eighteenth century, the Prince's group of instrumentalists compared favorably with those of other European courts. For example, when Hasse assumed leadership of the great Dresden Opera Orchestra in 1731, its membership included only six violinists, three violists, four cellists, two string bass players, three flutists, four oboists, three bassoonists, two hornists, and two cembalists.[16] It was the Dresden orchestra which had dazzled the young Frederick in 1728, and which was regarded by Rousseau in 1754 as the most artistically arranged and best disciplined in Europe.[17] Also, it was a fullfledged opera orchestra, not merely a chamber group like Frederick's. The excellence of the Prince's musicians is attested by Quantz, who was Frederick's "visiting teacher" during these years. Quantz was able to witness the building of the Ruppin-

[16] Mennicke, *Hasse und die Brüder Graun*, 270.
[17] Jean-Jacques Rousseau, "*Orchestre*," *Dictionnaire de Musique* (1823).

Rheinsberg orchestra while he was himself a member of the Dresden orchestra. In his autobiography he says that Frederick's musicians were "already a permanent organization during the years 1731–1740[18] in Ruppin and Rheinsberg—a group which charmed every composer and visiting concert artist. . . ."[19] The Rheinsberg orchestra, then, should not be considered less than a significant artistic group, in spite of its small size.

These musicians performed instrumental music by such composers as Hasse, Telemann and Handel. Occasionally an aria was sung by K. H. Graun or Franz Benda, or by a visiting singer; and, of course, flute compositions by Quantz and Frederick became more and more often a part of the programs.[20] The years at Ruppin and Rheinsberg were the most liberal of Frederick's musical life; never again would he enjoy the music of so many different composers. However, even at Rheinsberg there was a lack of rapport between the Prince and his instrumentalists; governing them was often a problem for him. Two letters written to Wilhelmina show this gap between patron and performers:

November 19, 1738: M. Benda, one of Apollo's children, is virtuous enough at present. I must praise his good conduct and that of his fellow musicians, although I am sure it is not going to last.[21]

November 26, 1738: I am sorry to hear, my dear sister, that a revolt has taken place among your musicians. This race of creatures is very difficult to govern; reigning over a group of musicians requires more care than the conduct of affairs

[18] This early date was an exaggeration. Frederick visited Ruppin only during the last month or two of 1731 and did not move there until 1732.
[19] Quantz, "Herrn Johann Joachim Quantzens Lebenslauf," Historisch-Kritische Beyträge, ed. by Marpurg, I, 249.
[20] Kothe, Friedrich der Grosse als Musiker, 5.
[21] Frederick the Great, Oeuvres de Frédéric le Grand, ed by Preuss, Vol. XXVII, Bk. 1, 58.

of state. . . . I am waiting for some new sedition among my own children of Euterpe.[22]

The probable reason for the discontent of Frederick's performers was their realization that Frederick William did not approve of them, and that they would not be officially recognized until after the King's death. Nevertheless, during the years at Rheinsberg this group continued to grow both in number and importance, and upon Frederick's accession it was finally legitimatized and became the core of the great Berlin Opera Orchestra.

SECOND PERIOD OF PATRONAGE, 1740–1756

On May 31, 1740, Frederick William died. In early July the new king sent Karl Heinrich Graun to Italy for the purpose of hiring singers;[23] also during July he sent word to his envoy in Paris to begin hiring dancers;[24] on October 26 he wrote Voltaire in Paris, directing him to engage the *Comödiant* La Noue and a French troupe of actors.[25] Frederick had made plans for the new opera house while still a prince at Rheinsberg, and had told the architect Knobelsdorf (who also built the mansion at Rheinsberg) to begin designs for it.[26] On October 27 Berliners read in the *Vossische Zeitung:* "According to report, a large room on the upper floor of the palace will be adapted for performances of the opera, and will be so used until a separate opera house, the plans for which are already made, shall be completed."[27] Thus the feverish activity of creating the Berlin Opera began immediately after Frederick became king.

22 *Ibid.,* 60.
23 Johann Mattheson, *Grundlage einer ehren-pforte,* 428.
24 Schneider, *Geschichte der Oper,* 60.
25 *Ibid.*
26 Thouret, *Friedrich der Grosse,* 42.
27 Schneider, *Geschichte der Oper,* 56.

It was taken for granted from the beginning that Frederick's singers would be Italian and his dancers and actors French. Accordingly, Graun's primary assignment on the trip to Italy was to bring back singers. Frederick gave him letters of credit on banks in Venice, Florence, and Rome, plus six thousand thalers in bills of exchange,[28] instructing him to offer salaries of no more than two thousand thalers a year to any single person.[29]

As soon as Graun left for Italy, the King and his architect began their search for a suitable site on which to build the opera house. By the last month of 1740 Frederick found himself engrossed in prosecuting the War of the Austrian Succession; but such was his eagerness to establish the Opera that his plans for it were carried out relentlessly. In early 1741, after months of indecision, he decided to demolish an old fort on the Linden-Allee and build the opera house on that site. Knobelsdorf's task was not an easy one. Not only was it necessary to tear down the fort and clear away the rubble, but a system of moats had to be filled in and the entire site required leveling. All of this preliminary work lasted months longer than he had anticipated.[30]

In the meantime, Graun auditioned singers in Venice, Bologna, Florence, Rome, and Naples. By the spring of 1741 he had spread the news of the new Berlin Opera throughout Italy and had sent to Berlin two female singers from Venice: Maria Camata (la Farinella) and Anna Lorio Campolungo.[31] When he returned in the summer, almost a year after his departure, more artists arrived with him. They were the male singers Giuseppe Santarelli from Rome, Giovanni Triulzi from Milan, Mattia Mariotti from Naples, Gaetano Pinetti and Ferdinando Mazzanti

[28] Mennicke, *Hasse und die Brüder Graun*, 458.
[29] Mattheson, *Grundlage einer ehren-pforte*, 428.
[30] Schneider, *Geschichte der Oper*, 56.
[31] Mennicke, *Hasse und die Brüder Graun*, 458.

from Brescia; the female singer Giovanna Gasparini from Bologna;[32] and the librettist, Giovanni Gualberto Bottarelli.[33]

Graun's arrival was an occasion of considerable interest to all the musicians of Berlin, especially the German singers who, in most of Germany as in this city, suffered because of the prevalent taste for Italian voices. Their cause was espoused by Johann Mattheson, the great Hamburg musician and writer. Resentful of Frederick's imports from Italy, he asserted that there was no need to bring Italian singers into the city at great cost when Berlin already possessed native singers of the first rank. To drive home his point he printed the following bitter outburst sent him by an anonymous contributor from Berlin:

> The great composer's first triumphs have been premature. Herr Kapellmeister Graun has come back from Italy empty-handed; aside from a few young children, who have only good voices and know nothing about music, he has brought practically no one with him. He wrote to his good Friend [Frederick] that he was making his needs known in the best courts of Venice, Florence and Rome; but he found that the best offerings of those places hardly compared with what was already available to him in the Berlin *Kapelle*. When will we give up our blind worship of foreigners and learn to judge our own countrymen fairly! If we sought the best voices in our schools, or selected from among young girls those who have singing talent, and then gave these students a livelihood while they studied with good teachers; if, when they had learned to sing, we paid them decent salaries—I wager that Germany would produce more fine musicians of both sexes than any other country in the world. But our Herr Kapellmeister is too comfortable to bother with teaching; he believes that his little imported mushrooms will ma-

[32] *Ibid.*

[33] A. E. Brachvogel, *Geschichte des Königlichen Theaters zu Berlin,* I, 98.

ture overnight into capable singers. Because of such circumstances, our best performers leave the country in shocking numbers, while wretched Italians are accorded great honor.[34]

There is no evidence that these objections by German musicians had any effect on Frederick.

Construction of the opera house had hardly started when the first Italian musicians arrived in Berlin. Frederick was away in Silesia, and had left the whole opera project in the hands of Knobelsdorf, naming him *Intendant der Königliche Gebaüde und Direktor der Musik* on May 30, 1741. The work of preparing the site had proved so difficult that actual construction did not begin until July 17, and the foundation was not complete until September 5.[35] The singers, then, had nothing at all to do for the first few months after their arrival. They were finally given an opportunity to display their talents when Frederick returned from Silesia. The King arrived in Berlin at about noon on November 11, 1741 and ordered a performance for seven o'clock the same evening.[36]

It was obvious that the first opera would not be produced for a long time if its production had to wait for the completion of the opera house. Frederick had foreseen the need for some kind

---

[34] *Beyträgen zur critischen Historie der deutschen Sprache, Poesie und Beredsamkeit*, XXV, 16.

[35] Mennicke, *Hasse und die Brüder Graun*, 459. The cornerstone was laid on September 5, probably by a member of the royal family. Curiously, no exact information is available on just who laid it. It could not have been Frederick, since he was in Silesia at the time. Cf. Schneider, *Geschichte der Oper (Pracht-Ausgabe)*, 17. The inscription read:

FRIDERICUS II / REX BORUSSORUM / LUDIS / THALIAE ET MELPOMENES / SORORUM / SACRA HAEC FUNDAMINA / PONIT / ANNO MDCCXLI DIE QUINTO / SEPTEMBRIS

The present building, finished in 1955, does not have an inscribed cornerstone. See note 53 of this chapter.

[36] Schneider, *Geschichte der Oper*, 67.

of temporary substitute and had ordered, as reported in the *Vossische Zeitung*, that a little theater in the Stadtschloss (called the *"Kurfürstensaal"* and built in 1686 in imitation of the royal theater in Versailles) be adapted for the production of opera. On December 13, 1741, in this *Interimstheater*, the first opera was given. Entitled *Rodelinda*, it was Graun's first operatic creation for Berlin. It consisted of twenty-four arias and almost no choruses. The principal parts were played by Gasparini, Santarelli, Mariotti, Farinella, Pinetti, Mazzanti, and Triulzi; the choruses were sung by boys from the Berlin *Gymnasium*, dressed in women's clothes. An orchestra of thirty-eight members, over twice the size of the Rheinsberg orchestra, was used in this opera: twelve violins, four violas, four cellos, three string basses, four flutes, two bassoons, two horns, four oboes, one theorboe, one harp, and harpsichord. There was a repetition of the performance on December 19. *Rodelinda* made a considerable impression on opera-hungry Berliners, if we are to believe one hearer's testimony:

> For the beginning there was a symphony in which fiery and gentle sections were opposed. This was such a masterpiece of full, pure harmony, such a many-sided, artful mixture of tones, that it seemed as if the Muses and the Graces had united to draw our Frederick out of his own heroic sphere and to themselves, where he could be held back from the rude cares of war. The bewitching voices of the singers, the naturalness and beauty of the action—everything was captivating to eye and ear. The whole spectacle, brought to such artistic perfection and executed with such skill, was received by the Monarch with high approval, and the public went forth from the theater lost in enchantment.[37]

[37] From *"Briefe zur Erinnerung an merkwürdige Zeiten und rühmliche Personen aus dem Zeitlaufe von 1740 bis 1778,"* quoted in Schneider, *Geschichte der Oper (Pracht-Ausgabe)*, 21.

This performance was hardly finished when Frederick instructed his musicians to prepare a new opera for January 6, the date of the marriage celebration of Prince August Wilhelm (Frederick's younger brother) and Princess Louise Amalia of Brunswick. For this abruptly announced occasion, Graun and his company managed to piece together a work consisting of two arias, one recitative and one duet, called "Venus and Cupid." Frederick wanted ballet with it, but the dancers had not yet arrived from Paris.[38]

In early 1742 Frederick went back to Silesia, continuing his war; but even in the field he pursued his plans for the Opera. On April 18 he wrote to Algarotti in Rome, asking him to engage the singer Pinti for "up to" four thousand thalers a year. At about the same time he sent his *Cabinets-Courier,* Pierino Spary, to Italy to hire more performers; for a similar purpose he also contacted his representative in Venice, Count Cataneo.[39] It was primarily through the efforts of these agents, rather than through the somewhat ineffectual visit of Graun to Italy, that Frederick was successful in engaging the more illustrious members of his troupe.

While the King was in Silesia, a financial crisis threatened to put a stop to the construction of the opera house. A mammoth order of wood arrived all at once, and Knobelsdorf's building budget was not adequate to pay for the order without stopping work altogether, so he refused payment. The hierarchy of authority in the ministry of finance had not yet been settled at this early stage of Frederick's reign, and no member of the ministry dared presume on the King's power by allocating funds in any unusual way. Finally the minister von Happe wrote to Knobelsdorf: "All I can do about this situation is to write to the King, telling him that there is no money for the payment,

[38] Schneider, *Geschichte der Oper,* 68–72.
[39] *Ibid.,* 74.

and that, due to lack of funds, construction must come to a halt."[40] Frederick eventually solved the problem by diverting funds meant for other causes into this project. It is ironic that the war for which he was largely responsible caused delays in building his opera house, not only because of his absence but also because of the wartime shortage of wood and other building materials.[41]

During the first week of August, 1742, the ballet master Poitier arrived with his dancers; with them were the actors for the *Schauspiel*.[42] Frederick happened to be in Berlin at the time, but he had to leave by August 20; so, in order to sample the talents of his new *"Puppen"* (a term he applied to all his actors, dancers and musicians) he had a performance of Crébillon's *Rhadamiste et Zenobie* staged on August 9, giving the actors and dancers hardly time to unpack.[43] The King's rapture over the rapid building-up of his artistic kingdom is almost as apparent in his letters of this period as his concern for the progress of the war: he discusses every detail regarding the singers and dancers, the decoration and machinery, the texts and musical scores, the schedule of rehearsals and performances. Each time he returned from the field to Berlin his artists had to produce impromptu recitals; back in Silesia he spent his spare time with plans for the Opera.

The Berlin public awaited the opening of the opera house with great anticipation. Frederick had made a public statement that the general public and soldiers would be admitted free of charge to the *Parterre*.[44] Mention of progress in construction

[40] *Ibid.*, 73.
[41] Brachvogel, *Geschichte des Königlichen Theaters*, 93.
[42] *Ibid.*, 98.
[43] Schneider, *Geschichte der Oper*, 74–75.
[44] Kothe, *Friedrich der Grosse als Musiker*, 9. This notice appeared in the Berlin newspapers on November 29: "Librettos of the opera which will be performed early next month in the Royal Opera House may be purchased from the widow Simon on Königstrasse, Herr Richard at the

appeared often in the newspapers; Knobelsdorf wrote a complete description of the new building for the *Berlinische Zeitung* of November 27, 1742.[45] Because of the danger of fire to the uncompleted structure, elaborate precautions were taken; handbills (one of which is extant) were posted throughout the city, warning Berliners "not to approach the opera house with burning torches under any circumstances, and especially not to go into the building with torches or coal-filled braziers or anything which might start a fire," on pain of immediate arrest.[46]

The opera house was at last opened on December 7, 1742, with Graun's *Cesare e Cleopatra*, but it was far from finished. It lacked exterior decoration, whole sections were still being worked on, makeshifts took the place of permanent installations, and the first audiences had to pick their way through piles of building materials. Construction was not fully completed for several years. Nevertheless, it was a magnificent building. Knobelsdorf's description of it in the *Berlinische Zeitung* contains many interesting details, only a few of which are mentioned here. Across the colonnaded façade was an inscription

castle, and Herr Cournon, the teacher of Italian, on Kronenstrasse. The cost is 8 Groschen each on ordinary paper and 12 Groschen each on fine paper." Cf. Schneider, *Geschichte der Oper* (*Pracht-Ausgabe*), 20.

[45] At about the same time, Knobelsdorf had the plans for the opera house engraved and bound into a book for limited publication. The dedication reads:

SIRE

I am honored to present to Your Majesty the plans for the Opera House, which You fashioned Yourself, entrusting their final execution to me. I ask You very humbly to receive them as evidence of my eagerness to fulfill, as well as I am able, the noble ideas of Your Majesty. This will always be my way of thinking, always accompanied by the profound respect with which I am, Sire,
Your Majesty's
most humble, submissive and obedient servant
Knobelsdorf

Cf. Schneider, *Geschichte der Oper* (*Pracht-Ausgabe*), 20.
[46] Schneider, *Geschichte der Oper*, 78.

honoring the King: *FREDERICUS REX APPOLONI ET MUSIS*. Adjacent to the theater was a large square which would accommodate a thousand carriages. A canal nine feet deep ran through the entire building, below the floor,

> from which, by means of two pumps, great quantities of water can be brought into reservoirs just below the roof. Through a system of pipes, this water can not only be used in decorative cascades and jets, but can be made to saturate the whole theater in case of fire.[47]

At the time of its construction, the theater was one of the longest and widest in the world. Knobelsdorf made sure that it would have proper acoustical qualities:

> . . . listeners note with wonder that musicians can easily create splendid effects there. Even when a singer is standing backstage, not only can his most delicate tones be heard equally well in the farthest balcony and on the main floor, but he can also hear the effect he produces and judge his own performance with exactness. Few theaters offer such advantages to singers.[48]

One of the most remarkable features of the building was its provision for the opera balls following performances. When the curtain fell on the last act, the *Fürsten* who were invited to the ball dined in a large room adjacent to the theater. While they were dining, the entire floor of the theater (the *Parterre*, where the public had stood during the performance) was raised by pneumatic jacks to the level of the stage.[49] The stage scenery

47 *Ibid.*, 81.
48 *Ibid.* J. S. Bach, on visiting this opera house, did not need to hear music there in order to note the acoustical qualities. See p. 245.
49 The floor was raised by twelve of these jacks, which were manually operated. In 1823 a laborer was killed by the handle of a jack after losing

and apparatus disappeared behind Corinthian columns; within niches in the walls, naiads sculptured from white marble began to pour cascades of water from their pitchers. The rococo ballroom thus created was divided into three parts. Its creator, Knobelsdorf, goes on to describe these parts in his article:

(1) The Corinthian section [the stage, before the raising of the floor], (2) the main floor, where on the boxes and portals there are gilded decorations against a broken background of white, all done in impeccable taste and producing a very beautiful effect, and (3) the Apollonian section, in which there is an entablature, supported by many satyrs, which surrounds the spectators.[50]

Distributed about the theater, among the caryatids, were statues and bas-reliefs of gods and mortals of antiquity: Apollo, Thalia, Melpomene, Daphne, Sophocles, Aristophanes, Menander, Euripides, Orpheus, Eurydice, Seneca, Varius, Terence, Homer, Vergil, Ovid, Horace, Anacreon, Pindar, Amphion, Arion, Achilles, Sappho. (One can well imagine what Berlin's clergymen must have thought of this pagan display.) The whole opera house was lighted by wax candles and tallow torches; a considerable portion of the cost of a production consisted of lighting expense.[51] Thouret estimates[52] that the total cost of the Berlin Opera House was approximately one million thalers.[53]

control of it. His body lay in the cellar until the masked ball overhead had ended. Cf. Schneider, *Geschichte der Oper*, 84. In the present building the floor of the orchestra pit can be raised or lowered hydraulically, but the *parterre* is immovable. See note 53 of this chapter.

[50] Schneider, *Geschichte der Oper*, 81.

[51] *Ibid.*, 82–86.

[52] *Friedrich der Grosse*, 43.

[53] This magnificent structure stood for a hundred years. On August 18, 1843, in spite of Knobelsdorf's ingenious reservoirs and pumps, it was destroyed by fire. Standing on its site today, on Unter den Linden in the eastern sector of Berlin, is a fourth opera house: The *Deutsche Staatsoper*. The second building, a copy of the first, was bombed in 1941 and imme-

Once the opera house was opened, the musical season settled quickly to a fixed routine. Grand opera was performed only during the carnival season, which usually began late in November and ended on March 27, the Queen Mother's birthday. During most of the weeks within this season the same schedule of festivities was observed: Sunday, *"grosse Cour"* at the Queen's residence (usually consisting of a banquet accompanied by a little playlet or musical performance, or followed by a ball); Monday, an opera, followed usually by a ball; Tuesday, a masquerade at the opera house; Wednesday, a play by the French troupe of actors, in one of the palace theaters; Thursday, a small version

---

diately rebuilt by order of Hermann Goering, only to be bombed again in 1945.

When the Communist East German authorities invited Erich Kleiber (conductor of the Berlin Opera before the rise of the Nazi party) to be general musical director of the East Berlin *Staatsoper,* Kleiber accepted the offer only after he had been promised that the *Staatsoper Unter den Linden* would be reconstructed "exactly as it was presented in 1743 by the '*Alte Fritz*' to the German people through his architect Knobelsdorf." Accordingly, the East German authorities spent a tremendous sum rebuilding the opera house almost exactly as Frederick had built it, and it was virtually finished by early 1955.

However, as the last touches were being added, an order was suddenly given that the inscription across the front of the building, FREDERICUS REX APOLLONI ET MUSIS, be removed. (According to an official East German publication, the first opera house was "the salon of a feudal regime, with no inner meaning for the people.") Kleiber was so incensed at this action that he immediately resigned. On March 16, 1955, he wrote to the Communist general manager that "the sudden tearing out of the inscription...from the Linden-opera is a desecration of a just-rebuilt monument. ...The same department or another, responsible for the mad order to remove the inscription 'within two hours,' will not refrain from intruding on my province and disturbing through its orders or guiding principles, my artistic work, thus far completely uninfluenced. My resolution to resign from my contract with the *Staatsoper,* is past recall. I would have liked to be faithful to the institution; alas, I had to recognize that the genius of the old *Staatsoper* cannot exist in the new house." On September 4, 1955, the opera house was opened, but without Kleiber. (Cf. Horst Koegler, "Berlin Controversy," *Opera News,* Vol. XIX [February 7, 1955], 31, and "New Life for Berlin Opera," *Opera News,* Vol. XIX [April 11, 1955], 21, 31; Joseph Wechsberg, "Behind the Golden Curtain," *Horizon,* Vol. I [November, 1958], 133.)

of the *"grosse Cour,"* this time in the apartments of the princesses; Friday, an opera, with or without a ball afterwards; Saturday, a night of rest.[54] Normally, two new operas were presented each season: the first was given repeatedly until New Year's Day, and on that day the second began its run.[55] The two most grandly celebrated yearly occasions were Frederick's birthday on January 24 and the Queen Mother's birthday on March 27. This schedule was not as strenuous as it seems to be, because it was not rigidly observed. During some weeks the festivities were reduced or omitted altogether, and Frederick spent his evenings in private orchestral concerts; celebrations were often arranged as the occasion demanded; and on many

---

Scrupulous care has been taken in this showplace of the East German government to avoid all references to the "feudal regime" of Frederick the Great. The inscription put in place of the one which was eradicated reads simply, *"Deutsche Staatsoper."* There is no inscribed cornerstone. Nothing exists in the entire building to make one think of the first building's creator. However, the East German authorities apparently realized that some historical figure would have to be given mention in the new structure, since it is a historical monument. They chose Knobelsdorf. (Knobelsdorf's name is a respected one in Berlin architecture, and he can, after all, be classified as a "worker," in spite of the fact that he was titled.) There is a bust of him in the lobby, and a large plaque on the front of the building which reads:

G. W. V. KNOBELSDORF / 1699–1753 / DEM GROSSEN ARCHITEKTEN / ZUM GEDACHTNIS. / SEINEN WERK SCHLUGEN BOMBEN / DES ZWEITEN WELTKRIEGES / SCHWERE SCHADEN. / SIE ZERSTÖRTEN AUCH SEIN GRAB. / DIE WIEDERHERSTELLUNG DES / OPERNHAUSES ALS EINES / DENKMALS DEUTSCHER KULTUR / IST EINE ZEICHEN UNSERES / DANKBAREN GEDENKENS / AN DEN BAUMEISTER UND / AUSDRUCK DES FRIEDLICHEN / AUFBAUWERKES. DEM DAS / SCHAFFEN DER WERKTÄTIGEN / UNTER FÜHRUNG DER / REGIERUNG DER DEUTSCHEN / DEMOKRATISCHEN REPUBLIK GILT. / BERLIN 1953

[54] C. F. Nicolai, *Beschreibung der königlichen Residenzstäte Berlin und Potsdam,* 396–97.
[55] Brachvogel, *Geschichte des königlichen Theaters,* 114.

Mondays and Fridays the operas were replaced by ballets, musical dramas, or revivals of works dating from earlier years.

The King's opera company produced these works between the opening date and the outbreak of the Seven Years' War in 1756:[56]

1742–43, carnival
> *Rodelinda;* music by Graun, libretto adapted from Rolli by Bottarelli
> *Cesare e Cleopatra;* Graun, Bottarelli
> *La clemenza di Tito;* Hasse, Metastasio

1743–44, carnival
> *Artaserse;* Graun, Metastasio
> *Catone in Utica;* Graun, Metastasio
> Repeat performance of *Rodelinda*

Summer of 1744: Repeat performances of *La clemenza di Tito, Artaserse* and *Catone in Utica*

1744–45, carnival
> *Alessandro nell' Indie;* Graun, Metastasio
> *Lucio Papirio;* Graun, Zeno

1745–46, carnival
> *Adriano;* Graun, Metastasio
> *Demofoonte;* Graun, Metastasio

1746–47, carnival
> *Cajo Fabrizio;* Graun, Metastasio
> *Arminio;* Hasse, Pasquini
> *Le feste galanti;* Graun, Villati

[56] This list is taken from Marpurg, *Historisch-Kritische Beyträge,* I, 79–84; *ibid.,* II, 271–72; and Schneider, *Geschichte der Oper,* 68–148.

1747–48, carnival

Repeat performance of *Le feste galanti*
Cinna; Graun, Villati (libretto adapted from Corneille)
Europa galante; Graun, Villati (libretto adapted from Mothe)

1748–49, carnival

Repeat performance of *Cinna*
Ifigenia in Aulide; Graun, Villati (libretto adapted from
  Racine)
Angelica e Medoro; Graun, Villati (libretto adapted from
  Quinault)

1749–50, carnival

Repeat performance of *Angelica e Medoro*
Coriolano; Graun, Villati (sketch of plot by Frederick)
Fetonte; Graun, Villati (libretto adapted from Quinault)

1750–51, carnival

Repeat performance of *Fetonte*
Mithridate; Graun, Villati (libretto adapted from Racine)
Armida; Graun, Villati (libretto adapted from Quinault)

1751–52, carnival

Repeat performance of *Armida*
Britannico; Graun, Villati (libretto adapted from Racine)
Orfeo; Graun, Villati (libretto adapted from du Boulai)

1752–53, carnival

Repeat performance of *Orfeo*
Didone abbandonata; Hasse, Metastasio
Sulla; Graun, Frederick (libretto translated from French
  prose into Italian verse by Tagliazucchi)

103

1753–54, carnival
>Repeat performance of *Sulla*
>*Cleofide;* Agricola, Metastasio
>*Semiramide;* Graun, Tagliazucchi (libretto adapted from
>Voltaire)

1754–55, carnival
>Repeat performance of *Semiramide*
>*Montezuma;* Graun, Frederick (libretto translated from
>French prose into Italian verse by Tagliazucchi)
>*Ezio;* Graun, Tagliazucchi

1755–56, carnival
>Repeat performance of *Ezio*
>*I fratelli nemici;* Graun, Tagliazucchi (sketch of plot
>by Frederick)
>*Merope;* Graun, Tagliazucchi (sketch of plot by Frederick)

The end of the carnival season did not mean an end to courtly entertainments. Throughout the summers informal dramatic or musical productions were given in the palace theaters, and Frederick enjoyed his private concerts whenever he desired them.[57] In the summer of 1747 the King began to have little *intermezzi* performed at Sans Souci. At first these were given by only two singers, one male and one female, but soon the number grew to five and became a permanent group under the direction of the *basso buffo* Domenico Cricchi. The little works performed by this group (and accompanied instrumentally by the ever present *Kapelle*) were usually untitled *pasticci* composed anonymously by court musicians—Graun, Quantz, Benda and others—and even partly by Frederick himself; the "*Serenata fatta per l'arrivo de*

[57] In September, 1750, at Potsdam, Voltaire himself took the part of Cicero in his *La Mort de César*. Cf. Alan Yorke-Long, *Music at Court*, 121.

la Regina Madre à Charlottenburg" of 1747 is an example. In
March, 1748, Pergolesi's *La serva padrona* conquered the Prussian court as it had conquered all of Europe.[58] This event would
seem to have announced Frederick's approval not only of *intermezzi, Schäferspiele,* pastorales, *serenate,* and the like, but also of
full-scale *opera buffa.* Such was not the case. The appearance of
La serva padrona in the Prussian court was an isolated incident;
the King considered all such works to be nothing more than a
frivolity, a fad which would soon pass. His own tiny *intermezzi*
continued, especially in the summers; but to Frederick they
remained on the level of "dumb stuff"—entertaining, but hardly
an art form.[59]

During the period from 1742 to 1756, when the Opera grew
and flourished, the opera house was always packed with spectators. In spite of Frederick's earlier announcement that the
public was to be admitted free, an invitation was usually necessary. Nevertheless, anyone who really wanted to attend could
gain admission by one little fraud or another, the most common
of which was simply to give the doorman a few *Groschen.*[60]
The main purpose of the invitations, in any case, was to keep
undesirables out of the audience; thus Burney is substantially
correct in saying that since the King was "at the whole expense
of this opera, the entrance is *gratis,* so that any one, who is

[58] Thouret, *Friedrich der Grosse,* 48.

[59] Thouret, in *ibid.,* 48, tells an amusing anecdote about the lighthearted
entertainments given by the King's little troupe of *intermezzo* singers:
A performance was scheduled for the night of April 1, 1748. On that
night the audience, consisting of the royal family and local petty princes,
was seated and ready. The curtain went up; Cricchi appeared on stage
and looked in a puzzling manner at the audience; everybody laughed.
Then Cricchi stepped forward and said in broken German, "Ladies and
Gentlemen, today is the first of April! Ha, ha, ha, ha!" The curtain fell,
and the performance was over.

[60] E. Frensdorff, *"Die Sängerin E. Mara am Hofe Friedrichs des
Grossens,"* Mitteilungen des Vereins für die Geschichte Berlins, Vol.
XXIV (January 12, 1907), 29.

decently dressed, may have admission into the pit."[61] The pit, or first floor, was reserved for the public. Since there were no seats in this section, the spectators here were obliged to stand for the entire performance. The first group of boxes was reserved for the use of the royal family and other important nobility; the boxes behind these and the balconies were reserved for minor nobility, visiting envoys, officials, and burghers. Frederick's seat was directly behind the conductor's stand, and so close that he could see the score from where he sat.[62]

The performances were begun with pomp. The audience was expected to be ready for the evening's entertainment by six o'clock. At that hour Frederick came striding in, wearing a resplendent uniform; at his appearance, a group of trumpeters and tympanists of the *Gens d'armes* and the *Gardes du Corps*, stationed in an elevated box near the stage, played a resounding fanfare. (Burney's wry comment on this display shows him to be the complete Englishman: "There is scarce a sovereign prince in Germany, who thinks he can [even] dine comfortably, or with proper dignity, without a flourish of drums and trumpets. . . .")[63] No one sat down until the King took his chair. As soon as Frederick and the portion of the audience having chairs were seated, the *Intendant des Spectacles*, watched by every eye in the theater, gave the signal for Graun to begin. Graun, wearing a red cloak (a mark of distinction also affected by the concertmaster) and a long white wig, would thereupon commence the overture.[64]

The average length of a performance, including ballet—which seldom had anything to do with the plot—between the acts and at the end, was three to four hours, although perform-

[61] Burney, *The Present State of Music*, II, 99.
[62] Nicolai, *Beschreibung der königlichen Residenzstäte*, 394.
[63] *The Present State of Music*, II, 101.
[64] Nicolai, *Beschreibung der königlichen Residenzstäte*, 397.

ances lasting five hours were not unusual.[65] When the curtain fell, those invited to the masquerade ball went into the dining room for a banquet while the floor was being raised and the theater transformed into a ballroom. After the banquet the King, dressed in a rose-colored cloak but without a mask, opened the ball by dancing a minuet. Music for the ball was provided by twenty-four oboists chosen from various regiments—perhaps Frederick's version of Louis XIV's twenty-four violins! This music, none of which still exists, was composed by Johann Gottlieb Janitsch, string bass player in the *Kapelle*.[66]

In 1754 Marpurg wrote the following summary of the activities of the Berlin Opera during its first twelve years of existence, showing the renown it had gained by that time:

> It has now been twelve years since our present king re-established the Berlin Lyric Stage, an artistic medium which, before his reign, had been dead since the death of Frederick I. During these twelve years the most skillful German players, Italian singers, and French dancers have been maintained with excellent salaries, and music in Berlin has been lifted to its former eminence.[67]

Marpurg also gives a list of Frederick's musical forces as of 1754 (he does not include the singers for the *intermezzi*):[68]

1. Karl Heinrich Graun, *Kapellmeister*
2. Johann Friedrich Agricola, court composer
3. Carl August, oboist
4. Carl Philipp Emanuel Bach, cembalist
5. Ernst Gottlieb Baron, theorbist

[65] Thouret, *Friedrich der Grosse*, 54.
[66] *Ibid.*, 55.
[67] *Historisch-Kritische Beyträge*, I, 75.
[68] *Ibid.*, 76–79.

6. Franz Benda, violinist
7. Joseph Benda, violinist
8. Balthasar Christian Friedrich Bertram, violinist
9. Joseph Blume, violinist
10. Ivan Böhm, violinist
11. Georg Czarth, violinist
12. Joachim Wilhelm Döbbert, oboist
13. Julius Dümmler, bassoonist
14. Engke, violist (first name missing)
15. Franz, violist (first name missing)
16. Johann Gottlob Freudenberg, violinist
17. Georg Heinrich Gebhard, (?)
18. Johann Gottlieb Graun, concertmaster[69]
19. Johann Caspar Grundke, violinist
20. Christian Ludwig Hesse, gambist
21. Hesse, violinist (first name missing)
22. Antonius Hock, cellist
23. Joseph Ignatius Horzizky, hornist
24. Johann Gottlieb Janitsch, bass violist
25. Koch, violinist (first name missing)
26. Georg Wilhelm Kodowsky, flutist
27. Samuel Kühlthau, bassoonist
28. Alexander Lange, bassoonist
29. Johann Joseph Friedrich Lindner, flutist
30. Ignatius Mara, cellist
31. Johann Christian Marks, bassoonist
32. Christian Mengis, hornist
33. Augustinus Neuff, flutist
34. Christoph Nichelmann, cembalist
35. Friedrich Wilhelm Pauli, oboist
36. Johann Joachim Quantz, chamber composer and flutist

[69] J. G. Graun took Franz Benda's place as concertmaster when Frederick became king. Benda regained his post when J. G. Graun died in 1771.

37. Johann Christoph Richter, bass violist
38. Friedrich Wilhelm Riedt, flutist
39. Christian Friedrich Schale, cellist
40. Johann Gabriel Seyfarth, violinist
41. Johann Georg Speer, cellist
42. Hans Jürgen Steffani, violist
    Female singers:
43. Giovanna Astrua, soprano
44. Giovanna Gasparini, soprano
45. Benedetta Agricola (Molteni), soprano
46. Anna Lorio Campolungo, contralto
    Male singers:
47. Giovanni Carestini, contralto
48. Antonio Uberi (Porporino), soprano
49. Paolo Bedeschi (Paulino), soprano
50. Antonio Romani, tenor
    Plus about a dozen other singers, all German, for sing-
    ing minor roles and strengthening the chorus.

The voice ranges of the leading singers were always in about
the proportion shown in the above list: The women were primarily sopranos, the men primarily *castrati*. Women with alto
voices and men with tenor voices were rarely used, and the only
use for basses was in the *intermezzi*.

The first female singer to gain prominence in the Berlin
Opera was the soprano Benedetta Emilia Molteni of Modena,
who made her debut in *Cesare e Cleopatra* (1743). When Burney
visited Berlin in 1772 he met this singer and admired her ability
even at that date.

> . . . she is now fifty years of age, and yet sings songs of
> *bravura*, with amazing rapidity . . . her compass extends from
> A in the base, to D in *alt;* and she has a most perfect shake

and intonation; she was born at Modena, and had instructions from all the great masters of her time; among whom she numbers Porpora, Hasse, and Salimbeni. . . . [70]

Benedetta Molteni was one of the first of the King's singers to suffer because of his rule that none of them should marry. In 1751 she married J. F. Agricola, Frederick's newly appointed court composer; Frederick punished them both by reducing their joint salary to one thousand thalers. He dismissed her when Agricola died in 1774, in spite of the intercession of Princess Amalia, and even though she could sing as well as ever. She died in obscurity a few years later.[71]

In 1748 Molteni's place as prima donna was usurped by the soprano Giovanna Astrua. Astrua had been engaged by Count Cataneo, the King's representative in Venice, for a salary of six thousand thalers a year.[72] She made her debut in *Cinna* (January, 1748). Of Astrua Frederick wrote, "This singer is really amazing; she produces arpeggios like the violin, she sings everything the flute can play, with infinite facility and quickness. Of all the voices ever created by nature, none like this one has ever before existed."[73] Astrua was prima donna until 1756, when her voice began to fail. Frederick gave her better treatment than he had given her predecessor: she was retired to Italy and given a pension. She died two years later.[74]

Several famous *castrati* sang at the Opera during this period before the Seven Years' War: Antonio Uberi (Porporino), Paolo Bedeschi (Paulino), Stefanino, Felice Salimbeni, and Giovanni Carestini. The first of these to gain outstanding recog-

[70] *The Present State of Music,* II, 93.
[71] E. van der Straeten, "Agricola, Benedetta Emilia," *Grove's Dictionary of Music and Musicians,* Vol. I.
[72] Yorke-Long, *Music at Court,* 116.
[73] Thouret, *Friedrich der Grosse,* 44–45.
[74] Yorke-Long, *Music at Court,* 116.

nition in Berlin was Porporino, who made his initial appearance in *Cesare e Cleopatra*. Frederick took great delight in Porporino's soprano voice, using him not only during the opera season but also in the summer productions.[75] The King even took it upon himself to "instruct" this singer in the art of performing adagios, and wrote out an elaboration of an aria from Hasse's *Cleofide* for him.[76] Porporino took his service to Frederick so seriously that he would sing for no one else, except in the services of the Catholic church. When asked to sing on one visit to Italy, he is said to have replied, "My voice is only for God and the King of Prussia."[77]

Porporino gave up his leading position to Felice Salimbeni when the latter made his Berlin debut (*Catone in Utica*, January, 1744). Apparently Salimbeni needed no further instruction upon his arrival in Berlin, because in Frederick's later opinion "he sang like an angel, with unlimited grace, delicacy and taste; such singers hardly exist any more."[78] He retained his leading position until the end of the 1749–50 season. By that time, since his voice had lost some of its brilliance, Frederick blamed him for the failure of *Coriolano* in the spring of 1750, and he was abruptly dismissed.[79]

The last outstanding *castrato* before the outbreak of the Seven Years' War was Giovanni Carestini, a singer who had performed under Handel and Hasse. Unlike his predecessors, all of whom were sopranos, Carestini was a contralto. The unusual range of his voice probably explains the rather cool reception given him at his debut in *Mithridate* (December, 1751). In spite of his highly praised performance in *Orfeo* (March, 1752), he

[75] *Ibid.*
[76] Thouret, *Friedrich der Grosse*, 45. This "pedagogical piece" is extant; see the list of Frederick's compositions.
[77] Thouret, *Friedrich der Grosse*, 47.
[78] *Ibid.*, 45.
[79] Yorke-Long, *Music at Court*, 117.

was never as celebrated as the soprano *castrati* had been; in addition, his poor health often interfered with his duties. He left Berlin in 1754.[80]

Throughout Frederick's patronage of the opera, the chorus was composed mainly of schoolboys, as it was in the operas of many other cities at that time. On the whole this practice hampered the education of the children in the chorus; but it was a primary vehicle for musical advancement, and Graun's complaints about the chorus' lack of skill caused the King to enact beneficial laws for better musical education. One of Frederick's *Cabinetsordres* of 1746, effecting the improvement of singing instruction in the schools, still exists:

> Having received many complaints of the decline in the art of singing, and the neglect of it in our gymnasiums and schools, His Majesty commands that the young people in all public schools and gymnasiums shall be exercised more diligently therein, and to that end shall have singing lessons three times a week. . . .[81]

The salaries paid by Frederick to his artists varied widely. The Italian performers were given the greatest remuneration: Astrua received six thousand thalers yearly, Salimbeni four thousand, Porporino two thousand.[82] Considering the trifling duties expected of these performers, their salaries were immense, especially as compared with those of the orchestra members. (The Italian dancer Barbarina received the highest salary of all Frederick's artists—seven thousand thalers yearly—but her circumstances in the life of the court were unique. See pp. 114–18.) The singers and dancers performed only twice a week, from

[80] *Ibid.*

[81] Gehring and Loewenberg, "Frederick II," *Grove's Dictionary*, Vol. III.

[82] Thouret, *Friedrich der Grosse,* 46.

the end of November through March. From May to October was a holiday which was seldom interrupted. On the other hand, the orchestra had to perform the year round, and not only at operas but also at the King's private concerts. Nothing illustrates better the penetration into Frederick's court of the "star system" than the tiny salary at which the great C. P. E. Bach, cembalist in the *Kapelle*, began his service to Frederick in 1740—three hundred thalers a year.[83]

The quality of the opera performances was never higher during Frederick's reign than during the period immediately preceding the Seven Years' War. Frederick's delight in the success of his enterprise is expressed in a poem which he wrote to his *Intendant*, Baron von Schwerts, in 1748:

Épitre XIV, à Schwerts, sur les plaisirs

Cherchez, me dites-vous, un spectacle nouveau!
Allez à ce palais enchanteur et magique
Où l'optique, la danse et l'art de la musique
De cent plaisirs divers ne forment qu'un plaisir.
Ce spectacle est de tous celui qu'il faut choisir;
C'est là que l'Astrua par son gosier agile
Enchante également et la cour et la ville
Et que Felicino[84] *par des sons plus touchans*
Sait émouvoir les coeurs au gré de ses accens;
C'est là que Marianne,[85] *égale à Terpsichore,*
Entend tous ces bravos dont le public l'honore:
Ses pas étudiés, ses airs luxurieux,
Tout incite aux désirs nos sens voluptueux.[86]

But the establishment which pleased the King so much was

[83] C. S. Terry, "Bach, Carl Philipp Emanuel," *Grove's Dictionary of Music and Musicians,* Vol. I.

[84] Felice Salimbeni.

[85] Marianne Cochois.

[86] Cited in Schneider, *Geschichte der Oper,* 121–22.

not without its difficulties. The performers, like the musicians of Rheinsberg, were often very hard to handle. Poitier, the *maître de ballet*, was one of the first offenders. On August 14, 1743, Frederick received a frantic note from two of his ballerinas, Cochois and Tessier: "We are forced to throw ourselves at Your Majesty's feet to beg protection from the ballet master. . . . This man is so tyrannical that he violates the terms of our contracts every day, saying that they mean nothing to him. . . . We will have to resign if Your Majesty permits him to continue abusing his title. . . ."[87] This note was accompanied by one from Baron von Schwerts, who assured the King that the complaint of the dancers was fully justified, adding anxiously that none of the disturbance was his fault.[88] Frederick tried at first to let the affair settle itself; but when it became apparent that Poitier was really impossible to deal with, he decided that dismissal was the only solution. When he gave the dismissal, Frederick justified his action to the public by writing an anonymous article for the *Spener'sche Zeitung* of August 22, 1743, in which he tells how Poitier's "thousand insolences" forced the directors of the Opera to "throw him out." In a letter to his minister Jordan dated two days earlier, Frederick says, "I have just given an article to the Berlin paper, in which Poitier is thrashed in the very best manner. I have already written for another ballet master—perhaps a foolish thing to do, since none exist who are better than Poitier . . . but we will live without Poitiers, and be able to divert ourselves none the less."[89]

Frederick's relationship with the dancer Barbarina created a disturbance which disrupted the functions of two governments, attracted the attention of the whole continent, and provided material for two centuries of anecdotes. It began in the

[87] *Ibid.*, appendix, *Beilage* XIII.
[88] *Ibid.*
[89] Schneider, *Geschichte der Oper* (*Pracht-Ausgabe*), 23.

spring of 1743, when Frederick, considerably annoyed that his prima ballerina had resigned as a result of the actions of Poitier, ordered his representatives in France and Italy to procure a new one. By November Count Cataneo had discovered Barbara Campanini, called Barbarina, in Venice, and had obtained the King's permission to hire her. As soon as she signed the contract, however, she changed her mind about going to Berlin. A more attractive offer had come up: that of going to England as the bride of a young English nobleman, Lord James Stuart-Mackenzie. When Frederick heard of this, he wrote directly to the King of the Republic of Venice, requesting that the ballerina who was now his servant by legal right be sent to him immediately; but the Venetian monarch refused to cooperate, since he considered such actions beneath the dignity of a government.

By this time Frederick's ire was aroused. He had heard glowing reports of Barbarina's reputation as a great artist and a great beauty, and he was in no mood to lose such a prize. Conveniently for him, it happened that at just this time a Venetian ambassador and his retinue were passing through the Prussian States. This gave him the solution to the problem. He placed an embargo on all the goods of this group, promising that the embargo would remain in effect until the Republic of Venice had promised to give him "satisfaction in the Barbarina affair."

This maneuver convinced the Venetian government that the King of Prussia was actually willing to risk an international incident over a dancer, so they complied with his demand: Barbarina was arrested and prepared for the trip to Berlin. From this part on the events seem like part of a cloak-and-dagger tale, but they are well-documented in official letters and reports in the Prussian *Geheimen Cabinets-Archiv*.[90] Barbarina was put

[90] Schneider collected most of these in 1851 and put them in the appendix of his *Geschichte der Oper*.

into a closed carriage during the night and conducted by an armed group of Venetian cavalry as far as the border between the Republic of Venice and Austria. At the border she was received by a representative of the Prussian envoy to Vienna, a Herr Mayer, whose task was to get her safely to Vienna, from where she would be sent on to Berlin. Herr Mayer had progressed only a few miles when he was met by Lord Stuart-Mackenzie and a group of hired helpers, who attempted to bribe him into giving up the dancer and might have done worse if Mayer had not been resourceful. With the help of local authorities he escaped both temptation and danger and reached Vienna without further incident.

But Stuart-Mackenzie had gone ahead to Vienna to try his luck with the Prussian envoy there. He was successful in getting permission to go on to Berlin—by a route different from that used by Barbarina's escort—where he sought to use the influence of his cousin, Lord Hyndford, who was English ambassador to Berlin at that time; but Hyndford, as well as the other members of Stuart-Mackenzie's prominent family, was firmly opposed to the marriage. As a last resort the young nobleman wrote Frederick an impassioned letter telling of his love for Barbarina and begging for her release from the contract. Frederick's answer is not extant, but subsequent events are informative enough: Stuart-Mackenzie went straight to Hamburg and sailed from there to England, alone.

Barbarina was finally ushered into the King's presence on May 8, 1744, after six months of strenuous effort which had been devoted merely to getting her to Berlin. She and Frederick conversed informally for a long while, and he readily forgave her truancy. On May 13 she danced before him for the first time, between the acts of a French play in the *Schlosstheater*. The sum of one group of anecdotes about the first few days of their acquaintance is that the young king was charmed by her intelligent conversation, intoxicated by the grace of her dancing, and thrown into a paroxysm of desire by her great beauty. Other anecdotes, however, would have it that Frederick's admiration for his new ballerina was more aesthetic than sensual. The latter are more in accord with the historical fact of Frederick's misogyny.

At any rate, Barbarina was warmly received by her new patron; and when she was presented to the public shortly thereafter, between the acts of Graun's *Catone in Utica*, the welcome given her, especially by the male members of the audience, was almost hysterical. Poems in German, French, and Latin appeared in the newspapers, celebrating her reign over the hearts of Berliners. Worshipers of all classes flocked to her, and she held court every day at her apartments in the Behrenstrasse. She was, of course, expressly forbidden to marry, like all the stars of the Opera; but many a young nobleman stood willing to risk banishment or worse for the privilege of making her his wife.

It is not known exactly when Frederick was advised to take her for his mistress, but the likelihood is that she was cold-bloodedly chosen for this position as soon as it became apparent that the public considered her one of the most seductive women in Berlin. A mistress for Frederick, in name at least, was needed to combat the scandalous rumors about his lack of masculinity, rumors founded on his well-known aversion to the opposite sex and his complete alienation from Queen Elizabeth. Frederick was quite willing to go through the needed motions: he sent Barbarina well-publicized invitations to dine with him alone; he applauded her at the Opera so energetically that the audience could not fail to note the particular significance of his applause; he had her painted by Vanloo, in revealing allegorical costume, for the ceiling of the *Schlosstheater* in Potsdam.

Barbarina's lifetime contract lasted not quite eight years. For this entire period she was the most dazzling star of the Berlin Opera; but even from the beginning of her service she had a way of abusing her privileges and eventually got into trouble over nonpayment of debts, in spite of her high salary. Her infractions of Frederick's rules for her conduct increased in proportion to his loss of patience with her. Finally, and inevitably, she fell in love again, this time with the privy councilor von Cocceji, son of the Lord High Chancellor. The old story was repeated: the prominent Cocceji family objected strenuously and asked the King to prevent the marriage. Frederick was glad to comply by imprisoning young Cocceji for a few months. However, for once the Conqueror of Prussia was unable to vanquish his enemy. As soon as Cocceji was released—Frederick could not, after all, keep the son of the Lord High Chancellor imprisoned indefinitely—he and Barbarina eloped. On their return to Berlin as a married couple there were more fireworks from the outraged family, as well as from the disobeyed monarch, but the struggle was over. The King's last action concerning this dancer, in November of 1751, was to have her husband banished to Glogau in Silesia. Greatly relieved, Barbarina followed him there—and Frederick must have been just as relieved to see her go, because he did not interfere.[91]

It can hardly be doubted that Frederick brought much of this trouble with performers on himself. His way of using imprisonment as a means of coercion hardly inspired confidence, and his almost unlimited power made artists hesitate to commit themselves to his service. In addition, his desire to have a per-

[91] Most of the details of Barbarina's relationship with Frederick can be found, well documented, in Schneider, *Geschichte der Oper* (*Pracht-Ausgabe*), 24–34. Troubles with Barbarina notwithstanding, there was no interruption, during these early years, in the steady stream of dancers going to Berlin. In April, 1754, Frederick wrote to Darget in Paris: "I still need a third pair of dancers. Can't you find me a daughter of pleasure with roguish eyes, a pretty face and a nice figure, who would like very much to caper in our theater in Berlin?" (Cf. Schneider, *Geschichte der Oper* [*Pracht-Ausgabe*], 35.)

sonal hand in every phase of the Opera was a constant irritant to his personnel. Although Baron von Schwerts was an *Intendant* of considerable ability, the King felt that he could not really trust anyone to look after his *"Puppen."* He coached singers personally, approved or disapproved costumes and scenery, hired and fired performers impulsively, rewrote or changed music or libretti, and believed that his singers and dancers were only children and had to be treated as such. In 1753, after a particularly unpleasant incident with the singer Astrua, he wrote to Fredersdorff: "The opera people are such *Canaillenbagage* that I'm sick of them a thousand times over."[92]

But the King had his magnanimous moments, too. Once during a rehearsal the tenor Romani, whose art Frederick admired but whose gluttony he deplored, was enjoying a bit of wine and a capon which he had filched from a near-by cabinet. Suddenly hearing Frederick's voice on the stage, he was seized with fright and hid in a wardrobe closet, still clutching the cabinet key and the bottle of wine. When his cue came up he was nowhere to be found; finally, after a search, he was discovered in the closet, besotted. Luckily for him, Frederick made only a smiling comment: "Ah, Monsieur Romani, the instrument of sin is also the instrument of punishment."[93]

While the King's singers developed into a significant company of performers, so did his orchestra. As Marpurg's list[94] shows, this group had grown by 1754 to a size which was quite impressive at that date—forty-two members. It compared favorably with the best orchestras in Europe; for example, the great Mannheim court orchestra created by Johann Stamitz had exactly forty-two members in 1756.[95] However, the entire mem-

---

[92] Frederick Burchardt (ed.), *Friedrich II. Eigenhändige Briefe an seinen geheimen Kämmerer Fredersdorff*, 43.
[93] Thouret, *Friedrich der Grosse*, 46.
[94] See pp. 107–109.
[95] Mennicke, *Hasse und die Brüder Graun*, 277.

bership played only at performances of the Opera. For most of the evening concerts a smaller group was used, seldom consisting of more than a suitable accompaniment for Frederick's flute playing: clavier, string quartet, string bass, bassoon.[96]

The soirées were regularly between six and nine in the evening, in the music rooms of one of the palaces or mansions in Potsdam or Berlin. Often the King and his musicians were the only audience for these concerts. When there was a larger group of listeners, it was usually made up of a few selected guests or members of the royal family. The music performed was almost never anything other than some concertos or sonatas for flute, with either Quantz or Frederick playing the solos. When Frederick played, Quantz beat time (he did not usually perform as an accompanist); when Quantz played, Frederick watched the score and rebuked those who made mistakes.[97] Karl Heinrich Graun had practically nothing to do with this facet of the King's musical entertainments; his only function after 1742 was as conductor and composer for the Opera.

It is perhaps not surprising that most of the lasting achievements of Frederick's musical patronage were brought about by the underpaid and unnoticed members of his orchestra, rather than the "stars" of his opera. It never occurred to the King that his native instrumental virtuosi represented a fresh artistic development, while his imported opera was merely the decaying copy of a worn-out art. This was, of course, true in other German centers of Italian opera during the eighteenth century. Burney shows once again an amazing sense of perspective in recognizing the importance of German instrumental music during his time:

> It is . . . certain that whatever will justify my rambling through France and Italy after the *materia musica,* or apol-

[96] Thouret, *Friedrich der Grosse,* 105.   [97] *Ibid.,* 104–106.

ogize for it, may with the same force and propriety be pleaded for my having visited Germany; for though Italy has carried *vocal* music to a perfection unknown in any other country, much of the present excellence of *instrumental* is certainly owing to the natives of Germany, as wind and keyed instruments have never, perhaps, in any age or country, been brought to a greater degree of refinement, either in construction or use, than by the modern Germans.[98]

The permanent individual accomplishments of Frederick's musicians will not be discussed until the final chapter of this book; therefore further details of the organization to which most of them belonged—the orchestra—will be deferred until then.

SUSPENSION OF PATRONAGE, 1756–1763 (SEVEN YEAR'S WAR)

The first forebodings of the damage that would be done to the Opera because of the Seven Years' War came late in 1754, when Frederick spent some of his opera budget for military supplies. The public first noticed a chill in the air on March 27, 1755: Frederick was so occupied with the hostile actions of Maria Theresa that he failed to appear at the opera house for the customary observance of his mother's birthday. On March 27, 1756, Graun's last opera was performed.[99] In early August one more *intermezzo* was staged at Potsdam. On August 28, Frederick left Potsdam at the head of his troops and crossed the border of Saxony a few days later, in the first action of the war.[100]

From March 27, 1756, to December 17, 1764, not a single opera was produced at the Berlin Opera House. March 27, 1757, was Sophie Dorothea's last birthday; in celebration of it an

[98] *The Present State of Music,* I, vi–vii.
[99] Thouret, *Friedrich der Grosse,* 58.
[100] M. Dubinski, *"Beiträge zum Musikgeschichte Berlins während des Siebenjährigen Krieges,"* Die Musik, XI, 137.

intermezzo was performed at Potsdam. She died on June 28. By the time Karl Heinrich Graun died, in the summer of 1759, many of the opera performers had left. Late in 1760 the roof of the opera house was struck by Russian cannon—a fateful pronouncement of the wartime state of royal music in Berlin.[101]

The following were the main musical events in Berlin and Potsdam during the war: March 27, 1757, an *intermezzo* at Potsdam; May 15, 1757, the first performance of K. H. Graun's famous *Te Deum,* commemorating Frederick's siege of Prague; January 24, 1759, an orchestral concert prompted by the Queen and honoring the visiting King on his birthday; January 24, 1763, an Italian cantata, sung for the same occasion by members of the opera troupe.[102] Naturally, all of Berlin was not musically so inactive during this time. The private theaters and opera houses actually profited by the fact that the Berlin Opera had closed its doors, and they even hired some of Frederick's musicians on a part-time basis. Sacred music, part of which was composed by K. H. Graun, Agricola, and C. P. E. Bach, continued at the churches. Many of the King's singers and instrumentalists found employment in the churches or the music rooms of the royal family; salaries were generally continued, although they were paid in depreciated paper money. None of this activity, however, was the direct result of Frederick's musical patronage. It would have been much the same if Frederick had ceased to exist.

THIRD PERIOD OF PATRONAGE, 1763–1786

From the end of the Seven Years' War until Frederick's death in 1786, the following operas were produced at the Berlin Opera House:[103]

[101] Thouret, *Friedrich der Grosse,* 59.
[102] Dubinski, *"Beiträge zum Musikgeschichte," Die Musik,* XI, 137–42.
[103] This list is taken from Schneider, *Geschichte der Oper,* 151–202.

1764-65, carnival
Repeat performance of *Merope*
Leucippo; music by Hasse, libretto by Pasquini (first performed at Dresden in 1751)

Summer of 1765: *Achille in Sciro;* Agricola, Metastasio (for the wedding of the Prince of Prussia)

1765-66, carnival
Repeat performance of *Achille in Sciro*
Lucio Papirio; Hasse, Zeno (first performed at Dresden in 1742; libretto used by Graun in 1745)

1766-67, carnival
Repeat performance of *Cajo Fabrizio*
Repeat performance of *Le feste galanti*

1767-68, carnival
Amor und Psyché; Agricola, Landi (for the wedding of Princess Wilhelmina)
Repeat performance of *Ifigenia in Aulide*

1768-69, carnival
Repeat performance of *Catone in Utica*
Repeat performance of *Orfeo*

1769-70, carnival
Repeat performance of *Catone in Utica*
Repeat performance of *Didone abbandonata*
Repeat performance of *Fetonte*
"Serenata fatta per l'arrivo de la Regina Madre à Charlottenburg," performed in the opera house (previously performed at Charlottenburg in 1747)

1770–71, carnival
    Repeat performance of the "Serenata"
    Repeat performance of *Montezuma*

1771–72, carnival
    Repeat performance of *Britannico*
    I Greci in Tauride; Agricola, Landi (for the visit of the
        Queen of Sweden and the Duchess of Brunswick)

1772–73, carnival
    Repeat performance of *I Greci in Tauride*
    Repeat performance of *Merope*

1773–74, carnival
    Repeat performance of *Arminio*
    Repeat performance of *Demofoonte*

1774–75, Carnival
    Repeat performance of *Semiramide*
    Repeat performance of *Europa galante*

1775–76, carnival
    Attilio Regolo; Hasse, Metastasio (first performed at
        Dresden in 1750)
    Repeat performance of *Orfeo*

Summer of 1776: Repeat performance of *Angelica e Medoro*
    (somewhat altered by Reichardt and Landi; for the visit
    of the Russian Grand Duke)

1776–77, carnival
    Repeat performance of *Angelica e Medoro*, altered version
    Cleofide; Hasse, Metastasio (first performed at Dresden,
        with Frederick in attendance, in 1728)

FREDERICK'S FLUTE CONCERT AT SANS SOUCI

From a painting by Menzel which now hangs in the Orangery of Schloss Charlottenburg

Reprinted in this book by permission of the Dahlem Museum, West Berlin

The listeners in the painting are (from left to right): Baron Jakob Friedrich von Bielfeld; Count Gustav Adolf von Gotter; Pierre de Maupertius; the Queen Mother, Sophie Dorothea (?); Princess Amalie; K. H. Graun; Princess Wilhelmina; Frederick; Countess Sophie Caroline von Camas; the Chevalier Chasot; C. P. E. Bach; J. G. Graun (?); Anton Hock (?); Hans Jurgen Steffani (?); Franz Benda; Quantz.

1777–78, carnival
  Repeat performance of *Rodelinda*
  Artemisia; Hasse, Migliavacca (music considerably altered
    by Reichardt; first performed in Dresden, 1754)

(interruption until December 1779 because of the War of the
  Bavarian Succession)

December 1779: Repeat performance of *Rodelinda*

(The carnival was closed on January 13, 1780 because of the
  death of Princess Amalia, so no other operas were performed
  during that season.)

1780–81, carnival
  Repeat performance of *Armida*
  Repeat performance of *I fratelli nemici*

1781–82, carnival
  Repeat performance of *I fratelli nemici*
  Repeat performance of *Coriolano*

1782–83, carnival
  Repeat performance of *Artaserse*
  Repeat performance of *Sulla*

1783–84, carnival
  Repeat performance of *Alessandro nell' Indie*
  Repeat performance of Hasse's *Lucio Papirio*

1784–85, carnival
  Repeat performance of *Cajo Fabrizio*
  Repeat performance of *Orfeo*

1785–86, carnival
   Repeat performance of *Artemisia*, altered version
   Repeat performance of *I Greci in Tauride*

As this list shows, almost all of the postwar productions were "reruns." The only new operas commissioned by the King from 1756 until his death thirty years later were the three composed by J. F. Agricola; and considering the harassment Agricola suffered at the hands of Frederick, the words "new" and "composed" are perhaps too strong to be used in describing these works.[104] With the exception of these three, every opera of this period dates from before the war and is by either Graun or Hasse.

When K. H. Graun died in 1759, Frederick did not appoint a new *Kapellmeister*, and immediately after the war he did not deign to give the title to any of his musicians. J. F. Agricola, who had joined Frederick's service in 1751, was appointed court composer and musical director of the Opera, but it was hardly a station of dignity. He had already earned the King's disfavor by marrying the singer Benedetta Molteni, and his patron had little faith in his ability. In addition, he was unsuited for the position, being more a composer of sacred music than of opera.

The marriage of the Prince of Prussia in the summer of 1765 roused Frederick to something like his old magnificence: for the first time since before the war he commissioned a new opera, *Achille in Sciro* by Agricola. The young *castrato* Concialini sang the title role (his first) with success, and became a mainstay of the Berlin Opera, remaining as such until 1796.[105] But the successful season of 1765 was not followed by similar triumphs. The King became increasingly conservative, begrudging every

[104] See the section on Agricola in chapter IV. The composers mentioned in this account of the opera's decline are included only for the sake of continuity. Like the important members of the orchestra, they will be discussed more fully in chapter IV.

[105] Thouret, *Friedrich der Grosse*, 90–91.

expenditure made for the Opera. For example, the production of *Amor et Psyché*, part of young Princess Wilhelmina's marriage celebration in 1767, was preceded by anxious notes like the following (from Frederick to Baron Pöllnitz, written to arrange for the services of Landi as librettist):

> I am enclosing a letter from the Abbé Landi. Concerning its contents, keep in mind that I want you to arrange everything connected with the opera in question, and to do it with the greatest possible economy. . . .[106]

For the production of *Ifigenia in Aulide* in 1768 there was not a single female singer available for the role of Ifigenia (sung in 1749 by Astrua). Frederick solved the problem by giving the role to the *castrato* Coli.[107] This was too much even for a public accustomed to eighteenth-century artificialities, and the performance was so widely ridiculed that Frederick finally published an edict prohibiting the writing of anything whatever about the Berlin Opera. The budget for every production was now cut to the bone, the ridicule continued, the performers and the management became irresponsible, the costumes and decorations were shabby, and Frederick gradually lost interest in the enterprise. He realized that his company of singers, dancers, and actors was going downhill, and had resigned himself to circumstances. In 1770 he wrote to the Landgravine of Hessen-Darmstadt:

> For seven uninterrupted years the Austrians, Russians, and French led me such a dance that I have somewhat lost my taste for dance in the theater, or at least have decided that I can no longer spend much money on it.[108]

[106] Schneider, *Geschichte der Oper, appendix,* 69.
[107] *Ibid.,* 158.
[108] Thouret, *Friedrich der Grosse,* 59.

During the same year Frederick even considered leasing the Opera to a private promoter. It was possibly through the intervention of Quantz, one of the few musicians able to be completely frank with Frederick, that the King did not do so. Quantz suggested that if the opera house were leased, the inscription honoring "Fredericus Rex" should be removed.[109]

Yet there was to be one more brief flowering of the Opera, caused by Frederick's appointment in 1771 of a new *directeur des spectacles*, Count Zierotin-Litgenau, and a new singer, Elizabeth Schmeling. The new director was an efficient manager in spite of Frederick's suspicions that he was stealing more than he was saving. (At the time of Zierotin-Litgenau's appointment Frederick also delegated to one of his ministers, a Herr Stiegel, the responsibility of keeping the costs of the opera and theater to a minimum. Herr Stiegel was the overseer of the overseers of the opera and theater.) The new singer, together with Concialini, was able to add youth and artistry to the efforts of the aging Porporino and Signora Agricola.[110] Elizabeth Schmeling was one of the most colorful personalities in the history of opera. The story of her dealings with Frederick, as told in her autobiography, gives interest to a depressing picture.

She was born in 1749, the daughter of a Kassel violinist. She played the violin at the age of four, toured Germany as a prodigy with her father, and played before the Queen of England at ten. However, because the violin was considered unladylike, Elizabeth became a singer; and by the time she was twenty she had performed in Vienna, London (under Paradisi),

109 *Ibid.*, 90.
110 In 1772 the visiting Burney commented on Frederick's singers: "The chief singers of this serious opera, in the female parts, are Mademoiselle Schmeling, Signora Agricola, and Signora Gasparini, seventy-two years of age; a time of life when nature seldom allows us any other voice than that of complaint, or second childhood," (*The Present State of Music*, II, 98). This was one of Burney's many inaccuracies: Signora Gasparini was sixty-five at the time.

Leipzig (under Johann Adam Hiller), and Dresden, all with great success. The compass of her voice was from f to e³; her sense of pitch was unfailing; she sang with great artistry, and with such power that her voice could easily be heard above the largest chorus or orchestra; Goethe immortalized her in a poem.[111] Yet when in 1771 her father brought her to apply for a position in the Prussian court, where a prima donna was badly needed, Frederick refused to hear her because she was German; he was convinced that she would have the *"accent tudesque"* which made German singers generally ineligible for the performance of Italian opera. His comment is famous: "I'd rather have the arias of my operas neighed by a horse than to have a German prima donna."[112]

Nevertheless, Frederick was eventually persuaded, mainly through the endeavors of Count Zierotin-Litgenau and Franz Benda, to give her a hearing. Schmeling gives a detailed, if rather immodest, description of this interview in her autobiography. When she arrived at Sans Souci the King was playing a concerto with an accompaniment of two violins and cembalo, while Quantz listened. After he had finished, he called her into his music room.

The King sat on a sofa with the general [Tauenzien], near his three Italian greyhounds—who started barking loudly when they saw me. The King called them to him, and I drew near in order to kiss the hem of his coat; but he would not allow me to do so. Instead he asked, "We will hear something from you?" I answered, "As Your Majesty commands," and turned to the harpsichord. At that time I was not anxious about gaining the King's approval, since I was

---

[111] Gertrud Elisabeth Mara (Schmeling), *"Eine Selbstbiographie der Sängerin Gertrud Elisabeth Mara,"* ed. by O. von Riesemann, *Allgemeine Musikalische Zeitung*, Vol. X (August 11–September 29, 1875), 497–98.

[112] Thouret, *Friedrich der Grosse*, 93.

planning to go to Italy for further study anyway; so I had not the slightest fear. Besides, I knew what I was doing. So I stood there quite calmly, looking at the large, beautiful paintings, as the ritornello of an aria was played; then I sang the aria through. The King said "bravo" several times, and at the end of the aria he came up to me, inquired about who my teachers were, and asked whether I could sing from written music. I answered yes, so he handed me the famous bravura-aria "Mi paventi, il figlio indegno" from Graun's opera *Britannicus*.

I looked through it, and then sang it, after my fashion, half again as fast as it had been performed by Astrua, my predecessor. The musicians had difficulty in keeping up with me; I believe they thought I was some kind of sorceress. The King appeared to admire my ability. The following evening I was called on to perform again, and so it went for six weeks. I was often on the point of obtaining permission to make my trip to Italy in order to perfect myself further there; but the King said that I had no need of study in Italy, and that if I did go it would only make my singing deteriorate. He was generally very gracious to me, almost gallant. I believe it pleased him, when we spoke with each other, to see me look straight into his big blue eyes rather than casting my eyes down like so many others, who always said that one could not bear his gaze.[113]

After her six weeks of impromptu performances, Schmeling was engaged as prima donna and given a contract promising her a salary of three thousand thalers for a two-year period (fifteen hundred thalers a year).[114]

Within a year, however, she began to have disagreements with her father—who had been engaged in the orchestra—which

---

[113] Frensdorff, *"Die Sängerin E. Mara," Mitteilungen des Vereins,* 28–29.
[114] *Ibid.*

eventually became so violent that Frederick ordered them to live apart from each other. Soon afterwards she became scandalously involved with one of the orchestra cellists named Mara, asked Frederick's permission to marry him, and was refused. When the two tried to escape from Prussia, the King arrested them and jailed Mara. Elizabeth's father, who by now had become obnoxious, offered to leave Berlin permanently if Frederick would allow his daughter to marry. The King at length agreed but only on the additional condition that she serve in the Berlin Opera for the rest of her life. Under these conditions the marriage took place, but Mme Mara was still unhappy in Berlin's atmosphere of musical decay and inactivity. She feigned sickness, sang performances while intoxicated, and continued to plan escape.

In 1774 Agricola died, and his place as court composer was taken temporarily by Karl Friedrich Fasch, who since 1756 had been C. P. E. Bach's assistant at the clavier. Fasch, in Frederick's eyes, did not even deserve the doubtful place of honor held by Agricola. Like Agricola, he was denied the title of *Kapellmeister;* his directorship of the opera, between 1774 and 1776, was uneasy, unhappy, and mutually unsatisfactory. It is rather surprising to learn that Fasch, after having done with Frederick's patronage, founded the famous *Singakademie* of Berlin.

Fasch was replaced as musical director in 1776 by J. F. Reichardt, the first person since the death of Graun to receive the title of *Kapellmeister*. Although Reichardt's title had dignity, there was little dignity in the tasks of rewriting which Frederick assigned him. Revising the works of others was hardly a fit occupation for the musician who later played an important part in the development of the *Lied* and the *Singspiel*, as well as being one of the most distinguished of eighteenth-century writers on music. Reichardt was only able to bear the oppressive musical rule of his patron by taking frequent leaves of absence and ended his service to Frederick by denouncing the deceased king's artistic policies:

> Everybody knows that the Italian opera in Berlin, which I directed for twelve years, sank to such a deplorable state during the last part of [Frederick's] reign that it became utterly worthless as an artistic medium.[115]

In July of 1776 Frederick was visited by the Russian Grand Duke Paul Petrovitch. For this important guest's entertainment, Frederick instructed his opera company, two months before the Grand Duke's arrival, to prepare a performance of Graun's *Angelica e Medoro* (libretto by Villati, adapted from Quinault), which had been given at the opera house in 1749. The King specified that Reichardt and Landi (the last of Frederick's librettists and one of the poorest, hired in 1767)[116] should compose a new prologue for this opera which would celebrate the genius of Prussia and Russia. He also specified that the opera be shortened, that it be adapted for performance in the small theater at Potsdam, and that the main aria, "*Nell' orror d'altra foresta*"—which Astrua had sung in 1749—be recomposed to suit the voice of Elizabeth Mara. Baron von Arnim, director of the *Schauspiel*, was given the responsibility of supervising the preparations. All these instructions threw the King's decaying troupe into such a desperate scramble, such a series of crises, that the whole story of the production would itself make a fine comic opera plot.

The first crisis occurred when Landi came to the realization that it would be impossible to squeeze the opera into such a small theater. He wrote a letter to Arnim on May 25:

> I take the liberty of asking you, Monsieur, to notify Sig-

[115] Schneider, *Geschichte der Oper*, 203.
[116] See p. 152.

nor Reichardt to cease his work on the parts of *Angelica e Medoro*, because it is going to be necessary to change the opera considerably. The more I read and reread the libretto, the more I perceive the impossibility of having this opera performed at Potsdam in its present state. How is it possible, in that little theater, to represent a ship and a storm at sea? Where are we going to put the towers, the drawbridges, the grottoes and all the other decorations? Since we will have to do without most of these, I must make major changes in the libretto—which will be so much the better, for in doing this I shall be able to shorten the performance time to less than two hours. However, I will arrange it so that if the opera happens to be given in Berlin during the carnival season, it can be staged with the usual decorations and magnificence. The task will be difficult, but I have dedicated myself to it. Working at my ordinary rate, I should be able to send you my manuscript, Monsieur, by the end of next week.[117]

In consequence of this letter, Frederick decided that he would rather have the performance in the opera house after all rather than mutilate it for the sake of a single production at Potsdam. Landi, then, had only to compose a prologue and make a few changes in the main body of the work. His prologue took the form of a duet, in which the Genius of Russia and the Genius of Prussia greet each other, exchange flatteries, and finish with a warm embrace.

Reichardt, eager to impress his new patron, took the revised libretto straight to Potsdam so that he could confer with Frederick about the music as he composed it. On arriving there he sent a letter to Baron von Arnim:

I am honored to report to Your Excellency that immediately on my arrival, soon after three o'clock, I had a very

[117] Schneider, *Geschichte der Oper* (*Pracht-Ausgabe*), 44.

gracious audience with His Majesty the King. His Majesty permitted me to listen while he played three excellent sonatas, the most interesting of which was one of his own compositions—just as you told me it would be. I remained with him for awhile after he finished playing. He told me that I should compose the music for the prologue here so that, as each bit is completed, I can play it for him. I shall begin tomorrow, and I should easily finish in three days; after that we must have rehearsals. I shall work with all possible speed.

The characters of the prologue will be sung by Signor Tosoni and Madame Koch. Before His Majesty named the latter, I suggested Signor Porporino; but His Majesty said that while Signor Porporino would be ideal for the part, it would not be suitable for him to sing it because of his having a role in the main body of the opera.[118]

In a few days Reichardt finished the prologue, as well as the aria which was to be sung by Mara, and it was all given Frederick's approval.

The second crisis was a result of Frederick's determination to spend as little money as possible on the production. On June 22 Herr Stiegel, whom the King had appointed as "budget-watcher" for the opera and theater, wrote the following message to Arnim:

I have settled everything with His Majesty regarding the opera and ballets, and this is the gist of his statement to me: Not one cent has been allocated for decorations. The making of any decorations whatever has been forbidden by His Majesty. Your Excellency will understand, I trust, that I cannot change this. *Your Excellency will therefore condescend* to use, for the first setting, the scenery from the garden made by Galliari [Frederick's stage decorator for a

[118] *Ibid.,* 45.

short while in 1773] and also the horizon which goes with it—or you could use the seaport garden as well. For the fourth decoration there is Mount Rhodope from *Orfeo*. For the palace in the final scene I will be quite satisfied if you will use the marble column properties, provided that it does not cost too much to have them set up. The decoration made by Verona [stage decorator at the time] is, just between us, a bit "crazy," and horribly in danger of catching fire. Concerning the prologue, we are in need of nothing except two costumes for Tosoni and Madame Koch. How they are to be dressed in order to represent the Geniuses of Russia and Prussia is a mystery to me; I leave it up to you. I believe the Cupid costume would do well for Tosoni, but whether Madame Koch is to be dressed as a man or as a woman is something the *Kapellmeister* must decide.

The apparatus for changing the trees is a minor consideration; Your Excellency may order that it be constructed. As for the ballets: we have already decided on just the costumes we will need, all of which will come from what we already have in the opera house; and now here comes Herr *Hermann* with two costumes for *Salamon* and *Desplaces*—for two hundred thalers. It is really impossible for me to accept these; I am ordered by His Majesty not to spend more money, and I dare not ask him for more. All I can say to Your Excellency about this is that they must dance in the best and cleanest costumes available from the wardrobe, *whether they are appropriate or not.*[119]

Baron von Arnim was upset and angered by this insolent advice from a bookkeeper on how to produce an opera. He objected violently, as much to Herr Stiegel's lack of tact as to his curtailment of the budget. But in only two days he received another message which repeated the statements of the first one; like it or not, he would have to give the Grand Duke a glam-

[119] *Ibid.*, 45–46.

orous picture of Royal Opera in Berlin without spending money in the process.

The third crisis was caused by Elizabeth Mara. Still unhappy, still trying to find a way to escape from the petrified musical life of Berlin, she was not particularly anxious to please her patron. In addition, she disliked Reichardt intensely, openly referring to him as an "arrogant egotist."[120] When Frederick sent her the aria composed by Reichardt and told her to study it, she sent it right back with a note saying that she could not sing such music. This made Frederick turn to his customary means of coercion: he wrote out a *Cabinetsordre* instructing that she be arrested and sent to the prison at Spandau. In the margin he wrote: "She is paid to sing and not to write." Baron von Arnim, fearing ruin of the whole enterprise, attempted to intervene in her behalf; but he was cut down by another *Cabinetsordre* to the effect that he had better keep his mind on the opera and leave affairs of state to cabinet ministers.[121]

The last crisis took place during rehearsals of the prologue, when what had been apparent to Reichardt from the beginning now became obvious to all the performers: Tosoni, the Genius of Prussia, was tall and robust-looking; Madame Koch, the Genius of Russia, was small and delicate, even rather timid. Grand Duke Paul was known to be violent, distrustful and easily offended. The difficulty was that nobody knew whether Frederick intended to insult the Grand Duke or not. Reichardt was afraid to ask because a month earlier the King had rejected his suggestion of Porporino for the part. Arnim was afraid to ask because he was already in trouble with Frederick over Mara. The problem was eventually solved by Reichardt: he staged a performance of the prologue at one of the evening

---

[120] Mennicke, *Hasse und die Brüder Graun*, 481. This title was not entirely undeserved; see the section on Reichardt in chapter IV.

[121] Schneider, *Geschichte der Oper (Pracht-Ausgabe)*, 45.

chamber concerts, hoping that the possibility of its being con-
strued as an insult to the Grand Duke would occur to Frederick, if it had not already occurred to him. This strategy was
successful; Frederick had not intended an insult, and immediately saw the necessity of making the two Geniuses the same
size. He ordered that Porporino, who was about as tall as Tosoni,
take Madame Koch's place in the prologue. The only remaining
difficulty was that Porporino feared that he would not be able
to learn the extra role in time. The King solved this problem
by ordering that Madame Koch, dressed in boy's clothes, should
stand near Porporino and sing the part while Porporino went
through the motions. Fortunately, this was not necessary; the
Genius of Russia learned his part in time, and Madame Koch
had only to stand near by "in case."[122]

In spite of all the crises, the King's troupe gave an acceptable
performance. Elizabeth Mara was not jailed and she sang in the
opera. Frederick probably never intended to send her to Spandau; according to several anecdotes, it was only necessary for
him to imprison her husband until she agreed to sing. The same
anecdotes tell us that she performed very artistically all the
parts of her role which had been composed by Graun, but de-
liberately spoiled the aria composed by Reichardt.[123] During
the following season Frederick half-heartedly sought a substitute for her; but Spandau was becoming almost as well known
as the Bastille, so he could find no prominent singers willing to
join his service.

In August, 1779, Elizabeth and her husband managed to
escape Berlin after several futile attempts, and Frederick was
no longer interested enough to have them brought back. The
man for whom she had endured so much now proved to be
unworthy, and they were separated. He was finally reduced to

[122] *Ibid.*
[123] *Ibid.*

playing the cello in a sailor's pub in Rotterdam. She went back to Berlin in 1803, then to Vienna, then to Russia—where she lost all her possessions in Napoleon's burning of Moscow—and finally back to Germany and Reval (now Tallinn), where she died in obscurity at the age of eighty-four.[124] Although she was probably the greatest German singer of her time, her real importance lies in the fact that she was a great eighteenth-century German singer who never went to Italy.

The outbreak of the War of the Bavarian Succession in 1778 struck the death blow to the King's French theater. Soon after the war began, Baron von Arnim received the following *Cabinetsordre* from Frederick:

> The events which are already taking place are merely a preparation for something more serious. We will do well to give up our pursuit of the theater, and that is why I must discontinue the appointments and pensions of all the French actors and actresses. Consequently, you are ordered to dismiss them.[125]

Less than two years later Elizabeth Mara was gone, and Frederick lost all interest in the Opera. The opera house by this time was so nearly empty during performances that the King often ordered entire companies of soldiers to attend, simply to have all the seats filled and to help keep the house warm. The soldiers brought their wives, and filled the entire house with such a stench of onions and tobacco that it was difficult for others to sit through the operas.[126] For the production of *Armida* in 1780 not a cent was spent on décor or costumes.[127] In spite of Frederick's decree against writing anything about the Opera, the

---

[124] Frensdorff, *"Die Sängerin E. Mara," Mitteilungen des Vereins,* 30.
[125] Thouret, *Friedrich der Grosse,* 101.
[126] Carl Lange, *Johann Friedrich Reichardt,* 19.
[127] Yorke-Long, *Music at Court,* 143.

newspapers were full of criticisms. Frederick attended the Opera for the last time during the carnival season of 1781–82, and never again set foot in the opera house.[128] The leading performers who remained were as old and worn as Frederick himself. In October 1781 a visitor to Berlin, the Marquis Luchesini, wrote to Italy: "For the next carnival it is impossible to have an acceptable voice without a repulsive figure to go with it."[129] In 1785 Reichardt wrote that Graun's *Orfeo*, reperformed that year, was "an old Italian hodgepodge."[130] The reason he was not jailed for this statement was probably because Frederick was simply not interested in the Opera any longer.

During the last two decades of Frederick's life the productions of opera in Berlin for paid admission became firmly entrenched. The King was literally surrounded with a vital development in German *Volksoper;* private theaters had already given *Singspiele* as early as 1743, and from 1771 to Frederick's death in 1786 no less than 101 different *Singspiele* were performed in Berlin.[131] But new developments in opera, as in instrumental music, had ceased to interest the King many years before; his orchestra and his opera company had to wait for a younger patron before they could advance into the nineteenth century.

[128] Schneider, *Geschichte der Oper,* 195.
[129] *Ibid.*
[130] *Ibid.,* 201.
[131] *Ibid.,* 204–10.

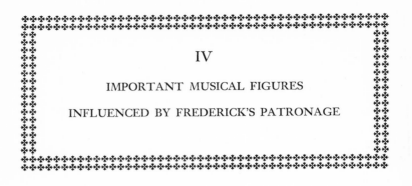

IV

IMPORTANT MUSICAL FIGURES

INFLUENCED BY FREDERICK'S PATRONAGE

T HE MOST FITTING MONUMENTS to the memory of a great
musical patron are not buildings or organizations or performances, but the lasting advancements in the art of
music brought about by individuals under his patronage. Frederick's vociferously expressed musical opinions affected vitally
the lives and the work of his artists, not only through his concrete actions but also through the pervasion of the Berlin atmosphere by his rationalistic spirit. The King's concrete actions
included choosing artists, giving commissions to composers,
accepting and rejecting compositions and productions, and determining artistic policies. The spirit of the *Aufklärung*, which
he represented above all, set the intellectual climate in Berlin
which resulted in an almost unprecedented amount of verbaliza-

tion on music and musical theory. Frederick had a direct influence on creators of music and an indirect influence on writers about music.

The number of musicians influenced by the King is, of course, indefinite; but fourteen musical personalities seem to deserve specific mention because of the importance or interest of their relationship to him: Karl Heinrich Graun, Johann Joachim Quantz, Carl Philipp Emanuel Bach, Franz Benda, Johann Gottlieb Graun, Johann Friedrich Agricola, Karl Friedrich Christian Fasch, Johann Friedrich Reichardt, Friedrich Wilhelm Marpurg, Christoph Nichelmann, Johann Philipp Kirnberger, Johann Adolph Hasse, Johann Sebastian Bach, and Gottfried Silbermann. In the following discussion these men are grouped according to the degree of their dependence on Frederick. K. H. Graun and Quantz are dealt with first because they were the main representatives of the King's opera and instrumental music, and were so vitally influenced by Frederick that their musical significance was determined by him. C. P. E. Bach, Franz Benda, and J. G. Graun,[1] grouped together as the most important of Frederick's chamber musicians, each produced great works which had only a slight connection with their assigned duties. Agricola, Fasch, and Reichardt are the next three composers discussed because they were K. H. Graun's successors as conductors; however, they had little else in common except the misfortune of being frustrated by their patron. Following these are Marpurg, Nichelmann, and Kirnberger, whose primary claims to fame rest rather uneasily upon their accomplishments as writers and theorists, as musical spokesmen of Frederick's philosophy of rationalism. Finally, Hasse, J. S. Bach, and Gottfried Silbermann, the only three who were not directly

---

[1] Since J. G. Graun's accomplishments as a performer and composer of chamber music were quite different from those of his more famous brother Karl Heinrich, these two brothers are discussed separately.

patronized by the King, are worthy of notice here simply because of their interesting and diverse associations with him.

K. H. Graun received a thorough education at the *Kreuzschule* in Dresden. In addition, he studied singing with the cantor Johann Zacharias Grundig, clavier with the cembalist Christian Petzold, and composition with the *Kapellmeister* Johann Christian Schmidt. His first important post was in the Brunswick court, from 1725 to 1735, as singer and assistant *Kapellmeister*. He achieved early success as a composer during the season of 1726–27, when his first Brunswick opera, *Sancio und Sinilde*, was performed. During the ten years at this court he composed six operas, all but one of which had German texts, but the music of all these works is just as Italian in style as his later operas. Ironically, too, his one opera of this period which is in Italian, *Lo specchio della fedeltà*, has the least satisfactory text of the six.

The occasion of this first Italian opera of Graun's was the marriage of Frederick and Elizabeth at Salzthal on June 12, 1733. The Prince had heard many favorable reports of Graun's music, and after the wedding he resolved that this composer should be one of his court musicians. Graun was given an occasion to resign when his patron Ludwig Rudolf died in 1735; in that year he accepted Frederick's invitation and moved to Ruppin. His position at first was only as singer and composer, but he became *Kapellmeister* within a few months.[2]

The few years Graun spent at Ruppin and Rheinsberg were unglamorous in comparison with his career after Frederick's accession. The musical activities fostered by the Prince were

[2] Carl H. Mennicke, *"Zur Biographie der Brüder Graun," Neue Zeitschrift für Musik*, Vol. VIII (1904), 130.

hardly operatic and made little use of Graun's major talent. He had been hopefully hired by Frederick, during the King's illness, for the main purpose of composing operas; but Frederick William's unexpected recovery and continuing existence made it necessary for Graun to bide his time with comparatively trivial activities. From 1735 to 1740 he produced only small compositions: about fifty chamber cantatas (each usually consisting of two arias with recitatives) and a few instrumental works. He gave the Prince lessons in composition, conducted the orchestra, sang an occasional aria, and waited for Frederick William to die.

Graun's "unauthorized" status came to an end in 1740. One of Frederick's first acts as King was to appoint him Prussian Court *Kapellmeister* at a salary of two thousand thalers a year.[3] The first duty of the now legitimate composer was the composition of a *Trauerkantate* for Frederick William's funeral ceremony. The text of this work, in Latin, was by a Berlin minister, Pastor Baumgartner. Since Frederick did not yet have singers in his court, it was necessary to borrow three Italian performers from Dresden; these three and Graun sang the cantata.[4]

The career of this composer is indistinguishable from the history of the Berlin Opera during its greatest eighteenth-century period, from 1740 to 1756. The tremendous establishment which the King had set up was devoted almost solely to the works of his musical director. Graun basked in the favor which Frederick had so generously bestowed, and in the renown which his position had given him. The King's preference for Italian opera was Graun's aesthetic guidepost, and he followed it well, though not without difficulty. Frederick never hesitated to suggest changes or to order that portions of the operas be rewritten; many of the arias in the extant dramatic works of Graun are

---

[3] A. Maczewsky and Alfred Loewenberg, "Graun, Karl Heinrich," *Grove's Dictionary of Music and Musicians*, Vol. III.
[4] Mennicke, *Hasse und die Brüder Graun*, 457.

second or even third versions. Graun was duly appreciative of his fame, eager to please, and even genuinely fond of his patron, but it was inevitable that he should find Frederick's dictates irksome.

On one occasion, the performance of his *Demofoonte* in 1746, his embarrassment at being "corrected" almost outweighed the musical pre-eminence which he enjoyed. The aria *"Misero pargelotto"* of this opera did not suit the King's fancy, and Graun was ordered to rewrite it. The second version was even less satisfactory to Frederick; and when Graun assured him that he had done his best, Frederick substituted an aria by Hasse. Nothing could have made Graun more uncomfortable, for he was constantly being reminded by Frederick of the Saxon composer's excellence and considered him a formidable rival. Unluckily for Graun, this aria was so well received by the public that it became almost a street song.[5]

For the opera *Lucio Papirio* (1745) Graun wrote his last French overture. All of his overtures after that date were Italian *sinfonia*,[6] according to Frederick's specification.[7] Frederick's dissatisfaction with the French overture, aside from being an evidence of his aversion for all "French" music, was largely based on his dislike of contrapuntal forms in general, which in turn originated in his, and Voltaire's, disrespect for all traditions of the immediate past. As it happened, Graun's discontinuance of this form was a general trend followed by most composers of his time; so Frederick's instruction was timely, if not tolerant.

The *sinfonia* composed by Graun are part of the large back-

---

[5] Müller-Blatteau, *"Karl Friedrich Zelters Rede auf Friedrich den Grossen,"* *Deutsche Musikkultur*, Vol. I (August–September, 1936), 172.

[6] The term "Italian sinfonia" (= "Italian overture") is used by the author to denote the operatic overture in three sections, fast–slow–fast, in primarily homophonic style, which was introduced in the late seventeenth century by Alessandro Scarlatti and was the immediate predecessor of the symphony.

[7] Mennicke, *Hasse und die Brüder Graun*, 111.

ground out of which came the first symphonies. In 1906 Karl H. Mennicke produced a very scholarly study, *Hasse und die Brüder Graun als Symphoniker*, in which the overtures and symphonies of these composers are evaluated. As might be expected, Mennicke shows that these works are among the ever-growing list of preclassical instrumental pieces leading to the classical symphony. Karl Heinrich Graun's chief contribution to symphonic structure is his adherence, in the first movements of his *sinfonia*, to the opening theme as a unifying factor. For example, the *Kopftheme* of the overture to *Ezio*, as shown in Fig. 19,[8] is reiterated throughout the movement, especially in the bass: first in D, then in B minor, then G, and so on; through this

Fig. 19.—K. H. Graun, *"Sinfonie"* from *Ezio*, first violin, measures 1–4.

method the movement gains unity. Graun's compositions resemble those of Hasse very closely (which explains Frederick's admiration of Hasse); this is especially true of his overtures. After an exhaustive study of the French and Italian overtures of these two composers, Mennicke concludes that

> An analysis of Karl Heinrich Graun's *sinfonia* will not keep us long, since these pieces by the Berlin composer of operas, like his French overtures, resemble the corresponding works of Hasse—in form and content—so closely that it is very easy to confuse a *sinfonie* by Graun with one by Hasse.[9]

One last mention should be made of K. H. Graun's overtures in connection with the quality of their opening themes. These

[8] Cited in Friedrich Noack, *Sinfonie und Suite*, 106.
[9] Mennicke, *Hasse und die Brüder Graun*, 199.

melodies are a good index to the fertility of Graun's imagination; a study of them shows that their composer's power of invention was wanting. Fig. 20 shows the *Kopfthemen* from the *sinfonia* of some of his operas.[10] In fairness to Graun, it must be remembered that it was often customary in his time to scribble anything that would suffice for an overture, because the audience seldom listened carefully to it; they were usually occupied with discussing the personalities they would see and hear when the curtain rose.

F IG. 20.—Opening themes from some of K. H. Graun's *Sinfonia*.

Like Hasse and other eighteenth-century Italian or Italianized composers, Graun was concerned with beautiful, singable

[10] Cited in Mennicke, *Hasse und die Brüder Graun*, 199–200.

melody above all; he was an outstanding melodist who knew how to write effortlessly and idiomatically for the voice. His operas were composed very rapidly: starting not long before the beginning of the carnival, he would usually write one aria a day, which he sketched in the morning and finished in the afternoon. He used manuscript paper on which a copyist had already written the text.[11]

Graun's operas are like the compositions of his patron in that they are products of an environment in which enlightenment and reason were foremost considerations, whether in philosophy, politics or art. They are straightforward, made according to a simple pattern, not subtle or irrational. The essence of Graun's formal principles is well stated by Paul Henry Lang:

> Carl Heinrich Graun . . . dominated opera in Berlin, but the dramatic works of this composer—and of most of the Italianized Germans—seem to have been entirely shaped on one well-established musico-dramatic last. They contain a good deal of pleasing and sound music, but the objective was to write well and fluently for the singers, to keep the orchestra occupied in an effective fashion, and to unite, in the important dramatic situations, all available means in a telling manner.[12]

This is the structure of Graun's *Ifigenia in Aulide* (1748), a formal plan closely followed in most of his operas:

First Act

Scene 1: (a) Secco recitative (b) accompanied recitative
(c) secco recitative (d) aria
Scene 2: (a) secco recitative (b) aria
Scene 3: (a) chorus (b) secco recitative (c) aria
Scene 4: (a) secco recitative (b) aria

[11] C. F. Zelter, *Karl Friedrich Christian Fasch*, 221.
[12] *Music in Western Civilization*, 459.

Scene 5: secco recitative
Scene 6: (a) secco recitative (b) aria (c) secco recitative (d) aria
Scene 7: (a) secco recitative (b) duet

Second Act
Scene 1: (a) secco recitative (b) aria
Scene 2: (a) secco recitative (b) aria
Scene 3: (a) secco recitative (b) aria
Scene 4: (a) secco recitative (b) aria
Scene 5: secco recitative
Scene 6: (a) secco recitative (b) trio
Scene 7: (a) secco recitative (b) accompanied recitative (c) secco recitative (d) aria
Scene 8: (a) secco recitative (b) accompanied recitative (c) secco recitative
Scene 9: (a) secco recitative (b) aria
Scene 10: (a) secco recitative (b) duet

Third Act
Scene 1: secco recitative
Scene 2: (a) secco recitative (b) aria
Scene 3: (a) secco recitative (b) aria
Scene 4: secco recitative
Scene 5: (a) secco recitative (b) aria
Scene 6: (a) secco recitative (b) aria
Scene 7: secco recitative
Scene 8: (a) secco recitative (b) aria
Scene 9: (a) march (b) chorus (c) chorus (d) orchestral interlude (e) accompanied recitative (f) aria (g) secco recitative (h) chorus

This composer's arias, duets, trios, and choruses generally

follow one of two forms: that of the *da capo* aria or (at Frederick's "suggestion") the cavatina.[13] The aria *"So, che giusto"* from *Ifigenia*, in *da capo* form, is perfectly indicative of the musical taste of the mid-eighteenth-century Berliner; it became so popular that it was sung everywhere. The first section of it is quoted in Fig. 21.[14] In this same opera, Graun is able to express sorrow eloquently, even for modern ears, in the chorus *"Mora, Mora, Ifigenia."* This chorus (Fig. 22) moved its original auditors deeply, and was quite well known.[15] In the last act of *Montezuma* (Fig. 23) Graun portrays the emotional reaction of Eupaforice (bride of Montezuma) to the burning of Mexico City by the Spaniards.[16]

Graun also composed the entr'acte and ballet music for his operas, but he did not include this music in his scores; consequently, only a few fragments of it are extant. One of these fragments is a "Musette" (Fig. 24) from the ballet music of *Orfeo*, first produced in 1752.[17]

The orchestra was handled as conservatively as possible by this composer. He was not an innovator, and his primary aim was simply to make use of all the resources which the King put at his command. He considered the string quartet the basis of the orchestra and was rather sparing in his use of woodwinds and brasses. The voices for which he composed included *castrati;* the leading male roles for most of his Berlin operas are in the soprano range. This single factor prohibits the modern performance of his operas, like most of the operas of his contemporaries. It is interesting and perhaps significant that five of Graun's six Brunswick operas give leading roles to basses.

The majority of the texts used by Graun were tragedies,

---

[13] See the section on Frederick's libretti.
[14] Cited in Thouret, *Friedrich der Grosse,* 73–76.
[15] *Ibid.,* 76.
[16] K. H. Graun, *Montezuma,* ed. by A. Mayer-Reinach, 214.
[17] Cited in Thouret, *Friedrich der Grosse,* 81.

Fig. 21.–K. H. Graun, Aria *"So, che giusti"* from *Ifigenia in Aulide*, measures 1–32 (piano reduction).

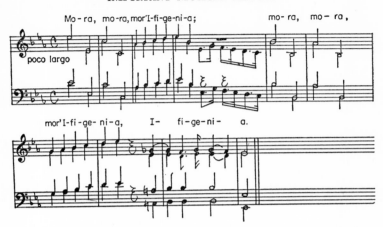

FIG. 22.—K. H. Graun, Aria *"Mora, Mora, Ifigenia"* from *Ifigenia in Aulide,* measures 1–10 (piano reduction).

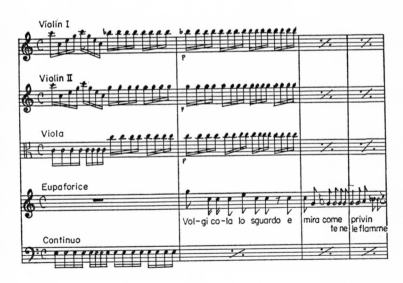

che ar-do-no la cit-tà per cenno mi – o

FIG. 23.—K. H. Graun, excerpt of an aria by Eupaforice, page 214 in Mayer-Reinach's edition of *Montezuma*.

written in imitation of their French counterparts. They dealt primarily with mythical subjects, epics of ancient times, and ancient history (Frederick's *Montezuma* is a noteworthy exception); their characters were gods, heroes, and kings. Four librettists were in Frederick's employ: Bottarelli, Villati, Tagliazucchi, and Landi. Not one of them was a poet of outstanding talent, although Tagliazucchi was perhaps more talented than the rest. The best texts for Graun's operas were those of Metastasio and Zeno,[18] used over and over by composers in all parts of Europe; but even these were usually "adapted" and ruined by the King's librettists. The mediocrity of Frederick's court poets was noticed by their contemporaries, and Villati was a particularly frequent target for criticism. Of Villati, Gotthold Lessing wrote: "In Herr Villati's operas there is little invention,

[18] See the lists on pp. 102–104 and 122–26.

organization, or verisimilitude. He gleans all his works from tragedies by other authors, and when he changes something, he spoils it."[19] The work of these librettists was not helped by Frederick's interference. Even the libretti in which he did not take a creative part were affected by his taste. Thouret was of the opinion that "not a single opera text came into Graun's hands without first being subjected to the criticism of the King."[20]

Fig. 24.—K. H. Graun, "Musette" from ballet music to *Orfeo*, measures 1-8 (piano reduction).

Graun's operas vary considerably in worth. *Ifigenia* was perhaps the most widely praised; in addition to *Ifigenia* Frederick had a particularly good opinion of *Cesare e Cleopatra*, *Cajo Fabrizio*, *Ezio*, and *Montezuma*.[21] None of Graun's operas were published during his lifetime. Strangely enough, he is known today not for his operas, but for two sacred works: *Der Tod Jesu*, a passion composed in 1755 to a text by Ramler, and

[19] Thouret, *Friedrich der Grosse*, 49.
[20] *Ibid.*, 49–50.
[21] *Ibid.*, 80.

Te Deum auf den Sieg bei Prag, a commemoration of Frederick's victory at Prague in 1756. These two works, which Graun was able to write only because the King's objection to sacred music was not rabid enough to prevent their composition, saved Graun from oblivion for two reasons: they were composed in complete freedom, not according to specifications; and they were free of the grotesque elements found in many eighteenth-century operas. *Der Tod Jesu* has been especially celebrated. It was sung annually in the Cathedral of Berlin from the year of its composition until late in the nineteenth century.[22] It is a work of considerably more boldness and technical interest than any of Graun's operas. For example, the harmonies of one recitative from this passion (Fig. 25) are far more radical than anything created by order of the King.[23]

Graun's deficiencies were noticed by at least some of the musicians of the eighteenth century. Reichardt criticized Frederick's composer while criticizing royal artistic policy:

> Graun merely worked according to his king's taste. Whatever did not please Frederick was struck out, even if it happened to be the best piece in the opera. Since the King adhered stubbornly to his own unchanging preferences, he could not allow Graun the slightest variety or freedom.[24]

And Burney, after wryly quoting a panegyric written to the memory of Graun (which uses such phrases as "creator of his own taste," "tender, soft, compassionate, elevated, pompous, and terrible, by turns," and "in the theatre inimitable"), describes the feelings of those who do not admire Graun, unmistakably placing himself on their side:

[22] Maczewsky and Loewenberg, "Graun, Karl Heinrich," *Grove's Dictionary.*
[23] K. H. Graun, *Der Tod Jesu,* No. 16 Recitative.
[24] Thouret, *Friedrich der Grosse,* 69.

FIG. 25.–K. H. Graun, No. 16 Recitative from *Der Tod Jesu*, measures 1–9.

Now to reverse the medal; it is denied, by the other party, that Graun was the creator of his own taste, which is the taste of Vinci; they deny, that he is ever pompous or terrible, but say, that an even tenor runs through all his works, which never reach the sublime, though the tender and graceful are frequently found in them; they are equally unwilling to subscribe to his great invention, or the originality of his ideas; and think that still more perfect models of sacred music may be found in the chorusses of Handel, and the airs and duos of Pergolese and Jomelli: nor can they well comprehend, how that composer can be called *inimitable*, who is himself an *imitator*.[25]

It is perhaps not coincidental that the years of glory for Graun and for the Opera ended at almost the same time, with the outbreak of the Seven Years' War in 1756 and Graun's untimely death in 1759. Frederick received the news of his composer's death while on the battlefields in Bohemia, surrounded by enemies. He is reputed to have said, "Eight days ago I lost my best field-marshal [Schwerin] and now my Graun. I shall create no more field-marshals or conductors until I can find another Schwerin and another Graun."[26] But he never found a substitute for Graun, because by the end of the war he had stopped searching.

JOHANN JOACHIM QUANTZ (1697–1773)

J. J. Quantz was the greatest German flutist, probably the greatest flutist, of the eighteenth century; yet he did not begin a serious study of the flute until he was over twenty years old. He was too much occupied with becoming a virtuoso on string bass, violin, oboe, and harpsichord. At the age of eight he played the string bass for festivals at his native Oberscheden (in Hanover). He studied harpsichord in Merseburg as an apprentice

---

[25] *The Present State of Music*, II, 228–29.
[26] Jeffrey Pulver, "Music at the Court of Frederick the Great," *Musical Times*, Vol. LIII (September 1, 1912), 600.

to Kiesewetter, and before 1713 he was practicing the violin as his main instrument and playing the solos of Biber, Walther, Albicastro, Corelli, and Telemann.[27] When he entered the service of the Polish court in 1718, he was hired as an oboist; but, not happy with the subservient role of the oboe, he soon began a study of the flute with Buffardin, flutist in the Dresden *Kapelle*.

During 1717 Quantz studied counterpoint with Zelenka and Fux in Vienna, where he was an assiduous and inquiring student of composition. In his autobiography he mentions the importance of his first contact with the violin concertos of Vivaldi:

> In Pirna, during this [early] period, I happened to see the violin concertos of Vivaldi for the first time. The completely new art embodied in these works made a powerful impression on me. Since then I have never stopped collecting them, and I now have a collection of considerable size. The magnificent ritornelli of Vivaldi have long served me as a worthy model.[28]

When the Polish ambassador went to Italy in 1724, Quantz was part of his entourage. In Rome he was able to continue his studies in counterpoint, this time under Gasparini. The two years he spent in Italy, from 1724 to 1726, were all-important to his musical development. One of his most interesting adventures while there was his introduction to Alessandro Scarlatti in Naples. Quantz was introduced by Hasse, who at that time was studying with Scarlatti and just beginning to endear himself to the Neapolitan public. In his autobiography Quantz tells the whole story of the meeting:

> I asked Herr Hasse to introduce me to his teacher, old Scarlatti; he readily consented. But when he went alone to Scar-

[27] Ruth Rowen, *Early Chamber Music*, 68.
[28] Willi Kahl (ed.), *Selbstbiographien deutscher Musiker*, 112.

latti and asked permission to introduce a flute-playing friend, the master answered: "My son (this is what he always called Herr Hasse), you know that I cannot bear to listen to wind instruments, because they all play out of tune." Nevertheless Herr Hasse persisted for a long time, and finally the old composer agreed to meet me. At the meeting, Scarlatti played first; his performance showed real artistry and understanding, although he did not have as much technique as his son [Domenico]. Then I played a solo, while he accompanied. I had the good fortune of winning his favor to such an extent that he composed some flute solos for me. He made my name known in several noble houses, and as a result of his influence I was offered a fine position in Portugal, at a high salary. However, I thought it advisable to refuse the offer.[29]

Back at Dresden in 1728—after having visited France and England on his way home—Quantz had the fateful meeting with the Crown Prince, and soon began his twice-yearly visits to the Prussian court for the purpose of giving his royal pupil lessons in flute and composition. It must have been during this period that he gained his remarkable influence over Frederick, an influence which was to make him one of the most powerful musicians in Germany. In a letter to Wilhelmina dated January 12, 1736, Frederick tells his sister that she will be visited by Quantz, and while warning her of the flutist's conceit, incidentally shows himself to be somewhat impressed by the force of Quantz's personality: "You will find Quantz's high opinion of himself the more insupportable in that it is really without foundation. The only way to bring his haughtiness to an end is not to treat him too much like a grand gentleman."[30]

Frederick certainly did not follow his own advice, for when

[29] *Ibid.*, 135–36.
[30] Frederick the Great, *Oeuvres de Frédéric le Grand*, ed. by Preuss, Vol. XXVII, Bk. 1, 37.

Quantz joined his service in 1741 he was given a salary of two thousand thalers yearly plus a bonus for every new composition and a hundred ducats for each new flute he produced.[31] For a German instrumental musician, this was an almost unheard-of salary; Quantz's annual pay at Dresden in 1728 had been 250 thalers.[32] During all the thirty-two years of his service to Frederick, he was treated "like a grand gentleman." The evening palace concerts were wholly in the hands of these two; Frederick was a tyrant over all the other musicians at the *Abendmusiken*. Only Quantz could criticize the King's flute playing, and only he dared compliment Frederick with an occasional "bravo." During one concert Frederick complained that one of his new flutes would not play in tune. Quantz tried it and found it perfect; but the King continued to have difficulty with the instrument, and Quantz finally remarked: "If a great man is able to hear and appreciate the truth, your Majesty will know that the fault is not in the flute, and where the fault is." Frederick stepped back and said vehemently: "What! Am I unable to bear the truth? Say what you have to say." Quantz replied, "I have often begged your Majesty to lay the flute on a table when you have finished playing and not to hold it in your hand or under your arm; but you hold it anyway, and the flute does not sound true simply because it is unevenly warmed." But Frederick insisted that the instrument was faulty. The next day he played on another flute. Quantz conducted the group as usual, but at the conclusion of the performance there was no "bravo." Eight days later Frederick approached Quantz at the beginning of a musical evening, and said in a respectful tone: "My dear Quantz, I have experimented with the flute in various ways for eight days, and have come to the conclusion that you

[31] Quantz, "*Herrn Johann Joachim Quantzens Lebenslauf*," *Historisch-Kritische Beyträge*, ed. by Marpurg, I, 248.
[32] *Ibid.*, 245.

are right. I will no longer let the flute become warm in my hand."[33]

The other musicians of the court were jealous of Quantz's power, even bitterly so. It is undoubtedly true that throughout his life in the Prussian court, this flutist was unfairly privileged. Reichardt called him a "dictator."[34] Burney saw immediately, during his visit in 1772, that Quantz was the most powerful musician in Berlin.[35] Kirnberger, for whom musical controversy seemed to be a major talent, criticized Quantz not only verbally but also in several of the Berlin musical periodicals. His most famous criticism concerned a characteristic of Quantz's flute pieces. Frederick was fond of triplet passages like this:

Fig. 26.—Triplet passage, as often found in J. J. Quantz's compositions for flute.

Therefore Quantz incorporated such passages into his compositions, and Kirnberger caustically remarked that Quantz's works could be recognized by their "sugar loaves." After one of Kirnberger's printed attacks, Quantz, incensed, asked the King to terminate Kirnberger's service. Frederick answered: "God forbid! We must be more intelligent than that. M. Quantz must write something against M. Kirnberger; thus we will keep an excellent man among us and have an interesting war of words."[36] C. P. E. Bach, the possessor of so much neglected genius, voiced an eloquent and sarcastic complaint:

Which is the most fearsome animal in the Prussian Mon-

[33] Thouret, *Friedrich der Grosse*, 109–10.
[34] Mennicke, *Hasse und die Brüder Graun*, 482–83, citing Reichardt, *Musikalische Monatschrift* (1792).
[35] *The Present State of Music*, II, 154.
[36] Kothe, *Friedrich der Grosse als Musiker*, 27–28.

archy? It is Madame Quantz's lap-dog. He is so terrifying
that Madame Quantz quails before him; Herr Quantz, in
turn, is afraid of Madame Quantz; and the greatest of all
monarchs fears Herr Quantz![37]

A good indication of the relative status of Frederick's orchestra members is given in this anecdote by Franz Benda: Once
during a performance of one of the King's sonatas, the forbidden melodic interval of a diminished fifth was heard. Quantz
cleared his throat loudly; Bach repeated the interval discreetly
in the accompaniment; everybody else looked at the floor. Later
Frederick corrected the passage and remarked jokingly to
Benda, "We must not aggravate Quantz's cough."[38]

The respect which the King felt for Quantz was genuinely
returned. In his autobiography Quantz speaks of his patron's
musical contributions in very complimentary words:

Of our royal music in general: The intelligent choice and
charming taste exercised in theatrical composition; the various excellent singers (those we once had and those we still
possess); the good orchestra, which was already a permanent
organization during the years 1731–1740 in Ruppin and
Rheinsberg—a group which charmed every composer and
visiting concert artist, and which, moreover, has grown since
the beginning of our king's reign to one of the most famous
in Europe; the large number of prominent instrumental
virtuosi who have made great personal achievements in
music—all this, I say, has made itself so widely known and
celebrated that it is really superfluous for me to write about
the individual merits of any of His Majesty's musical
organizations.[39]

[37] Georg Müller, *Friedrich der Grosse, seine Flöten und sein Flötenspiel,* 9.
[38] Thouret, *Friedrich der Grosse,* 109.
[39] Quantz, *"Herrn Johann Joachim Quantzens Lebenslauf,"* *Historisch-
Kritische Beyträge,* ed. by Marpurg, I, 249.

The importance of Quantz's improvements of the flute and his contributions to its literature can hardly be overstated. At the beginning of the eighteenth century the transverse flute was an instrument of considerable crudity, lacking both agility and accuracy of intonation. It generally had only a single (closed) key (E flat), and was tuned by changing its middle joint for one shorter or longer. Quantz's first improvement was made during his short stay at Paris in 1726;[40] he added another closed key and hole next to the E flat key which, when opened, produced a tone slightly higher than the regular E flat (that is, "D sharp") and enabled him to play more perfectly in tune such things as the common chords of E flat and B. This invention was quite useful during his time, when compositions were written in a limited number of keys; but it was not a lasting improvement for obvious reasons.

Quantz's second invention, the sliding head joint, was made in 1752.[41] He describes it in his autobiography:

> At about this time I was able to invent the sliding head joint of the flute, by means of which it is possible to change the pitch of the instrument by as much as a half step in either direction, without changing the middle joint and without sacrificing purity of tone or accuracy of intonation.[42]

This method of tuning the flute has continued to the present day. In Quantz's flutes, in order to keep the tonal advantages of a uniform bore, the cavity left when the joint was drawn

---

[40] Georg Müller, *Friedrich der Grosse, seine Flöten und sein Flötenspiel*, 6.

[41] Henry Macaulay Fitzgibbon, *The Story of the Flute*, 41, states that there is no evidence supporting the popular belief that Quantz also invented the adjustable head cork.

[42] Quantz, "Herrn Johann Joachim Quantzens Lebenslauf," *Historisch-Kritische Beyträge*, ed. by Marpurg, 1, 249.

out was filled with wooden rings, of which the flutist kept a supply in various widths.[43]

Quantz also increased the bore of his instruments, giving them an especially resonant tone in the low register; because of this characteristic his flutes became known as *"Berliner Flöte,"* and any particularly resonant flute was said to have a *"Berliner Stimmung."*[44] His flutes were later improved by Grenser, Ziegler, Meyer and others before they were superseded by the Boehm flute in the middle nineteenth century.[45] Quantz's instruments, like most flutes built between about 1650 and the time of Boehm, had conical bores which, while not affording great accuracy of intonation, produced a sweet, expressive tone not possible on a cylindrically bored instrument like the Boehm flute. (Since Boehm's time the disadvantages of the cylindrically bored flute have been partially remedied by such improvements as the parabolic head joint.)

Frederick played an important role as patron in urging his flutist to produce better instruments. Quantz bored most of the finger holes himself and supervised the making of the flutes very carefully,[46] because the King was a difficult customer to please, one who demanded full value for each hundred ducats he paid his flute-maker. Frederick imported whole tree trunks, mostly ebony, just for making flutes, and in his eagerness to find flutes meeting his exact specifications he bought also from other artists and makers.[47] Two of his letters, written in Silesia, show how particular he was about his instruments:

To Fredersdorff, October 6, 1745: "Quantz is going to make

[43] Fitzgibbon, *The Story of the Flute,* 39–40.
[44] Schwarz-Reiflingen, *"Friedrich der Grosse als Flötist,"* *Allgemeine Musikzeitung,* Vol. LXVI (1939), 478.
[45] *Ibid.*
[46] *Ibid.*
[47] Georg Müller, *Friedrich der Grosse, seine Flöten und sein Flötenspiel,* 8–9.

two new flutes for me, very unusual ones; one will have a strong tone and the other will blow very lightly and have a sweet upper register. He will have them ready for me when I return."[48]

To Tratenau, October 9, 1745: "I have tried Quantz's new flutes, but I find that they are not very good. I have given him one to take care of which is better. Give it to me in Berlin when I arrive there."[49]

Quantz was no less a trail blazer in the matter of solo flute literature. When he began his composing career, solo compositions for transverse flute were almost nonexistent, since only a handful of composers before his time had seriously interested themselves in this instrument. Jacques Hotteterre (died *c.*1761), chamber musician at the courts of Louis XIV and Louis XV, had composed a considerable assortment of flute pieces. The Belgian Jean Baptiste Loeillet (1653–1728) had written some sonatas, as had the French flutist Louis Mercy (1690–1750). Michel Blavet (1700–1768), a native of Besançon, was widely recognized for his playing, as well as for his sonatas and duets; and Frederick had tried in vain to engage him for service in the Prussian court. Then came Quantz and, of course, J. S. Bach, whose sonatas for transverse flute date from 1747.

Similarly, few adequate instruction books for this instrument, or even for the recorder, existed before Quantz's time. Hotteterre's *Principes de la Flûte Traversière ou Flûte d'Allemagne, de la Flûte-à-bec ou Flûte Douce,*[50] *et du Hautbois,* published in 1707 by Ballard in Paris, gives a great deal of instruction, but no musical examples. In 1712 Hotteterre produced his

[48] *Ibid.,* 8.

[49] Frederick the Great, *Oeuvres de Frédéric le Grand,* ed. by Preuss, Vol. XXVII, Bk. 2, 130.

[50] Both *"Flûte-à-bec"* and *"Flûte douce"* = recorder, or *Blockflöte.*

Art of Preluding on the Transverse Flute. This work was copied
and augmented a few years later by Michel Coretti and entitled *Méthode pour apprendre aisément à jouer de la Flûte
Traversière.* The earliest English instruction book for flute now
in existence, written by Peter Prelleur and published by Bow
Church Yard in 1730–31, is entitled *The Modern Musick-Master
or the Universal Musician, containing the Newest Method for
Learners in the German Flute as Improved by the Greatest
Masters of the Age.* This book deals not only with flutes of
various kinds, but also with violin, oboe, and harpsichord. The
music in it consists chiefly of a collection of airs from Handel's
operas, plus a few minuets, rigadoons, and other dance pieces.
It was an artistically assembled work and was very popular in
England. Quantz's *Versuch* followed it as the next major instruction book for flute.

The *Versuch einer Anweisung die Flöte traversière zu
spielen,* finished in 1752, is Quantz's magnum opus.[51] It would
be a misrepresentation to refer to this work as merely a flute
method, since only about a fifth of it is devoted specifically to
flute playing; it covers every phase of performance and composition and is an invaluable commentary on eighteenth-century
musical practice. Perhaps the best way to give an idea of its
contents is to list its major sections:

I. Short history and description of the transverse flute
II. Holding the flute, and placing the fingers
III. Fingerings; range of the flute
IV. Embouchure of the flute
V. Notes, time values, rests, and other musical signs
VI. Use of the tongue in playing the flute

[51] The edition whose page numbers are referred to here was made
by Arnold Schering (Facsimile edition, published in Kassel by Bärenreiter-
Verlag, 1953).

Under the above headings some surprising subjects are discussed: the relationship between kinds of musical programs and the sizes of the rooms in which they are performed (pp. 169–70); how to modernize old figured bass accompaniments, substituting simple intervals for the compound intervals represented by the old "high figures" (pp. 234–35); the advantages of the newly invented pianoforte (pp. 230–31); the technical clumsiness of most cellists at that time (pp. 212–13); the importance of not thinking of the viola as a "second-class" instrument, and of insisting "that a violist must be quite as good a player as a second violinist" (p. 207). Every vocal and instrumental form and device in common use at that time is defined and described from the standpoint of both performer and composer, and leading composers of the various forms are introduced to the reader (pp. 239–334). It is an invaluable work, the foundation of modern flute technique, worth far more than Quantz's compositions. It was enthusiastically received even in its own time, and can truly be said to be a product, in every sense of the word, of Frederick's patronage.

The compositions of Quantz cover a wider range of media and forms than do those of his royal pupil; he is more a part of the Baroque period than Frederick; his melodies are freer, his technique more facile. But his forms are basically the same; his harmonies and melodies are innocuous, if not monotonous; and a single unchanging ideal is followed from year to year, from composition to composition—an ideal fostered and followed by his patron. The major portion of Quantz's compositions consist of some 150 flute sonatas and about 300 flute concertos. None of these was published during his lifetime. They were intended for the entertainment of the King, and their publication was prohibited by him.[52]

The concerto *"pour Potsdam"* which is number 182 in this collection is amply illustrative of Quantz's powers as a creator of concertos. It begins with a *tutti* (Fig. 27).[53] This is a well-unified movement, because within the thirty-one measures of the opening *tutti* Quantz presents his three main thematic materials. The opening theme (Fig. 28) is the core of the movement, and is used to begin most of the solo passages. Second in importance is the triplet figure, with its accompanying emphasis of the rhythm ♩♩ (Fig. 29). This triplet figure serves primarily as a connecting device between ritornelli, while the rhythm ♩♩ is considered to be of sufficient weight to begin one of the *tutti*. Ranking third in importance as a motive in this movement is the Lombardic figure ♫. , which appears in various guises from beginning to end. The movement ends,

<hr />

[52] Thouret, *Friedrich der Grosse*, 111. Since the end of World War II, Quantz's compositions in manuscript, which were housed in the *Königlichen Hausbibliothek* in Berlin, have been missing.

[53] J. J. Quantz, *Concerto for Flute, Strings, and Basso Continuo*, ed. by Walter Upmeyer.

Fig. 27.—J. J. Quantz, Concerto No. 182, first movement, measures 1–8.

as it began, in D Major, having made only a few carefully regulated modulations.

The materials of the short but expressive second movement, consisting of four main ideas, are presented within the first few measures (Fig. 30). The four ideas are marked by brackets and

Fig. 28.—J. J. Quantz, Concerto No. 182, first movement, measures 1–2 of first violin part.

Fig. 29.—J. J. Quantz, Concerto No. 182, first movement, measures 3–4 of first violin part.

numbered. The opening theme (1) is the heart of the movement, and is the primary material of the solo flute. This theme bears a striking rhythmic resemblance to the opening theme of the first movement. The Lombardic motive (4) is also present again. This movement ends in G Major.

This concerto, rather languorous until now, finally comes alive in the last movement (Fig. 31). If the running sixteenth-notes in the sixth measure are not counted as a distinct motive, it can be said that virtually the entire presto is based on its opening theme (1). Only two other ideas are introduced, and these briefly (Fig. 32).

After his visit to the Prussian court in 1772, Burney wrote this about Quantz:

> M. Quantz, after studying counterpoint, which he calls music for the *eyes*, during six months under this master [Gasparini], went to work for the *ear*, and composed solos, duos, trios, and concertos; however, he confesses, that counterpoint had its use in writing pieces of many parts; although he was obliged to *unlearn* many things, in *practice*, which *theory* had taught him. . . .[54]

[54] *The Present State of Music*, II, 183–84.

Fig. 30.—J. J. Quantz, Concerto No. 182, second movement, measures 1–8.

Fig. 31.—J. J. Quantz, Concerto No. 182, last movement, measures 1–6.

Fig. 32.—J. J. Quantz, two secondary ideas in the last movement of Concerto No. 182.

Fig. 33.—J. J. Quantz, Sonata for three flutes, first movement, measures 1–23.

This unconcern of Quantz's for counterpoint is perfectly illustrated in the opening section (Fig. 33) of a sonata for three flutes.[55]

The music of Quantz continued to please Frederick because it was unchanging. During one of the campaigns of the Seven Years' War, the King said to his reader De Catt: "Now, if you would like to hear a new solo by Quantz I will play it . . . I tried it after dinner. It appeared to me to be superior to what I have had of him in this kind: this man does not grow old."[56]

[55] J. J. Quantz, *Sonate für drei Flöten*, ed. by Erich Doflein.
[56] De Catt, *Frederick the Great, the Memoirs of his Reader*, trans. by Flint, I, 178.

But time has proved that Frederick's continued praise for his flutist was based on his own petrified taste. Burney was less prejudiced in his judgment of Quantz:

> His music is simple and natural; his taste is that of forty years ago; but though this may have been an excellent period for composition, yet I cannot entirely subscribe to the opinions of those who think musicians have discovered no refinements worth adopting since that time.[57]

Frederick's great respect for Quantz continued undiminished until Quantz's death in 1773. In a churchyard at Potsdam the King had a monument built to honor his musician's memory, and as a last essay at composition he personally sketched the last movement of an uncompleted sonata by Quantz (which Agricola finished). Of the second movement, Quantz's final creation, he said to Benda: "It is easy to see that Quantz has departed from the world with good thoughts."[58]

CARL PHILIPP EMANUEL BACH (1714–1788)

During recent years there has been a steadily increasing interest in the life and works of C. P. E. Bach (usually called Emanuel Bach during his lifetime), second son of J. S. Bach and probably the greatest of all Frederick's musical servants. He has come out from under his father's shadow to be recognized as an original genius whose works not only supply many of the formal, technical, and aesthetic sources of classic and romantic music, but are in themselves great and provocative works of art. One of the major blots on Frederick's record as a patron is his neglect of this musician, a neglect which Emanuel Bach was fortunately able to overcome.

[57] *The Present State of Music,* II, 157–58.
[58] Lenzewski, *Die Hohenzollern in der Musikgeschichte des 18. Jahrhunderts,* 27.

Born in Weimar, Emanuel was a fine clavier player and an accomplished composer at an early age, before Johann Sebastian sent him to Leipzig and Frankfurt to study philosophy and law. In clavier and composition the only teacher he ever had was his father.[59] Upon graduation in 1738 Emanuel decided to settle in Berlin, but had hardly arrived there when he was given an opportunity to travel through Europe with a young nobleman. However, just before the trip was begun, he was called to Rheinsberg by Frederick, and the trip was canceled. Since he did not formally enter Frederick's service until 1740, just what his status was until that time is uncertain. In his autobiography he is intentionally vague about this matter: "Because of certain circumstances I was not engaged by his Prussian Majesty until 1740. . . ."[60]

In 1740 he was hired as first cembalist at a salary of three hundred thalers, and "had the pleasure of personally accompanying the first flute solo which His Majesty played as King."[61] The salary at which he began his service never improved very much. In 1756 it was raised to five hundred thalers—just in time to be depreciated in value by the war—and after the war it was raised again when Emanuel began casting about for another position; but it was nothing like the sums paid to the King's favorites.[62] Emanuel's main task was the same throughout his stay at the Prussian court, which lasted until 1767: accompanying Frederick's flute playing. From the beginning there was an antagonism between the King and his accompanist, which Emanuel did little to alleviate. This son of Johann Sebastian Bach was not subservient enough to make a good accompanist for any flutist, royal or not, whose tempos were erratic. He is said to have remarked that Frederick's being King did not auto-

[59] Kahl (ed.), *Selbstbiographien deutscher Musiker*, 34.
[60] *Ibid.*, 35.
[61] *Ibid.*
[62] Karl Geiringer, *The Bach Family*, 339.

matically make him a great musician;[63] and on another occasion, when a guest, complimenting Frederick's performance, exclaimed, "what rhythm," Bach replied dryly, "what rhythms."[64]

It could not have been possible for this sensitive and brilliant musician to avoid being frightfully bored at times with the task of accompanying the same works by the same two composers year after year.[65] The monotony of his position was somewhat relieved when Christoph Nichelmann, one of his private pupils, was appointed second cembalist in 1744, although this appointment was an occasion for Emanuel's embarrassment: Nichelmann was given a salary twice the size of his.[66] When Nichelmann left in 1756, his place as second cembalist was taken by Karl Friedrich Christian Fasch, who was a bit less stubborn than Bach and able to adjust his accompaniments more successfully to the King's rubato performances.[67]

One of Emanuel's greatest disappointments was Frederick's failure to appreciate his compositions. Frederick, dedicated to the preservation of the cautious and correct aesthetic of Graun and Quantz, was repelled by the impetuous musical expressions of his cembalist. Burney suggests a further reason for Bach's neglect:

> . . . his majesty having early attached himself to an instrument which, from its confined powers, has had less good music composed for it, than any other in common use, was unwilling, perhaps, to encourage a boldness and variety in composition, in which his instrument would not allow him to participate.[68]

[63] Terry, "Bach, Carl Philipp Emanuel," *Grove's Dictionary*, Vol. I.
[64] W. J. Mitchell, "Introduction" to *Essay on the True Art of Playing Keyboard Instruments* (by C. P. E. Bach), trans. and ed. by W. J. Mitchell, 6.
[65] See p. 45.
[66] Geiringer, *The Bach Family*, 340.
[67] Zelter, *Karl Friedrich Christian Fasch*, 14.
[68] *The Present State of Music*, II, 262.

In 1750 Bach asked for the cantorship at Leipzig, hoping to take his deceased father's place, but was not hired; and in 1753 he considered moving to Zittau for a position there.[69] After the Seven Years' War, as the musical atmosphere of the court became more and more stifling, his discontent increased. When his godfather Georg Philipp Telemann died in 1767, Emanuel applied for his position as musical director of the five principal Protestant churches of Hamburg. Telemann, before his death, had recommended him, and he was offered the position. But persuading the King to accept his resignation turned out to be a major task requiring repeated requests; finally Emanuel pleaded ill health and obtained his release.[70] Upon his departure from Berlin, the Princess Amalia, who recognized his talent, graciously appointed him her *Kapellmeister von Haus aus*.[71] He assumed his new position on November 3, 1767.

The busy company of the burghers in Hamburg, the freedom from court protocol, and the stimulation of the intelligentsia with whom he mingled were a tonic to Emanuel. There were, of course, disadvantages in his new position, chief among which seemed to be the indifference of the musically sated Hamburgers; but the atmosphere was one of creation rather than decay.[72] He remained in this post, a productive, cheerful, and independent citizen of a great musical city, until his death in 1788.

C. P. E. Bach, like his contemporaries, had ruthlessly rejected the learned contrapuntal style of baroque music and the architectural orientation of its forms in favor of the light and elegant accompanied melody, the surface detail of the rococo. He referred to canons, for example, as "dry and despicable

[69] Terry, "Bach, Carl Philipp Emanuel," *Grove's Dictionary*.
[70] Rudolf Steglich, "*Karl Philipp Emanuel Bach und der Dresdener Kreuzkantor Gottfried August Homilus im Musikleben ihrer Zeit,*" *Bach-Jahrbuch*, Vol. XII (1915), 41.
[71] Kahl (ed.) *Selbstbiographien deutscher Musiker*, 35.
[72] Burney, *The Present State of Music*, II, 251.

pieces of pedantry," notwithstanding his respect for the "learned style" of his father.[73] In observing these principles, Emanuel was following what became known as the *galanter Stil*. When he added to this style the incipient influences of irrationalism, the literary *Sturm und Drang* with which he found himself surrounded, the result was the *Empfindsamer Stil* in its highest manifestation. Thus the main works of this composer, though chronologically and formally preclassical, contain a streak of passionate romanticism.

Emanuel's artistic creed is partially contained in his autobiography. The following passage shows him to be at heart a revolutionary and a romantic:

> Where I have avoided the all-too-common uniformity of composition and musical taste, where I have adopted into my style as much of the best, from as many different sources as possible, where I have strived for meaning above all, I believe it will be noticed, as good things generally are. Even though such good things might appear only rarely in my compositions, their existence must be admitted. . . . My main concern during the past few years has been to compose for and to play the clavier in a singing style, bearing in mind its inability to sustain tones. This is not an easy matter if we are not to leave the ear empty or kill the noble simplicity of song with too much noise.
>
> It seems to me that music must first of all stir the heart, and that this will not be accomplished on the clavier through mere knocking, drumming or arpeggiation—at least not by me.[74]

His manner of playing, too, marks him as a musician whose aim was the expression of emotion. Burney describes an evening of music at Emanuel's home in Hamburg:

[73] *Ibid.*, 252.
[74] Kahl (ed.), *Selbstbiographien deutscher Musiker*, 43–44.

After dinner, which was elegantly served, and cheerfully eaten, I prevailed upon him to sit down to a clavichord and he played with little intermission till near eleven o'clock at night. During this time he grew so animated and *possessed,* that he not only played but looked like one inspired. His eyes were fixed, his underlip fell, and drops of effervescence distilled from his countenance. He said that if he were to set to work frequently in this manner he should grow young again.[75]

In about 1767 the poet Gerstenberg of Copenhagen, one of the leading spirits of the period of *Sturm und Drang,* wrote to this composer that true instrumental music, especially clavier music, should give utterance to precise feelings and subjects. He hoped that Emanuel, whom he described as "a musical Raphael," could accomplish this.[76] Emanuel had already done so. In following the requirement of precision, of course, he showed himself to be still a child of the age of rationalism, and it is this rationalistic quality which prevents his keyboard works from being called purely romantic; but the emotional feeling in many of them is of such strength that they give their composer full credit for being the founder of modern expressive piano style. The doctrine of *Empfindsamkeit,* when followed by a Quantz, was little more than a restatement of baroque pathos; when followed by Emanuel Bach, it showed him to be one of the great creative geniuses of the eighteenth century.

C. P. E. Bach is known (thus far) less for his compositions in general than for two specific technical advancements: the systematization of keyboard technique and the early development of sonata form. His system of keyboard playing is set forth in the epoch-making *Versuch über die wahre Art das Clavier*

---

[75] *The Present State of Music,* II, 251.
[76] Romain Rolland, *A Musical Tour through the Land of the Past,* trans. by Bernard Miall, 79.

zu spielen, written in 1753. Unlike the *Versuch* of Quantz, which deals with every imaginable musical subject, Bach's treatise is almost exclusively about keyboard performance. Its main divisions consist of the following:

I. Fingering
II. Embellishments
III. Performance
IV. Intervals and their Signatures (i. e., figured bass numerals and accidentals)
V. Thorough Bass
VI. Accompaniment
VII. Improvisation

This book is particularly valuable in matters of fingering, embellishment, the doctrine of *Empfindsamkeit,* and figured bass. In the discussion of fingering, Emanuel shows his debt to his father (especially in the use of the thumb), but he also provides the foundation for modern keyboard fingering; and the chapter on embellishment is a valuable guide, even today, to the proper performance of eighteenth-century music.

The ancestry of Bach's *Versuch* consists mainly of Mattheson's *General-Bass Schule,* Heinichen's *General Bass,* Neidt's *Musikalische Handleitung,* and Couperin's *L'Art de toucher le clavecin.* None of these works was as practical, thorough, and modern as Bach's, none so important to succeeding generations of keyboard players. Of Emanuel's influence through this treatise, Mozart said (quoted by Rochlitz): "He is the father, we are the children. Those of us who do anything right, learned it from him. Whoever does not own to this is a scoundrel."[77] Haydn, who was probably influenced by Emanuel Bach more

[77] Mitchell, "Introduction" to *Essay on the True Art of Playing Keyboard Instruments* (by C. P. E. Bach), 4.

than by any other composer, called the *Versuch* "the school of all schools."[78] And Beethoven, after listening to an audition by the young Czerny in 1801, said to Czerny's father: "The boy has talent; I shall take him as my own student and teach him. Send him to me once a week. Be sure to procure Emanuel Bach's instruction book on the *True Art of Playing Keyboard Instruments*, so that he may bring it to his next lesson."[79]

Bach's *Versuch* became famous as an instruction book almost immediately after its publication. William J. Mitchell, the translator and editor of a valuable English edition of it, estimates that one thousand to fifteen hundred copies of each part (it was divided into two volumes) were sold during the second half of the eighteenth century. Lest this figure be unfavorably compared with modern ones, Mitchell points out that there were only 602 subscribers to Göschen's publication of the series of Goethe's works from 1787 to 1790, and that "the *Jena Litteratur Zeitung*, a very popular and widely read journal of the time, achieved its success on issues of 2000 copies. . . ."[80] After this treatise was published, a rash of instruction books appeared which plagiarized it freely, and Emanuel was obliged in 1773 to write an open letter of protest, in the *Hamburger unpartheiischer Correspondent*, against the abuses of his ideas.[81]

The second specific technical advancement for which Emanuel Bach is known is his contribution to the development of early sonata form, particularly in works for keyboard. In spite of his romantic leanings he had a very orderly mind; trained in law and philosophy, he took delight in such matters as business and finance.[82] It was natural, then, that this penchant for logic and order, combined with a disrespect for traditional

[78] *Ibid.*, 2.
[79] *Ibid.*
[80] *Ibid.*, 2–3.
[81] *Ibid.*, 3–4.
[82] Geiringer, *The Bach Family*, 345–46.

forms, should produce formal innovations in his compositions.

Bach's six *Preussischen Sonaten,* which appeared in 1742 as the first product of Frederick's patronage of him, became widely known for their unique qualities and played a role of great importance in influencing the next generation of composers, notably Haydn. They exhibit both the expressive power of Emanuel's version of *Empfindsamkeit* and a fully delineated classical sonata form, complete in every respect (though often with truncated recapitulations). The first movement of Sonata number 4 in this group is an excellent example of his use of sonata form.[83] It opens in C minor (Fig. 34). In the eighth measure the

Fig. 34.—C. P. E. Bach, fourth Prussian Sonata, first movement, measures 1–3.

second principal theme, obviously derived from the first, is announced in F minor (Fig. 35). A third principal theme in E

Fig. 35.—C. P. E. Bach, fourth Prussian Sonata, first movement, measures 8–9.

[83] C. P. E. Bach, *Preussischen Sonaten,* Nos. 4–6, *herausgegeben von* Rudolf Steglich.

flat Major appears in measure 21 (Fig. 36). The entire exposition is only thirty-one measures long.

Fɪɢ. 36.—C. P. E. Bach, fourth Prussian Sonata, first movement, measure 21.

In the beginning of the development, the first and second themes, especially the triplets found in them, are the source for a passage in the relative major key (E flat), modulating to the dominant minor key (G) (Fig. 37). The first few notes of

Fɪɢ. 37.—C. P. E. Bach, fourth Prussian Sonata, first movement, melody line of measures 32–41.

the second theme are used sequentially in the development section (Fig. 38). The recapitulation, which consists of only eleven

FIG. 38.—C. P. E. Bach, fourth Prussian Sonata, first movement, measures 42–45.

measures, is built on the third principal theme and the triplet passages of the first and second themes, ending in C minor.

Deriving one melodic idea from another and combining ideas, as illustrated in this movement, was a favorite device used by C. P. E. Bach. In development sections he sometimes dissected and reassembled themes. Thus, although his themes are often contrasting in character, they are unified by this combination of their various parts.

The adagio movement of the sixth Prussian Sonata shows that by the early 1740's Emanuel was divorced from the baroque aesthetic, at least in his piano works, and was striving successfully to rise above the shallow *galanter Stil* of many of his contemporaries. In the passage shown in Fig. 39, the grating

FIG. 39.—C. P. E. Bach, sixth Prussian Sonata, second movement, measures 12–17.

dissonances caused by delayed resolutions are typical of his efforts to avoid platitudes.[84]

Emanuel was undoubtedly influenced by the operatic activity which surrounded him during his seventeen years in the Prussian capital. Certainly operatic in style are his instrumental recitatives, an example of which appears in the andante movement of the first Prussian Sonata (Fig. 40).[85] Aside from the

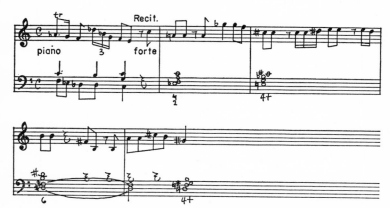

Fig. 40.—C. P. E. Bach, first Prussian Sonata, second movement, measures 3–7.

influence of these recitatives on Frederick, it would not be an exaggeration to claim their influence on Beethoven as well, considering Beethoven's use of this form and his interest in Emanuel's compositions.[86]

One of Bach's most striking and beautiful expressions of *Empfindsamkeit* is the C minor fantasia contained as one of

[84] *Ibid.*

[85] *Ibid.*, Nos. 1–3.

[86] Examples of instrumental recitative in Beethoven's compositions: The piano sonatas (op. 30, no. 1, first movement; op. 31, no. 2, first movement; op. 110, third movement) and the ninth symphony (beginning of the fourth movement).

FIG. 41.—Beginning of a C minor fantasia by C. P. E. Bach, showing Gerstenberg's two texts.

the *Probestücke* in the final chapter (dealing with improvisation) of his *Versuch*, 1753 edition. For the sake of rhythmic flexibility, the composer omits bar lines in the first and last sections. The poet Gerstenberg was so impressed with the beauty of this short piece that he attempted twice to make it a kind of cantata by adding text, once on Hamlet's monologue and a second time on the last words of Socrates as he empties the cup of poison. Since Emanuel was definitely influenced by dramatic forms, these literary attempts by his admirer were not aesthetically unreasonable (Fig. 41).[87]

In the history of the symphony, the term "sinfonia" falls into disuse with the works of C. P. E. Bach. His three-movement (without minuet) orchestral pieces are independent instrumental forms which deserve to be called symphonies in the fullest sense of the term. He composed about nineteen of them; only four were published during his lifetime (in 1780, by Schwickert in Leipzig). These four, called *"Orchester Sinfonien mit zwölf obligaten Stimmen,"* are master examples of their genre. They are scored for string orchestra, two flutes, two oboes, two horns, bassoon and harpsichord. The opening theme of the first one is shown in Fig. 42.[88] This theme, flanked by

FIG. 42.–C. P. E. Bach, D Major Symphony (1780), first movement, measures 1–7 (piano reduction).

several less important ones, is the subject of the entire movement. There is a real exposition, development, and recapitulation, and the movement ends with a dramatic bridge passage modulating to E flat Major. The second movement shows Emanuel's conservative side; it is merely a tender adagio without new devices (Fig. 43).[89] The final movement of this symphony is a presto (Fig. 44).[90]

In 1814 Reichardt wrote this statement in the *Allgemeine*

[87] Cited in Geiringer, *The Bach Family*, 357.
[88] Cited in Noack, *Sinfonie und Suite*, 110.
[89] *Ibid.*
[90] *Ibid.*

FIG. 43.—C. P. E. Bach, D Major Symphony (1780), second movement, measures 1–4 of first violin part.

Musicalische Zeitung, describing Emanuel Bach's symphonies: "One heard with rapture the original and bold course of ideas as well as the great variety and novelty in forms and modulations. Hardly ever did a musical composition of higher, more daring, and more humorous character flow from the soul of

FIG. 44.—C. P. E. Bach, D Major Symphony, last movement, measures 1–6 of first violin part.

a genius."[91] Reichardt's opinion was a common one in the early nineteenth century; Emanuel's music, like his *Versuch*, was prized by the composers of that generation. It is not surprising that the finale of Beethoven's second symphony is related thematically to the opening movement of the third of Bach's published symphonies (Fig. 45).

FIG. 45.—Similarity of two themes by C. P. E. Bach and Beethoven.

[91] Cited in Geiringer, *The Bach Family*, 368.

C. P. E. Bach belongs to the vast rank of innovators lost in the results of their own innovations. Perhaps more than any other North German composer of his period, he deserves to be brought fully to light as a musician of genius. Burney recognized his worth when he visited him at Hamburg in 1772: "Hamburg is not, at present, possessed of any musical professor of great eminence, except M. Carl Philipp Emanuel Bach; but he is a legion!"[92] Perhaps Burney also had in mind the legion of compositions of all types which were produced by Bach, truly great works which, it seems certain, will be more fully appreciated by future generations.

> Those who credit him with the "invention of the sonata form" do not know that this worthy son of another great musician was the composer of more than two hundred clavier works, fifty-two clavier concertos, eighteen symphonies, much chamber music and church music—including twenty-two settings of the Passion—and some two hundred and fifty songs. With the exception of some of the aforementioned piano sonatas, a few brilliant clavier fantasies and concertos, one or two symphonies of provoking originality, and a handful of songs of haunting beauty, nothing is known, not only to the public but to scholars as well. When his works are better known we shall recognize Carl Philipp Emanuel Bach as the outstanding master of the late rococo, of preclassical times, a master who triumphed over the weaknesses of the art and atmosphere of his own period.[93]

FRANZ BENDA (1709–1786)

In his colorful autobiography the violinist Franz Benda tells the story of how, by accident, his illustrious patron first heard him, and the result of the "audition":

[92] *The Present State of Music,* II, 245.
[93] Lang, *Music in Western Civilization,* 597.

I arrived in Ruppin on April 17, 1733, and was given a room in one of the guest-houses. During the same day, as I was practicing a bit, His Royal Highness the Crown Prince happened to stroll by. He stood listening for awhile, then sent a messenger to find out who I was. I went down immediately and presented myself. His Highness graciously invited me to join him in a *soirée* for that evening, where he personally accompanied me on the clavier. This was the beginning of my service to him, which continues to this day.[94]

In this casual way Benda began an engagement that was to last for fifty-three years.

This violinist's wanderings before the beginning of his Prussian service make his autobiography read like a storybook. He was born in Alt-Benatek, Bohemia, son of a town musician who made his living playing the oboe in an inn. As a child he studied singing in the town school and learned violin from his father; when his voice changed at the age of fifteen, he undertook the violin in earnest. The first violin literature which he studied seriously was the Vivaldi violin concertos. His only formal teachers were a M. Konyczek of Prague, whose lessons lasted ten weeks, and a blind Jewish fiddler named Lebel who was employed at another inn in Alt-Benatek. Before his twenty-fourth year he had served as a singer in the inn where his father played, the Dresden churches, the Dresden court, and the opera and churches of Prague; and as a violinist he played in the Dresden court (a position which Quantz, while at Dresden, helped him to secure), the Prague court, the court of a minor Viennese prince, a church in Prague, and the court at Warsaw.[95] Then came his fateful visit to Ruppin in 1733.

[94] "*Auto-Biographie von Franz Benda*," ed. by C. Freiherr von Lebebur, *Neue Berliner Musikzeitung*, Vol. X (August 6–August 27, 1856), 260.
[95] *Ibid.*, 251–60.

From the start of Benda's residence at Ruppin there was a close relationship between him and the Prince in spite of their frequent differences, and this mutual respect continued until both Benda and Frederick died in 1786. Benda was permitted to visit the neighboring courts of minor nobility, and seemed to have a way of winning esteem and affection for himself wherever he went. Soon after he arrived at Ruppin he became ill, and Frederick magnanimously gave him a vacation in Carlsbad. When he visited the Bayreuth court during this vacation, Wilhelmina presented him with a golden snuff box and his own horses for the trip.[96] Returning from a similar trip to Bayreuth, he stopped at Dresden and persuaded his brother Johann, also a violinist, to come with him to Ruppin; Frederick was happy to engage Johann in the *Kapelle*.[97]

In 1734 Franz's family in Bohemia was forced to seek refuge from persecution because of their Protestant faith, but were unable to obtain governmental permission to leave Bohemia. Their problem was solved by Frederick, as Franz relates:

> During 1734 my father visited me in Ruppin. One day he sneaked into the Crown Prince's house so that he could listen to the music. The Crown Prince happened to see him, and asked me if I had brothers who were musicians. My answer was "yes."[98]

As a matter of fact, almost the entire Benda family was composed of musicians. Frederick obtained permission from Leopold I, the Bendas were able to leave Alt-Benatek and settle in Prussia, and one more violin-playing Benda was added to the *Kapelle:* Franz's brother Georg.[99] Frederick thus compensated

[96] *Ibid.*, 268.
[97] *Ibid.*, 260.
[98] *Ibid.*
[99] *Ibid.* Georg Benda actually occupies a more important place in music history than Franz, because he was the first successful composer

for his poor treatment of such artists as Elizabeth Mara and Benedetta Agricola.

At Ruppin Franz was able to study music systematically for the first time, with both Johann Gottlieb Graun and Karl Heinrich Graun. He describes his early relations with these brothers in his autobiography:

> Until this time I had never heard a violinist whose playing —especially of adagios—impressed me quite as much [as J. G. Graun's]. I diligently sought his friendship, and he was happy to give it. He was kind enough to work very hard with me on a couple of adagios; I learned many things from this. When I undertook the composition of some violin solos, he helped me considerably in writing the basses. . . . A year later [1735] the famous Kapellmeister Graun was engaged. He had a great deal of affection for me; we lodged together for awhile. He gave me much instruction in composition, and under his tutelage I was able to compose some concertos.[100]

The competition between Franz Benda and J. G. Graun for the chair of concertmaster is rather puzzling. At Ruppin and Rheinsberg, Benda was concertmaster; but J. G. Graun was given the position when Frederick became king, possibly through the influence of K. H. Graun. When J. G. Graun died in 1771, Franz once more became the leading first violinist. Apparently the two violinists played equally well, although Benda is perhaps better known.

An astonishing number of Bendas and their relatives eventually played violin for the King. Besides Franz, Johann, and Georg, there were Franz's son—Franz, Junior—who came into

of melodramas. However, his first melodrama, *Ariadne*, was not composed until 1774, after he had long been *Kapellmeister* at Gotha (since 1750); so he can not be included as one of Frederick's important artists.
    [100] P. 260.

the orchestra in 1741; Karl Herman Heinrich, another son, who joined the King's service in 1762; a third son, Friedrich Wilhelm, who began his service in 1782; plus Franz's son-in-law and two of his nephews.[101] Johann died in 1752; Georg left in 1749 to become *Kapellmeister* at Gotha. Only Franz and Georg were outstanding musicians and composers.

Although Franz Benda created much excellent music, his primary fame rests on his abilities as a violinist and teacher. In addition to instructing his sons and nephews, he was the teacher of Leopold August Abel (brother of Karl Friedrich), Johann August Bodinus, Johann Friedrich Kiesewetter, Friedrich Wilhelm Rust, Joseph Fodor, Franz Adam Veichtner, Carl Haack, Karl August Pesch, and Johann Peter Salomon.[102] The length of this list and the names in it show that Franz Benda was truly the founder of the North German school of violin playing.[103]

As a performer Franz was held in high regard by his contemporaries. Johann Adam Hiller had this to say of his playing:

His tone is one of the loveliest, fullest, and most agreeable; his technique is equal to any difficulty that can be imagined. But his noble singing style—the characteristic of his playing which is most natural to him—has been the main reason for his great success.[104]

When Burney called on him in 1772, he was favorably impressed in spite of Benda's age:

He performed to me an admirable solo, of his own composition, *con sordino;* his hand, he said, wanted force sufficient

101 Andreas Moser, *Geschichte des Violinspiels*, 325–26.
102 *Ibid.*, 328.
103 The term "Berlin School" is sometimes used to denote the followers of Benda's methods. It is also used to denote eighteenth-century composers of songs in Berlin (from about 1750 to about 1810).
104 Quoted in Thouret, *Friedrich der Grosse*, 126.

to play without. The gout has long since enfeebled his fingers; however, there are fine remains of a great hand, though I am inclined to suppose him to have been more remarkable at all times for his feeling than his force. His style is so truly *cantabile*, that scarce a passage can be found in his compositions, which it is not in the power of the human voice to sing; and he is so affecting a player, so truly pathetic in an *Adagio*, that several able professors have assured me that he has frequently drawn tears from them in performing one.[105]

His style is not that of Tartini, Somis, Veracini, nor that of the head of any one school or musical sect, of which I have the least knowledge: it is *his own*, and formed from that model which should be ever studied by all instrumental performers, *good singing*.[106]

Looking back over his service to Frederick, Benda makes these remarks in his autobiography:

Today, April 17, 1763, I finish the fifty-third year of my life, still in service to His Majesty. It is no small source of satisfaction to me that I have had the good fortune to remain in the employ of our truly great Frederick. Through all these years I have accompanied him in flute concertos at least ten thousand times.[107]

The happy situation between him and his patron, their almost equal life spans, and their death in the same year are interesting particulars about a great king and a humble musical servant, showing the personal as well as musical kinship between the two. Of Benda's devotion to Frederick, Reichardt says:

[105] *The Present State of Music*, II, 129.
[106] *Ibid.*, II, 141.
[107] P. 269.

Benda venerated the King with such sincerity that every misfortune of Frederick's was a similar misfortune for him. He was convinced that he would not outlive the King, and, sure enough, he died a few months before him, at about the time that the doctors pronounced Frederick's illness incurable.[108]

After much hedging and apologizing, Benda gives in his autobiography a list of his compositions as of 1763: "Eighty violin sonatas, fifteen concertos, some *sinfonia* and a considerable number of capriccios. . . ."[109] This is the output attributed to him today, although only a few of his works were ever published. His solo violin sonatas are the most important part of his compositions. Their importance is based not only on their intrinsic worth, but also on the valuable information they afford on the subject of eighteenth-century performance practice (ornamentation, in Benda's case). Benda did not restrict his *ad libitum* ornamentation to slow movements, in the manner of Telemann and Corelli; instead, like Geminiani, he performed every movement in an ornamented version. This embellishment consisted of substituting fast runs for single notes or groups of notes, changing the direction of runs, substituting arpeggios for scales, changing registers, underlining a theme with double stops, and so on, in endless variety.

Fortunately for the cause of research in *Aufführungspraxis*, thirty-three of Benda's violin sonatas in manuscript, which were found by Hans Mersmann in the Berlin *Staatsbibliothek*, included notated versions of both the original violin part and the violin part with embellishments as Benda performed them. These sonatas are fitting examples for the rules on ornamentation contained in such eighteenth-century textbooks as those

[108] Quoted in Thouret, *Friedrich der Grosse*, 127.
[109] P. 269.

by Quantz, C. P. E. Bach and Leopold Mozart. Most of the embellished versions were probably written down by Benda's pupils after his death.[110] In some cases there were two degrees of embellishment, as is shown in the adagio movement of the first of these sonatas (Fig. 46).[111] In fast movements, the melodic

FIG. 46.—Two degrees of ornamentation, as performed by Franz Benda.

elaboration was more moderate and more faithful to the contours of the original (Fig. 47).[112] Double stops were a somewhat different device of elaboration, and were combined with ordinary devices, as in Fig. 48.[113]

A good example of an allegro by Franz Benda is that contained in his A minor sonata (Fig. 49), first movement (MS 1315 in the Berlin *Staatsbibliothek*).[114]

Finally, one of Benda's sonatas in A Major provides an exam-

110 Andreas Moser, *Geschichte des Violinspiels*, 324.

111 Cited in Hans Mersmann, "*Beiträge zur Aufführungspraxis der vorklassischen Kammermusik in Deutschland*," *Archiv für Musikwissenschaft*, Vol. II (1920), 111.

112 *Ibid.*, 113.

113 *Ibid.*, 117.

114 *Ibid.*, 126.

FIG. 47.—Moderate elaboration of fast movement, as performed by Franz Benda.

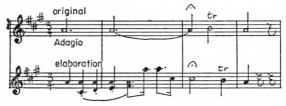

FIG. 48.—Melodic ornamentation by means of double stops, as performed by Franz Benda.

ple (Fig. 50) of the kind of slow movement which he performed so artistically.[115]

Benda's violin works can be considered a counterpart of C. P. E. Bach's keyboard pieces, in that they not only provide models of eighteenth-century performance practices and techniques, but are works of art which should be heard for their own sake. Like the keyboard compositions of Bach, they deserve to be rescued from obscurity.

[115] Franz Benda, *Sonata in A Major for Violin and Piano,* ed. by Alfred Moffatt.

FIG. 49.—Franz Benda, Sonata in A minor, first movement, measures 1–13.

JOHANN GOTTLIEB GRAUN (1703–1771)

This prolific and able composer of instrumental music is overshadowed today by his famous brother, Karl Heinrich Graun, just as he was overshadowed during their lives; but even a cursory examination of the music of these brothers shows that Karl Heinrich's greater reputation was caused more by the taste of the times than by the superiority of his music over that of Johann Gottlieb.

J. G. Graun was born in Wahrenbrück one year before Karl Heinrich. Like his brother, he attended the *Kreuzschule* in Dresden, singing in the boys' choir under Johann Zacharias Grundig.

197

FIG. 50.—Franz Benda, Sonata in A Major, andante, measures 1–9.

J. G. Pisendel was a member of the Dresden court orchestra from 1712, and Johann Gottlieb was his pupil in violin and composition. In 1718 both brothers were graduated from the University of Leipzig; in 1723 they went to Prague together. At just that time, 1723, the great Giuseppe Vivaldi began his three-year period of service to Count Kinsky in Prague, and Johann Gottlieb was able to study with him for a while. Soon afterward Johann Gottlieb returned to Dresden and secured his first employment as a violinist in the Dresden court orchestra. In 1726 he became concertmaster of Merseburg. When J. S. Bach visited there in the same year, he showed his confidence in Graun by having the fifteen-year-old Wilhelm Friedemann study with him.[116] (Bach's esteem of J. G. Graun is further illustrated by the fact that he copied two of Graun's trios. The C minor trio by Graun which appears in Riemann's *Collegium Musicum* was taken by Riemann from a copy which Bach had made.)[117] Graun went to Arolsen in 1731 as chamber musician to Prince von Waldek, but was called to Ruppin by Frederick only a year later.[118]

Although there was little direct personal relation between Frederick and J. G. Graun, this violinist was highly respected by Frederick and by his fellow-musicians. Princess Amalia was especially interested in him; present-day knowledge of his compositions—particularly his symphonies—is largely a result of their easy availability in the neatly copied collections of his works which she made herself.[119] When Frederick came to power, J. G. Graun was made concertmaster, deposing Franz Benda. Burney, hearing the orchestra in 1772, attributed its excellence to the high quality of the strings, as trained by the recently deceased J. G. Graun.[120]

[116] Philipp Spitta, *Johann Sebastian Bach*, trans. by Clara Bell and J. A. Fuller-Maitland, III, 227–28.

[117] Hans Mersmann, *Die Kammermusik XVII. Jahrhunderts bis Beethoven*, 159.

[118] Mennicke, "*Zur Biographie der Brüder Graun*," *Neue Zeitschrift für Musik*, Vol. VIII (1904), 131.

[119] Mennicke, *Hasse und die Brüder Graun*, 208.

[120] *The Present State of Music*, II, 229.

Graun's contemporaries regarded him as a competent, though not very progressive, composer. Their judgment was based on two characteristics of his music: a comparative immunity to the spirit of *Empfindsamkeit* and a frequent usage of counterpoint. For example, he was one of the last composers of French overtures—apparently Frederick was satisfied with ordering only Karl Heinrich to stop composing in this form. (Because of his contrapuntal leanings, his works were naturally criticized by Burney; but Burney's categorical rejection of counterpoint makes this criticism meaningless.)[121] However, there is another important characteristic to be found in J. G. Graun's music, the true progressiveness of which could not have been recognized by most of his contemporaries: many of his ninety-six symphonies show clearly-defined characteristics of sonata form. Moreover, they are orchestrated for unusually full ensembles, and use the winds in a highly original style. Thus J. G. Graun was actually a two-sided composer, able to create both polyphonic overtures and homophonic symphonies, and to show all shades of the old and the new in these forms as well as in his concertos, trios, and sonatas.

An example of this musician's ability to ignore musical trends can be found in a French overture of 1768 (Fig. 51), written only three years before his death. It is far from rococo

FIG. 51.—J. G. Graun, a French overture of 1768, measures 1–4 (piano reduction).

[121] *Ibid.,* 230.

refinement and surface manipulation, and shows a rhythmic solidity, a pompous vigor which is plainly baroque. One might easily mistake it for an overture by Lully.[122]

On the other hand, a symphony composed in 1762[123] (according to Breitkopf's catalogue of his works) has almost every feature of classical sonata form in its first movement, except—as in many of C. P. E. Bach's works—a complete recapitulation. It begins with an incisive first theme (Fig. 52). The second pri-

FIG. 52.—J. G. Graun, G Major Symphony (1762), first movement, first primary theme (piano reduction).

mary theme, in the dominant key, has a cantabile quality (Fig. 53). The exposition closes with a modulation back to the tonic key and a repetition of the first theme.

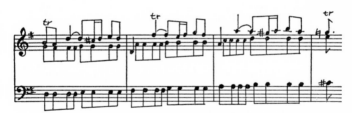

FIG. 53.—J. G. Graun, G Major Symphony, first movement, second primary theme (piano reduction).

[122] Cited in H. J. Moser, *Geschichte der Deutschen Musik*, II, 273.
[123] The parts of this symphony which are quoted here are cited in Mennicke, *Hasse und die Brüder Graun*, 210–15.

FIG. 54.—Treatment of first primary theme in development of J. G. Graun's G Major Symphony (piano reduction).

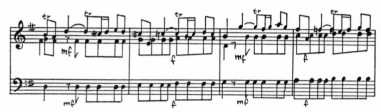

FIG. 55.—Treatment of second primary theme in development of J. G. Graun's G Major Symphony (piano reduction).

A regular development follows, in which no new themes appear, and in which the first theme is treated as shown in Fig. 54. The second theme appears in the development in the form shown in Fig. 55 (the dynamic markings are the composer's).

The recapitulation lacks only one feature of "regular" sonata form: a restatement of the second theme in the tonic key (the second theme does not appear at all in this section).

The opening themes in the symphonies (*sinfonia*) of K. H. Graun suffer by comparison with those of his less famous brother. Figure 56 presents some of the *Kopfthemen* of J. G. Graun's other symphonies.[124]

As a last musical example, one of J. G. Graun's trios in F Major is cited here (Fig. 57) to show how baroque and rococo traits are often present at the same time in some of his compo-

[124] Cited in *ibid.*, 209.

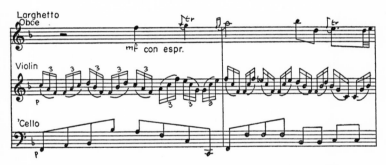

FIG. 56.—Opening themes of some of J. G. Graun's symphonies.

FIG. 57.—J. G. Graun, Trio in F Major, first movement, measures 1–2.

sitions.[125] The first movement, almost—but not quite—an expression of the *Empfindsamer Stil*, begins by displaying a typical German trait of Graun's time: giving the melody to a wind in-

[125] Hugo Riemann (ed.), *Collegium Musicum*, XXIV. (The additional piano part supplied by Riemann is omitted, as are also his unusual phrasing and expression marks.)

FIG. 58.—J. G. Graun, Trio in F Major, second movement, measures 17–20.

strument while the violin is relegated to the task of accompaniment.

The second movement (Fig. 58) is a binary allegro, like the fast movements of Frederick's flute sonatas, but displaying a contrapuntal independence of parts.

A combination of homophony and polyphony is shown in the third movement, a *Siciliano* (Fig. 59). Phrases are begun in imitative style, but the imitation is immediately abandoned for a more homophonic texture until the process begins again in the next phrase.

This trio is an exception in that it has four movements (Graun's trios are usually in three movements, fast–slow–fast).

FIG. 59.—J. G. Graun, Trio in F Major, third movement, measures 1–8.

The fourth movement (Fig. 60) a binary allegro like the second, uses the oboe in original fashion.

FIG. 60.—J. G. Graun, Trio in F Major, last movement, measures 27–34.

JOHANN FRIEDRICH AGRICOLA (1720–1774)

The early training of Agricola was very similar to that of Emanuel Bach. He commenced his music study as a young child. At the University of Leipzig he studied law from 1738 to 1741, and during that time also learned organ and composition with J. S. Bach. But at this point the two careers began to diverge, and their final results were quite dissimilar. Emanuel Bach surmounted the obstacles which Frederick placed in his path; J. F. Agricola, a capable and versatile—but submissive—musician, allowed his life and his music to be directed and corrected in every detail by the King.

From 1741 to 1751, in Berlin, Agricola studied composition with Quantz and gave private lessons in keyboard playing and singing. By 1749 the learned Berlin atmosphere had affected him, just as it did most musicians, and he wrote and published two pamphlets on French and Italian taste under the pseudonym of "Flavio Amicio Olibrio." In the summer of 1750 his first *intermezzo, Il filosofo convinto in amore,* was performed at Potsdam with considerable success. In 1751 Frederick appointed him a court composer, and in that summer an equally successful *intermezzo* of his was produced at Potsdam: *La ricamatrice divenuta dama.* This early favor was lost, however, when in the same year he married one of the singers of the opera, Benedetta Molteni, against Frederick's wishes, and their joint salary was reduced to one thousand thalers (Molteni's single salary had been fifteen hundred thalers before the marriage).

Agricola's activities in Berlin were many-sided. At the first performance of Graun's *Tod Jesu* in 1755, he sang the tenor part. He continued his private teaching of voice and his organ playing throughout a career of composing and conducting for Frederick. In 1757 he published a translation, with additions and notes, of Tosi's *Arte del Canto figurato,* which, according to Burney, was "regarded as the best book on the subject. . . .[126] (Burney also wrote this of Agricola in 1772: "He is regarded as the best organ-player in Berlin, and the best singing master in Germany.")[127] Agricola's incidental music for a performance of Voltaire's *Semiramis* in 1767 was highly praised, especially by Gotthold Lessing, who had a genuine admiration for him.[128] In 1768 Agricola assisted Adlung in the preparation of his famous *Musica mechanica organoedi,* one of the classic works on musical instruments. By this time he was well known as a writer of articles and pamphlets on every phase of music. With all this activity and in spite of his duties as court composer and conductor, he was able to compose a great deal of church music—his favorite medium—and to contribute to Berlin's rising reputation as a center of *Lied* composition with his odes and drinking songs.

When Graun died in 1759, Agricola was appointed musical director of the Opera (without the title of *Kapellmeister*), a position for which he was totally unsuited. The few operas which he composed were poor imitations of the style of Graun, and Frederick openly showed his contempt for them. After hearing the rehearsals of Agricola's *Amor und Psyché* in October of 1767, Frederick wrote this note to his attendant Pöllnitz: "You will tell Agricola that he must change all of Coli's arias—they are worthless—as well as those of Romani, plus the recitatives, which are deplorable from one end to the other."[129] Early in 1772 the King was visited by the Queen of Sweden and the Duchess of Brunswick. For the entertainment of these guests he ordered Agricola and Landi to compose a new opera. The result of their labors, entitled *Oreste e Pylade,* was so fervently

---

[126] *A General History of Music,* II, 950.
[127] *The Present State of Music,* II, 91–92.
[128] Friedrich Blume, "Agricola, Joh. Friedrich," *Die Musik in Geschichte und Gegenwart,* Vol. I.
[129] Mennicke, *Hasse und die Brüder Graun,* 479.

condemned by Frederick that the entire work had to be re-written and even retitled (its final title was *I Greci in Tauride*).[130] Agricola, in short, was one of the several talented and intelligent composers whose careers were distorted by Frederick's patronage. As he grew older he became more resigned to the puppet role which the King had given him, and to the loss of his self-respect as a musician. Reichardt referred to him irreverently as "old fat Agricola, who drank monstrous quantities of beer."[131]

All but a small fraction of Agricola's works remain in manuscript. Two published works give an adequate picture of his ability as a composer: the drinking song *Der Wettstreit*[132] and the larghetto movement from his *Sonata per Cembalo F-dur*.[133] Although Agricola belongs to the older school of Berlin song composers—the "first Berlin School"—there is a tinge of the early romantic *Lied* in *Der Wettstreit* (Fig. 61).

Similarly, the larghetto from the sonata in F Major (Fig. 62) shows a composer of imagination who, while not as bold as Emanuel Bach, certainly is no longer attached to the style of his great teacher, Johann Sebastian Bach.

KARL FRIEDRICH CHRISTIAN FASCH (1736–1800)

K. F. C. Fasch was born in Zerbst, son of the great composer and *Kapellmeister* Johann Friedrich Fasch. Taught by his father, Karl learned to play clavier and violin while very young, and was sent to Strelitz at the age of fourteen to continue his musical studies under Hertel. In 1751 Franz Benda visited

130 Schneider, *Geschichte der Oper*, 169.
131 Kohut, "Johann Friedrich Reichardt," *Neue Musikzeitung*, Vol. XXIV (November 27, 1903–January 8, 1904), 6.
132 Contained in Max Friedländer, *Das Deutsche Lied im 18. Jahrhundert*, Vol. I, Bk. 2, 91–92.
133 Contained in Kurt Hermann (ed.), *Lehrmeister und Schuler Joh. Seb. Bachs*, II, 26–27.

FIG. 61.—J. F. Agricola, *Der Wettstreit* (poem by Hagedorn).

Fig. 62.—J. F. Agricola, F. Major Sonata, larghetto, measures 1–9.

Strelitz for the purpose of playing before the court there. Linike, the old court cembalist who was to accompany him, could not manage the part for left hand in the accompaniment composed by Benda. A substitute accompanist was called in, the only one in Strelitz who could perform to Benda's satisfaction: Karl Fasch, then only fifteen years old. In Benda's subsequent visits, Karl was his accompanist.[134]

When Nichelmann was dismissed from the post of second court cembalist at Berlin in 1756, Benda remembered Karl Fasch and recommended him as a replacement. Although Karl was only twenty at the time, Frederick offered him the position at

[134] Zelter, *Karl Fasch*, 6–12.

a salary of three hundred thalers a year. This was a great honor for the young musician, but his father was disappointed; he had wanted Karl to succeed him as *Kapellmeister* at Zerbst, and, being a deeply religious man, he was appalled at the irreligious atmosphere of the Prussian court. Nevertheless Johann Friedrich gave his permission, but only after he had obtained a promise from his friend Emanuel Bach that Karl would be watched over and protected.[135]

For the first four weeks at court the new second cembalist listened to Emanuel Bach's accompaniments, accustoming himself to the King's style of playing. At the end of this period Bach took a leave of absence, and the accompaniments were Karl's responsibility. He discharged them well, showing a flexibility which was quite adequate for accompanying Frederick's changeable tempos. On one occasion during this early part of his service, he made the mistake of complimenting Frederick's playing with a "bravissimo," thus usurping Quantz's privilege. The performance stopped; the King glared at Fasch and ordered him to leave. Fortunately, when it was explained to Frederick that Fasch was new and did not know any better, the embarrassed musician was allowed to return.[136] Although his accompaniments were satisfactory in every way, he never succeeded in gaining much of the King's respect. He had a way of being too polite and was unable somehow to make his flattery sound like anything but flattery.

Fasch's service was begun at the worst possible time. He was hardly settled in the new post before the Seven Years' War began, bringing musical life at court to a standstill. His salary, paid in paper money, soon depreciated to a fifth of its former value. Like Emanuel Bach, he turned to teaching as a means of augmenting his income; but unlike Bach, he had not had an

[135] *Ibid.*, 12–13.
[136] Fitzgibbon, *The Story of the Flute*, 190.

opportunity to become established before the war and underwent serious financial hardships. Naturally, during this period he was able to improve himself only with difficulty, and so lost his most productive years.

The effect of the war on this musician was particularly tragic, because he lost his courage also. His health was never very good, and the many little enterprises which he promoted for extra income did not spare him much energy for pursuing a creative musical life. With a damaged sense of proportion, he began spending time on fruitless projects. He prided himself on the card houses which he constructed to exact scale without using any fastening material except the cards. Each morning after breakfast he went through a mental exercise (multiplying various numbers by themselves according to a system he had invented) in order to see if he was "fit to work"; if an error was made during this exercise, the whole day was ruined. He kept a complete register of all the events of every European war, complete with maps and tables, together with the names and locations of ships, armies, and individual officers. The old card game called "Patience" was one of his major interests, and he spent many hundreds of hours alone, becoming an expert player. Some of his activities were perhaps more worthwhile: he composed canons (among which was a canon for twenty-five real voices), which earned him the friendship and admiration of Kirnberger; he wrote thousands of figured bass examples for the use of his students; he interested himself in such diverse subjects as medicine and surgery, chemistry, architecture, mathematics, drawing, and especially languages.[137]

During 1760, in winter quarters at Leipzig, Frederick found time for some playing and sent for Fasch to accompany him. Fasch went to Leipzig for several months and had to give up teaching during that period, which further increased his finan-

137 Zelter, *Karl Fasch*, 15–19.

cial difficulties. When he saw how Frederick's playing had deteriorated and what an old man the King had become since the beginning of the war, he began to think about the possibility of finding other employment. In the spring of 1761 he was allowed to return to Berlin, but by that time he had spent all of his money. The following winter Frederick again sent word for Fasch to join him, this time at Dresden; but Fasch was without funds, and as the King did not send money for the trip, he remained in Berlin.[138]

When the war ended in the spring of 1763, Fasch, like the other musicians of the court, was bitterly disappointed to learn that Frederick had no intention of compensating him for his wartime financial losses. Instead of complaining, as Emanuel Bach did, he merely bore his misfortune with patience and made further plans for quitting the King's service. Since the previous winter he had been composing a number of sonatas, concertos and *sinfonia* for the purpose of showing his ability to prospective employers. He made known his intentions to Bach, who persuaded him to stay; but his discontent continued to grow, and in 1767 (the year Bach left) he applied formally for his release. Again the chronology of events worked for his disadvantage; Frederick was vexed at Bach's resignation, and refused at first even to acknowledge Fasch's application. Fasch applied a second time and received his answer in the form of a question: Why had he not joined Frederick in Dresden when ordered to do so? Fasch did not dare answer that he had had no money for travel and had spent his pitiful hoard on the trip to Leipzig, so he simply said that he wanted a higher salary and left himself without further excuse. The King then agreed to give him a raise, provided that he tell who was the instigator of the "plot" which was causing so many of the musicians to be discontented. Of course, Fasch knew of no plot, so Frederick was eventually sat-

[138] *Ibid.*, 19.

isfied with giving him a lump sum of a hundred thalers, promising more later. When this was done Fasch allowed himself to be persuaded by Bach and his other friends to remain in the position.[139]

The two seasons (1774–76) or Fasch's interim conductorship of the opera were hardly a period of advancement for this ill-used musician. He lacked executive ability, was too sympathetic with the old performers, and had no personal taste for opera. For his extra duties he received not a penny of extra pay; in 1778 his salary was four hundred thalers a year. Although the perpetual grind of poverty made it impossible now for him to resign in spite of his discontent, after 1776 Frederick's cessation of flute practice at least gave Fasch enough leisure for composing. In 1783 he accepted Karl Friedrich Zelter as one of his pupils, a musician who became an important composer as well as his biographer. In the last few years of Frederick's reign, Fasch's health declined rapidly until he was at last confined to bed. Eventually, however, he improved enough to resume his composition.[140]

When Frederick died in 1786 and the new king surprised Fasch by continuing his salary (but leaving it at four hundred thalers), the effect was amazing: Fasch acquired a zest for life. It seemed that Frederick's death had lifted a terrible burden from his shoulders. He burned his card houses, his maps, his lists of ships, and even many of his compositions, and plunged into a study of musical theory. In the summer of 1789, at the age of fifty-three, he held a casual meeting of a group of singers, at which he conducted performances of vocal music for solo and ensemble. There were more meetings, and by 1791 this group had become a permanent organization of twenty singers. In 1794 its membership numbered sixty-four; in 1800, the year

[139] *Ibid.*, 19–21.
[140] *Ibid.*, 21–27.

of Fasch's death, one hundred and twenty-eight. Although Fasch had not specifically intended it, during the last eleven years of his life he had founded the world-famous Berlin *Singakademie*, by simply following his own artistic impulses for the first time.[141]

Fasch gives an excellent demonstration of his musical imagination in his *Ariette avec Variations*, first published in 1782.[142] It is a simple binary piece for clavier upon which fourteen sectional variations are built (Fig. 63).

JOHANN FRIEDRICH REICHARDT (1752–1814)

Reichardt was the most broadly educated musician in Frederick's employ. He was trained in keyboard playing by C. G. Richter and in violin by Veichtner before taking a degree in philosophy from the universities in his native Königsberg (under Kant) and Leipzig. From 1771 to 1774 he traveled extensively, visiting Berlin, Dresden, Vienna, Prague, Brunswick, and Hamburg, making himself known to the intelligentsia in all those places and writing an account of his travels—*Briefe eines aufmerksamen Reisenden*—which was immediately published and gave him an early reputation as an able writer.

He returned to Königsberg in 1774 and accepted a government position (which he had secured through the influence of one of his violin pupils, a church official), though it was his intention to pursue a musical career as soon as a suitable opportunity presented itself. His opportunity came late in 1775, when he heard by chance that Agricola had died months before, that the King was seeking a new *Kapellmeister*, and that none of the applicants for the position had been able to satisfy Fred-

---

[141] *Ibid.*, 27–34.
[142] K. F. C. Fasch, *Ariette Avec Variations, herausgegeben von* Ludwig Landshoff.

Music at the Court of Frederick the Great

FIG. 63.—K. F. C. Fasch, *Ariette,* with the beginnings of some of its variations.

erick's requirements.[143] Reichardt was astute enough to realize that what Frederick wanted was a composer who could emulate Hasse and Graun, and he was enough of an opportunist to throw himself wholeheartedly into the project of securing the position, even using flattery and downright misrepresentation. On September 26, 1775, he sent the King an opera, *Le feste galanti*, which he had composed several years earlier in deliberate imitation of Hasse and Graun, together with the following note:

> Sire!
> I am taking the risk of sending Your Royal Majesty an opera which I have composed, using Hasse and Graun as my models. A great connoisseur might decide whether the composer of this work deserves to be given the position of honor once held by Graun. In deepest respect . . .
> Königsberg, Sept. 26, 1775.
J. F. Reichardt.[144]

In the next mail from Berlin, Reichardt received this *Cabinetsschreiben:*

> His Royal Majesty of Prussia, our Most Gracious Master, wishes to inform the musician Reichardt of Königsberg in Prussia that he shall withhold judgment on the opera sent him until a performance of it is given. In this way it shall be determined whether and how well the cause of Hasse and Graun is served.[145]

The trial performance of the opera must have pleased Frederick, because Reichardt was given the title of *Kapellmeister* two months later, at the age of twenty-three. In his autobiography Reichardt confesses that he had tossed this opera into a

143 Carl Lange, *Johann Friedrich Reichardt*, 15–16.
144 *Ibid.*, 16.
145 *Ibid.*

corner "because it seemed to be too 'Graunish,' too 'Hasseish' —that is, it betrayed too plainly the fact that both these composers had been my models. . . ."[146] But he knew that this very fault would cause Frederick to approve it, and so used it to win the position.

Fasch gave up his interim directorship to Reichardt during the 1775–76 carnival season. Reichardt's first duty as conductor was at a performance of Hasse's *Attilio Regolo*. From the moment he assumed leadership of the Opera, he was faced with an unending series of frustrations. He was not as easily manipulated as Fasch had been and insisted on composing in a style quite unlike that of his "trial" opera; consequently his own works were not performed and his chief duty consisted of rewriting parts of the eternal standard repertoire of Hasse and Graun. As it became increasingly obvious that his operas would probably not be produced at the Berlin Opera House until after Frederick's death, Reichardt turned to other pursuits. He composed in every form, wrote articles for the Berlin musical periodicals, and produced a steady flow of books on musical subjects. His songs on poems of Goethe and other poets began to appear. The Berlin impresario Döbbelin was very happy to give Reichardt's first *Singspiele* in the flourishing public opera houses.

In 1782 Reichardt tried once more to have his music performed by the Royal Opera. He chose Frederick's libretto to *Sulla* as the subject of a proposed work, and wrote an obsequious letter about it to Frederick on October 7, just before the beginning of the 1782–83 carnival season:

> . . . the masterly poetry of the opera *Sulla* fills me with such enthusiasm that I venture to beg Your Royal Majesty for the great honor of being allowed to compose new music to it in time for the forthcoming carnival. Perhaps in so doing

146 Kohut, "Johann Friedrich Reichardt," *Neue Musikzeitung*, 6.

I shall be able to demonstrate, for once, that I am not entirely unworthy of the well-being and profitable instruction bestowed so generously upon me by Your Royal Majesty. I remain ever your most devoted and humble servant Reichardt.[147]

But this time Frederick was offended by such gross flattery, and in a *Cabinetsordre* he angrily refused Reichardt the permission he sought. His feelings were further elucidated in one of the marginal notes which have supplied researchers with so much personal information about him: "He shall not compose any operas; evidently, he does not understand this, or does not choose to understand. He shall do only what I tell him to do."[148]

During the 1782–83 season Reichardt was able to take a leave from the King's decaying establishment. He visited Klopstock and Lavater, both of whom were his close friends, in Baden; watched Galuppi at work in Venice; met Gluck in Vienna and was as much an inspiration to Gluck (for the cause of opera reform) as Gluck was to him; and heard, also in Vienna, the symphonies of Haydn.[149] Early in the summer of 1783 he returned to Berlin and his monotonous duties. During this year he founded an organization for the purpose of performing unknown works, naming it the *Concert Spirituel* in imitation of the famous Paris organization. Less than two years later he applied for another leave, which Frederick granted; and in February 1785 he departed for England. The English court received him enthusiastically; on March 25, as part of the Handel Festival (its second year), his *Passione di Gesu* and his *Sixty-Fifth Psalm* were performed at Buckingham Palace with great success.[150]

147 Mennicke, *Hasse und die Brüder Graun*, 480.
148 *Ibid.*
149 Lange, *Johann Friedrich Reichardt*, 19–22.
150 *Ibid.*, 24.

Early in April, declining the English king's invitation to stay another year, Reichardt left London for Paris, the city which Gluck's music had conquered. Here he found himself completely at home; his own music was warmly received, and he began work on two operas: *Panthée* and *Tamerlan*. However, he was barely able to finish one act in each before having to return to Berlin in October for the coming carnival season. Almost immediately upon his arrival in Berlin, Reichardt applied for still another leave, which he wanted to begin at the close of the carnival. In his application he stated that he was to receive 30,000 livres for completing and producing in Paris the operas which he had begun there. Once again Frederick sent Reichardt a *Cabinetsschreiben* granting him the leave, but reminding him that 3,000 livres were equal to only about eight hundred thalers. (In his careless reading of Reichardt's application the King had mistaken the number 30 for the number 3.) On the last day of the carnival season, January 24, 1786, Reichardt left Berlin. In Magdeburg and Hamburg he finished *Tamerlan*, and arrived in Paris on March 23. Contract difficulties delayed the rehearsals of his opera, however, and before *Tamerlan* could be performed, Frederick died on August 17 and Reichardt had to return immediately to Berlin. He was commissioned by the new king, Frederick William II, to write a *Trauerkantate* for Frederick's funeral, which he finished in seven days and nights. This work, entitled *Cantus Lugubris*, is among his best.[151]

Reichardt kept his position in the Prussian court for a time. His new patron was quite liberal, his works were performed at last, and he was allowed to travel; but as an enterprising writer and man of the world, he was in sympathy with the French Revolution, and let his feelings be known. Once while playing cards with the new king, he is said to have exclaimed: "We must cut

[151] Kohut, "Johann Friedrich Reichardt," *Neue Musikzeitung*, 21.

off the heads of all kings!" Not surprisingly, then, he fell into disfavor by 1791 and was dismissed in 1794.[152]

When Frederick William II died in 1797, Reichardt returned to Berlin and to his varied life as a composer and writer. During the first few years of the nineteenth century he was a guiding force of several musical periodicals—notably his *Musikalische Kunstmagazin*, a romantically-colored journal which gained him enemies as well as friends—and was active in connection with Fasch's *Singakademie*. In 1806 he took refuge from the invading French, going to his native Königsberg. When Jerome Napoleon threatened to confiscate his Berlin property, Reichardt became the Frenchman's court conductor in Kassel; but because of his dissenting political beliefs he was granted an indefinite leave of absence. Reichardt spent part of this leave in Vienna in an unsuccessful attempt to produce his operas and *Singspiele;* during the last few years of his life he resided in Giebichenstein.

While Frederick was alive, and because of Frederick, Reichardt was not able to achieve real success as a composer of opera; therefore his operas cannot in any way be considered a result of Frederick's patronage. It is for his songs, however, that this composer is primarily known; and although Frederick understood nothing of the great developments in the composition of *Lieder* which took place during the last years of his life, he was at least disinterested enough to allow Reichardt to make a beginning at becoming one of the leading representatives of *Lied* composition in Germany. Reichardt, as much a littérateur as a composer, found the art song a perfect medium for honoring the poems of his literary associates, especially the poems of his lifelong friend Goethe. During the last years of the eighteenth century and the first years of the nineteenth, the "second Berlin School" of song composition, led by Reichardt, J. A. P. Schulz,

[152] *Ibid.*

and Karl F. Zelter, brought the German *Lied* to the first apex of its notable place in romantic music.

The song in Fig. 64 is quoted, then, not as an example of music composed in the Prussian court, but as an illustration of the creative life which Reichardt was able to lead after being freed from Prussian shackles. The poem is one of Goethe's most well-known.[153]

FRIEDRICH WILHELM MARPURG (1718–1795)

During the whole of Frederick's reign Berlin was a hub of musical theory, a city known for its preoccupation with words about music rather than with music itself. Burney's description of its musical climate was accurate in every respect:

> Musical controversies in Berlin have been carried on with more heat and animosity than elsewhere; indeed there are more critics and theorists in this city, than practicioners; which has not, perhaps, either refined the taste, or fed the fancy of the performers.[154]

This learned atmosphere was an indirect result of the same spirit of rationalism that had prompted the work of the Encyclo-pedists and the reforms of Frederick. Since the *Aufklärung* was the greatest force in the King's life, it was only natural that it should also be a force in the artistic life of his kingdom. Almost every leading Berlin musician felt compelled to produce at least one book on some facet of music. The treatises of Emanuel Bach and Quantz were outstanding contributions, as valuable today as in the eighteenth century; but the writings of too many Berlin musicians amounted only to mere verbiage.

Three musicians patronized by Frederick were largely re-

[153] Contained in Friedländer, *Das Deutsche Lied*, Vol. I, Bk. 2, 206.
[154] *The Present State of Music*, II, 225.

FIG. 64.—J. F. Reichardt, *Italien* (poem by Goethe).

sponsible for Berlin's reputation as a center of pedantism: Friedrich Wilhelm Marpurg, Christoph Nichelmann, and Johann Philipp Kirnberger. Of these three, Marpurg was the most powerful and the least pedantic; in fact, his reputation as an erring theorist is almost counterbalanced by his valuable writings and criticisms on the general musical life of his time. He was well educated (Burney calls him "a man of the world"),[155] articulate, and conscientious.

Marpurg never earned his sole livelihood as a practicing musician. His first important position, from 1746 to 1749, was as secretary to General von Rothenburg in Paris, and he was engaged by Frederick in 1763 as councillor of war and director of the royal lottery. However, he always found time to pursue his musical interests. In Paris he became well enough acquainted with Rameau to consider himself an authority on Rameau's theories (which he never really grasped), and in Berlin he was able to earn a national reputation as a musical littérateur.

He wrote rapidly and prolifically.[156] These are his most important literary productions: *Der Critischer Musicus an der Spree* (1749–51), the first periodical in history to be devoted to reviews of musical compositions; *Abhandlung von der Fuge* (1753–54), his most popular work, which appeared in many later editions; *Historisch-Kritische Beyträge zur Aufnahme der Musik* (five volumes, 1754–62, 1782), a vast collection of his writings on almost every conceivable musical subject, including a contemporary account of the activities of the Berlin Opera;[157] *Handbuch bey dem Generalbasse und der Composition* (three parts, 1755–58), in which he advanced what he thought were the theories of Rameau; and *Kritische Briefe über*

[155] *Ibid.*, 106–107.

[156] In one section of the *Historisch-Kritische Beyträge*, Marpurg lists six "*verschiedene neue Bücher*"; three are his own works.

[157] The format of the *Historisch-Kritische Beyträge* is similar to that of a magazine. In Volume II (*c.*1755), pp. 575–76, an advertisement by Carl Philipp Emanuel Bach appears. In it he advertises for sale the copper engraving plates of his father's *Art of the Fugue*, assuring readers that through it they can learn "*eine gute Fuge zu machen*," and offering it at "*eine billigen Preis*."

die Tonkunst (1759–63), another periodical somewhat like his earlier *Critischer Musicus*.

In many of his writings, Marpurg shows considerable judgment and intelligence. *Der Critischer Musicus*, for example, contains an article which presents some of his theories of *Empfindsamkeit* very adroitly:

> The rapidity with which the emotions change is common knowledge, for they are nothing but motion and restlessness. All musical expression has as its basis an affect or feeling. A philosopher who explains or demonstrates seeks to bring light to our understanding, to bring clarity and order to it. But the orator, poet, musician seek more to inflame than enlighten. With the philosopher there are combustible materials which merely glow or give off a modest, restrained warmth. Here, however, there is but the distilled essence of this material, the finest of it, which gives off thousands of the most beautiful flames, but always with great speed, often with violence. The musician must therefore play a thousand different roles; he must assume a thousand characters as dictated by the composer. To what unusual undertakings the passions lead us! He who is fortunate, in any respect, to capture the enthusiasm that makes great people of poets, orators, artists will know how precipitately and variously our soul reacts when it is abandoned to the emotions. A musician must therefore possess the greatest sensitivity and the happiest powers of divination to execute correctly every piece that is placed before him.[158]

Marpurg was one of the first writers on music who dealt with it from a thoroughly practical standpoint. That is, he concentrated on actual music, performers and performances rather

---

[158] F. W. Marpurg, *Der Critischer Musicus an der Spree*, September 2, 1749, cited by W. J. Mitchell in an editor's footnote to C. P. E. Bach's *Essay*, 81.

than paying a great deal of attention to the theoretical specula-
tions left over from medieval music theory which, until the
period of his writing, were essential to a "proper" understanding
of any musical matter.

The *Handbuch bey dem Generalbasse und der Composition*
appeared in two editions, was translated into French, and probably found considerable use in England.[159] Because of its popularity, a general understanding of Rameau's theories was delayed
a few more years. Marpurg not only attempted to propound
the ideas of Rameau in this book, but also added his own "corrections." Since he understood the great Frenchman's discoveries very imperfectly to begin with, reading his *Handbuch* was
almost a guarantee of never understanding Rameau. He could
never actually comprehend the principle of the fundamental
bass or of chord inversion, and he promoted theories of his own
which seem to be the result of a desire just to write something
—anything—on the subject which seemed original. His "added-
third" theory of chord generation is an example. According to
this idea, the chord of the seventh consists of three thirds added
together; the chord of the ninth is obtained by adding a third
below the seventh chord; the eleventh chord consists of a fifth
added below this seventh chord; the thirteenth chord is composed of a note a seventh below added to the seventh chord. The
gaps left below the seventh chord and the added note, in the
case of the eleventh and thirteenth chords, are "filled" by Marpurg quite arbitrarily:

> In the chord of the eleventh, we must remember that be-
> tween the fundamental note and the fifth below a third must
> be inserted in order that the chord may be properly under-
> stood. This six-part chord, however, is of little use in its
> complete state. . . . The chord of the thirteenth arises when,

159 Matthew Shirlaw, *The Theory of Harmony*, 316.

to a chord of the seventh, a seventh is added below. . . . It must be remembered that between the fundamental note [of the seventh chord] and the seventh [below], two thirds must be supposed, in order that the chord may be properly understood. The chord in its complete form . . . cannot be used.[160]

It would be unjust to judge Marpurg solely by his unfortunate *Handbuch*, and to forget that many of his other writings are quite valuable today, as they were in his own time. Compared to the importance of his work as a writer, his few compositions are inconsequential. If the example of his music (Fig. 65) lacks inspiration, then, it should be remembered that he was not seriously in the running as a composer.[161]

CHRISTOPH NICHELMANN (1717–1762)

Nichelmann is the most obscure member of the *Kapelle* having any lasting significance in connection with Frederick's patronage. Little is recorded of his relationship with the King, probably because this relationship never reached the level of personal interest on the part of either Nichelmann or Frederick.

This musician, born in Treuenbrietzen, Brandenburg, received almost the same early training as that given to Agricola. After studying clavier in his native city with unknown teachers, in 1730 he entered the *Thomasschule* in Leipzig as first treble in the boys' choir, under J. S. Bach.[162] He studied clavier there not with Johann Sebastian, but with Wilhelm Friedemann Bach (Wilhelm Friedemann was twenty years old in 1730).[163]

[160] *Handbuch bey dem Generalbasse und der Composition,* cited in Shirlaw, *The Theory of Harmony,* 312–14.
[161] Contained in Friedländer, *Das Deutsche Lied,* Vol. I, Bk. 2, 90.
[162] "Nichelmann, Christophe," *Biographie Universelle des Musiciens,* 2nd ed. by François J. Fétis, Vol. VI.
[163] Spitta, *Johann Sebastian Bach,* III, 248.

Fig. 65.—F. W. Marpurg, song *Der Junge Freier* (poet unknown).

In 1733 Nichelmann went to Hamburg, where he heard and studied the operas of Keiser, Telemann, and Mattheson. Going to Berlin in 1738, he became a composition student of Quantz (as Agricola was to do three years later); when the opera was established, he learned vocal writing with K. H. Graun. The

229

first six of his sonatas for clavier appeared soon afterward, and he began to be well known in Berlin for both his playing and his composing. When his father died, Nichelmann's financial support was cut off, and he decided to seek employment in England and France. However, when he arrived at Hamburg on his way out of Germany, he received an order from Frederick to return to Berlin, together with an offer of employment in the *Kapelle*.[164]

When Nichelmann entered Frederick's service as second cembalist in 1744 his main duty was to alternate with Emanuel Bach in accompanying the King. Caught up in the literary-musical activities of his contemporaries, by 1755 he had finished *Die Melodie nach ihren Wesen sowohl als nach ihren Eigenschaften*, one of the few treatises ever written on the subject of melody. He showed the manuscript of this book to Marpurg, who wrote the following notice in the *Historisch-Kritische Beyträge*:

> The King's chamber musician, Herr Nichelmann, will shortly have a work published which deals with melody. This is a subject which eminently deserves scholarly treatment. Herr Nichelmann has long ago demonstrated, with beautiful, tasteful, and widely-appreciated specimens of melody, that he is fit to write such a book.[165]

Fétis, also, had a good opinion of this work, though with reservations: ". . . the subject is treated here in a serious, if perhaps overly pedagogical, manner. One can find good things in this work; Nichelmann shows that he is well acquainted with philosophy, and he establishes solidly the relationships between melody and harmony."[166]

[164] "Nichelmann, Christophe," *Biographie Universelle*.
[165] Vol. I, 147–48.
[166] "Nichelmann, Christophe," *Biographie Universelle*.

One Berliner's appetite for controversy was whetted by this treatise, because an anonymous pamphlet appeared immediately after its publication which criticized Nichelmann's views on melody in the most sarcastic terms. It was signed with the pseudonym "Dunkelfeind" and was entitled *Gedanken eines Liebhabers der Tonkunst über Herrn Nichelmann Tractat von der Melodie. . . .* Nichelmann threw himself into the fray like a true Berliner, answering with an anonymous pamphlet entitled *Die Vortreflichkeit des Herrn C. Dunkelfeind über die Abhandlung von der Melodie ins Licht gesetzt von einem Musikfreunde. . . .*[167]

In 1756 Nichelmann was dismissed from Frederick's service. Although the specific reason for this action by the King is unknown, the commencement of the Seven Years' War was probably the deciding factor. Nichelmann remained in Berlin and managed to exist by giving lessons. He continued to compose keyboard pieces, and his songs were given considerable notice —along with those of Agricola, Kirnberger, the Grauns, Quantz, and others—in Marpurg's *Historisch-Kritische Beyträge.* He died in 1762, still a fairly young man.

The songs written by Nichelmann show the plain, dry style characteristic of the first eighteenth-century *Lieder* in Berlin ("first Berlin School") and contain few of the romantic features of the songs of such later court musicians as Reichardt and C. P. E. Bach. His drinking song entitled *Die Unwahrheit* (Fig. 66) shows an additional characteristic that was typically *Berlinische:* It is composed in two voices, melody and unfigured bass.[168]

Nichelmann's writing for orchestra is well demonstrated in a harpsichord concerto in A Major.[169] This work (Fig. 67)

[167] *Ibid.*

[168] Contained in Friedländer, *Das Deutsche Lied,* Vol. I, Bk. 2, 92–93.

[169] Christoph Nichelmann, *Concerto for Continuo and Strings,* ed. by Carl Bittner.

FIG. 66.—Christoph Nichelmann, *Die Unwahrheit* (poem by Lieberkühn).

shows a composer who has not fallen behind the trends of his time.

JOHANN PHILIPP KIRNBERGER (1721–1783)

Frederick's rationalistic philosophy affected Kirnberger in the same way that it affected Marpurg: by providing a learned climate in which theorists could flourish.

In Saalfeld, Thuringia (his birthplace), Kirnberger learned the rudiments of music; while still quite young he studied organ in Gräfenroda with Kellner, and in 1738 began lessons in violin with Meil of Sondershausen. At Sondershausen he was taught Bach's fugues by the court organist Heinrich Nikolaus Gerber (father of Ernst Ludwig and a pupil of J. S. Bach). Gerber recommended him to J. S. Bach, with whom he studied from 1739 to 1741. From 1741 to 1750 he was court clavierist for several minor princes at Leipzig, Lvov, and various cities in Poland, and toward the end of this period he was also musical director at a nunnery in Lemberg. In 1750 he went to Dresden and resumed his study of the violin under Zickler, for the purpose of securing a position as a violinist in Frederick's orchestra; after a year of study he was engaged.

Kirnberger remained in the King's orchestra as a violinist from 1751 to 1758. In all probability, Frederick hardly knew he existed. There are no records of any personal dealings between the two during this time. When, in 1758, Princess Amalia asked that Kirnberger be allowed to quit Frederick's service and become her court composer and teacher, Frederick readily granted her wish.[170] Until his death in 1783, Kirnberger was in the service of the Princess.

As a former pupil of J. S. Bach, Kirnberger considered him-

[170] Richard Münnich, *"Friedrich der Grosse und die Musik,"* Zeitschrift für Musik, Vol. CIII (August, 1936), 915.

FIG. 67.—Christoph Nichelmann, Concerto in A Major, third movement, measures 48–69.

self an authority on "learned" music, and was the chief Berlin guardian of the Baroque aesthetic. Naturally, many of his contemporaries thought of him as merely reactionary. Burney, the counterpoint-hater, did not hesitate to criticize him:

> Kernberger (1721–83), of Berlin, lately deceased, was a scholar of Seb. Bach, and possessed of great musical learning. His knowledge of counterpoint, and of all the laws and subtleties of canon and fugue, were indispensable. But in his compositions he is often dry and crude, and perpetually striving at new passages and effects, with which his invention did not very liberally supply him.[171]

Nicolai delivered a commentary on Kirnberger which was equally devastating to his musical principles, his theoretical work, his compositions, and his ability as a performer:

> Kirnberger has many good musical ideas, not only concerning analysis but also on the subject of composition; he deserves full credit as a theorist. But he is unable personally to bring any of his ideas to good musical fruition, perhaps because of insufficient talent. His aim is not to see good music performed, but merely to find music containing "errors" so that he may make learned—and often violent—statements about the mistakes of others. As a performer he has practically no skill at all, except when playing his own compositions; his sense of rhythm is especially uncertain.[172]

Marpurg, on the other hand, considered Kirnberger an important and gifted musician, a master of contrapuntal writing, a model to be followed.[173] This opinion, held by Marpurg in

---

[171] *A General History of Music*, II, 957.
[172] Mennicke, *Hasse und die Brüder Graun*, citing C. F. Nicolai, *Anekdoten von König Friedrich II. von Preussen . . .*, VI, 163.
[173] Siegfried Borris, *Kirnbergers Leben und Werk*, 21.

spite of bitter disagreements with Kirnberger, would probably have been shared more widely if the vogue for rejection of counterpoint had not been so widespread.

In any case, Kirnberger is most significant today as a theorist, not as a composer; and his reputation in the field of musical theory is based as much on his mistakes as on his contributions. The *Kunst des reinen Satzes* is Kirnberger's most important work. In Forkel's opinion it was "the first logical treatise on harmony;"[174] but Forkel does not give proper mention to the antecedence of Fux and Rameau, because Kirnberger's treatise does little more than repeat the contrapuntal rules of Fux and the harmonic discoveries of Rameau. In his discussion of Kirnberger, Matthew Shirlaw, the twentieth-century Scottish theorist, shows that many of Kirnberger's theoretical writings were the results of original thinking and at least served to correct some of the misconceptions perpetrated by Marpurg.[175] When Kirnberger wrote that "Rameau has filled this theory [of harmony] with so many absurdities as to cause one fairly to wonder how such extravagance could ever have found acceptance among us Germans," he was criticizing Marpurg's version of the Rameau system.[176] Unlike Marpurg, and like Rameau, he rejects harmonies of the ninth, eleventh, and thirteenth and recognizes only triads and seventh chords. However, Rameau's theories of fundamental bass and harmonic progression escaped Kirnberger, just as they had escaped Marpurg.

It would be difficult to unearth many reasons for changing Kirnberger's reputation as a pedant. His editions of some of J. S. Bach's works, his analyses of preludes and fugues from the *Well-Tempered Clavier*, and his articles on music in Sulzer's

---

[174] Johann N. Forkel, *Johann Sebastian Bach*, with notes and appendices by Charles Sanford Terry, 102.

[175] *The Theory of Harmony*, 317–25.

[176] *Ibid.*, 318, citing the preface to Kirnberger's *Die wahren Grundsätze zum Gebrauch der Harmonie* (1773).

Théorie des beaux-arts do not show him to be musically more creative than he is depicted in his works on musical theory. He did not have the redeeming insight or breadth of Marpurg, nor was he more than a mediocre performer or composer.[177] Burney said of him: ". . . in his late writings, he seems to be more ambitious of the character of an algebraist, than a musician of genius."[178] In 1781 Kirnberger requested that he be allowed to dedicate his *Über die Grundsatze des Generalbasses* to Frederick. Frederick refused because he felt, with justification, that the art of writing and playing figured bass had been dealt with adequately enough already.[179]

Kirnberger's songs show him to be a member of the "first Berlin School" of *Lied* composers. They are hardly discernible from the naïve little songs and odes of Nichelmann, except perhaps for a bit more independence of voices. Kirnberger's *Rheinweinlied* is quoted here (Fig. 68).[180]

This composer's best writing was for the clavier, and although his keyboard pieces were remarkable chiefly for their "correctness," they show a composer skilled in his craft. The prelude quoted here, for example (Fig. 69), illustrates Kirnberger's indebtedness to J. S. Bach.[181]

JOHANN ADOLPH HASSE (1699–1783)

The King of Prussia did not lack models to follow in his creation of the Berlin Opera. When he came to the throne, the operatic eminence of such musical centers as Dresden, Bruns-

[177] In his *Anleitung zur Singecomposition mit Oden,* Kirnberger naïvely asserts that many ancient Greek melodies actually continued to live in the form of Protestant chorales. Cf. Friedländer, *Das Deutsche Lied,* Vol. I, Bk. 1, xliv.

[178] *The Present State of Music,* II, 213.

[179] Thouret, *Friedrich der Grosse,* 40–41.

[180] Contained in Friedländer, *Das Deutsche Lied,* Vol. I, Bk. 2, 149.

[181] Contained in *Le Trésor des Pianistes,* X, 15 (31).

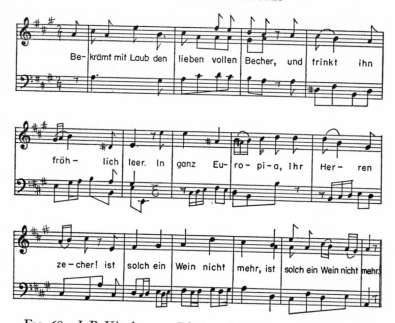

FIG. 68.—J. P. Kirnberger, *Rheinweinlied* (poem by Claudius).

wick, Vienna, and Hamburg was already well established. In Frederick's eyes the most brilliant of these, and the one whose rivalry he felt most keenly, was Dresden. He had not forgotten his dazzling visit there as Crown Prince in 1728, when he saw a splendid production of Hasse's *Cleofide;* and throughout his life he was jealous of Dresden's Italianate magnificence. Frederick even attempted to persuade some of the Dresden artists, among whom were Hasse, the decorator Giuseppe Bibiena, and the *castrato* Bindi, to join his service in Berlin. He was partially successful with Bibiena, who from 1751 to 1756 divided his talents between the two cities.[182]

[182] Yorke-Long, *Music at Court*, 123.

Fig. 69.—J. P. Kirnberger, D. Major Prelude, measures 1–11.

Although Hasse was never formally patronized by Frederick, the King's vast admiration of his music was of great importance in Berlin. Hasse was the most famous dramatic composer in Europe. From the time of his youth in Venice he had been idolized by the Italians, who fondly referred to him as *"il Sassone"*; in England he was considered the foremost creator of Italian opera, and his German nationality was hardly given a thought; in Germany he was the symbol of rescue from "learned" (contrapuntal) music. Burney's opinion of him was typical:

> The merit of Signor Hasse has so long, and so universally been established on the continent, that I have never yet conversed with a single professor on the subject, who has not allowed him to be the most natural, elegant, and judicious composer of vocal music, as well as the most voluminous now alive; equally a friend to poetry and to the voice, he discovers as much judgment as genius, in expressing words, as well as in accompanying those sweet and tender melodies, which he gives to the singer. Always regarding the voice, as the first object of attention in a theatre, he never suffocates it, by the learned jargon of a multiplicity of instruments and subjects; but is as careful of preserving its importance as a painter, of throwing the strongest light upon the capital figure of his piece.[183]

Hasse certainly excelled in his art. He was a favorite pupil of Porpora and of Alessandro Scarlatti. His understanding of Italian diction was remarkable; his melodies were inventive, charming, and above all, singable; his recitatives fulfilled both dramatic and musical requirements equally well. But he was also a German of his time, and his operas are almost as "correct" and unadventurous as those of K. H. Graun. This conservative aspect

[183] *The Present State of Music,* I, 238-39.

of his music was, no doubt, a major reason for Frederick's admiration of him. Hasse had an even more facile technique than Graun; he and his equally facile collaborator, the librettist Metastasio, were able to conceive and produce operas with amazing speed. Their *Achille in Sciro*, for example, was written, set to music, staged, and performed within eighteen days.[184]

Frederick first became personally acquainted with Hasse during January, 1742, at a performance in Dresden of Hasse's *Lucio Papirio*.[185] On October 7, 1745, Frederick entered Dresden as conqueror; for that same evening he ordered a performance of Hasse's *Arminio*. The performance pleased him greatly, especially that of Hasse's wife, the celebrated Faustina. The Prussian king stayed in Dresden nine days, requiring Hasse to supervise a nightly musical performance at court. Frederick's high regard for his Saxon favorite was expressed at the end of his "visit" to Dresden: Hasse was rewarded with a diamond ring for himself and a thousand thalers for distribution among the members of his orchestra.[186] For the lavish production of his *Didone abbandonata* at the Berlin Opera in 1753, Hasse was brought to Berlin and bedecked with honors as a singer and composer. By a strange twist of fate, during Frederick's bombardment of Dresden in 1760 all of the manuscripts assembled by Hasse for a complete edition of his works (which was to be financed by the Polish king) were destroyed.[187]

Since Frederick preferred Hasse's music even to Graun's, he naturally chose from Hasse's operas the one aria which he liked more than anything else in the literature of opera: "*All'onor mio rifletti*" from *Lucio Papirio* (Fig. 70).[188]

[184] Rolland, *A Musical Tour*, 207.
[185] Thouret, *Friedrich der Grosse*, 60.
[186] Alfred Loewenberg, "Hasse, Johann Adolph," *Grove's Dictionary of Music and Musicians*, Vol. IV.
[187] Yorke-Long, *Music at Court*, 134.
[188] Cited in Thouret, *Friedrich der Grosse*, 61–62.

Fig. 70.—J. A. Hasse, aria *"All'onor mio rifletti"* from *Lucio Papirio*, measures 1–12 (piano reduction).

JOHANN SEBASTIAN BACH (1685–1750)

Frederick the Great never had any real musical influence on J. S. Bach; but Johann Sebastian's visit to Potsdam and Berlin in 1747, his activities while there, and the great monument of music which he produced as a result of this visit all make up a part of music history which is so important that it deserves mention in any discussion of Frederick's patronage.

Bach had visited his son in Berlin once before, during the summer of 1741, and had probably met Frederick then. Frederick knew of Johann Sebastian's consummate genius as a performer, though he had little taste for his music, and he was curious to know more of this venerable musician. He often expressed, then, a desire to see *"der alte Bach,"* and Emanuel wrote his father of the King's wishes. Accordingly, J. S. Bach made a second trip in the spring of 1747 for the purpose of visiting Emanuel and his patron.[189]

He reached Potsdam on the evening of May 7. The King and his musicians were about to begin an evening concert when a chamberlain entered the music room and handed Frederick a list of the passengers who had just arrived in a coach. Frederick glanced at the list and exclaimed, "Gentlemen, old Bach has arrived."[190] He sent a messenger to Emanuel's lodging immediately, and Johann Sebastian was required to come in his traveling clothes. The cantor and the King greeted one another. The orchestra members put up their instruments. For the remainder of the evening Frederick and his musicians followed Bach from one room to another in the palace, listening to his extemporizations on each of the King's new Silbermann pianofortes. During the course of the evening Johann Sebastian suggested that Frederick give him a subject on which to extemporize a fugue. Frederick stepped to one of the pianofortes and played a subject that is a tribute to his musicianship and has become the most often-quoted example of a king's musical imagination (Fig. 71).

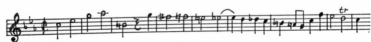

FIG. 71.—"Royal theme" of the *Musical Offering.*

According to a contemporary report, Bach's extemporaneous fugue on the King's subject was of such artistry "that not only His Majesty was pleased to show his satisfaction thereat, but all those present were seized with astonishment."[191]

189 C. S. Terry, *Bach,* 249–52.
190 C. S. Terry, "Bach, Johann Sebastian," *Grove's Dictionary of Music and Musicians,* Vol. I.

On the following day, Frederick had Johann Sebastian perform on all the organs in the churches of Potsdam, and that
night another extemporaneous fugue, in six parts, was played
for the King's pleasure. From Potsdam Bach went to Berlin,
where he inspected the new opera house (no opera was playing
at the time). As he walked through the building in the company
of friends, he took notice of some acoustical phenomena there
which Knobelsdorf might have been surprised to know about.
Spitta obviously enjoys describing this incident:

> It seems almost fabulous when the historian of this won-
> derful man is obliged to mention one more of his many gifts;
> but it is nevertheless true that Bach's keen judgment had
> penetrated the mysteries of the conditions of building which
> were favorable to acoustics; he detected everything that was
> advantageous or detrimental to musical effects in the opera-
> house at Berlin, and without hearing a note of music in it,
> he saw at a glance all that others had learned by experience.
> He also pointed out to his companions in the dining-room
> attached to the opera-house, an acoustic phenomenon which,
> as he supposed, the architect had probably not intended to
> produce. The form of the arches betrayed the secret to him.
> When a speaker stood in one corner of the gallery of the
> hall—which was longer than square—and whispered against
> the wall, another person, standing in the corner diagonally
> opposite, with his face to the wall, could hear what was said
> though no one else could. Bach detected this at a glance,
> and experiment proved him to be right.[192]

Before terminating his visit Bach made it known that he
planned to make use of Frederick's theme in a work which
would do justice to it.[193] When he returned to Leipzig he set

[191] From *Spener'sche Zeitung*, Berlin, May 11, 1747; cited in Paul
Nettl, *The Book of Musical Documents*, 125.
[192] *Johann Sebastian Bach*, III, 232–33.
[193] Nettl, *The Book of Musical Documents*, 125.

to work at once, and on July 7, just two months after his visit, he sent the King the first part of *The Musical Offering,* elegantly engraved and bound. This part consisted of six canons, a *fuga canonica,* and a three-part ricercar, all on the "royal theme." The ricercar was acrostically inscribed *Regis Issu Cantio Et Reliqua Canonica Arte Resoluta.* Upon reflection, apparently, Bach decided that this first offering was not enough, and sent in addition a trio sonata (for flute, violin, and continuo), the great six-part ricercar, and three more canons. One of the canons in augmentation was inscribed *Notulis crescentibus crescat Fortuna Regis;* on another, composed in ascending modulation, was written *Ascendenteque Modulatione ascendat Gloria Regis.*

This work and a similar one written two years later, *The Art of the Fugue,* sum up the contrapuntal art of three centuries. Perhaps Frederick's theme was doubly honored, because the subject of *The Art of the Fugue* is quite similar to that of *The Musical Offering* (especially in inversion) (Fig. 72).

FIG. 72.—J. S. Bach, subject of *The Art of the Fugue.*

Nevertheless, no evidence exists that Frederick ever heard performed any part of his Offering—not even the trio sonata, whose flute part was composed with the hope that it would be played by the King himself. Furthermore, Charles Sanford Terry says that he was unable to find any record, at the *Preussischen Haus-Archiv,* of Bach's having received a gratuity or gift in return for this work.[194] But if Frederick did not properly appreciate Johann Sebastian Bach, we can hardly accuse him of perverseness; he merely shared a widespread lack of enthusiasm for all the "learned contrapuntalists."

[194] Terry, *Bach,* 253.

GOTTFRIED SILBERMANN (1683–1753)

Although the pianoforte was invented by Bartolommeo Cristofori of Florence in 1709 and brought by him to a considerable degree of refinement, and although Jean Marius of Paris and Christopher Gottlieb Schröter of Dresden also built early pianofortes, the first commercially successful producer of these instruments was Gottfried Silbermann, a builder of keyboard instruments in Klein-Bobritzsch, Saxony. Two of the main reasons for his success were the disapproval of J. S. Bach and, years later, the approval of Frederick the Great.

Silbermann first submitted his instrument, a slight modification of the Cristofori pianoforte, to Bach in 1726. Bach's reaction to it was told by J. F. Agricola in 1768, in a note to Adlung's *Musica mechanica organoedi:*

Herr Gottfried Silbermann had at first made two of these instruments. The late Kapellmeister Johann Sebastian Bach had seen and played upon one of these. He had praised the tone of it, indeed wondered at it, but had objected that it was too weak in the upper part, and that it was much too hard to play. Herr Silbermann, who could not endure having his work blamed, took this very ill. For a long time he was angry with Herr Bach for it. Nevertheless his conscience told him that Herr Bach was not altogether wrong. So he thought it best—to his great credit let it be said—not to make any more instruments like these, but to try all the harder to correct the defects that Herr Johann Sebastian Bach had pointed out. He worked at this for many years. And that this was the true reason for this delay I doubt so much less, as I have heard it candidly confessed by Herr Silbermann himself. At last, when Herr Silbermann had really hit upon many improvements, especially with regard to the action, he again sold one to the Prince of Rudolfstadt. . . . Shortly afterwards the King of Prussia ordered one of these instruments, and, as he was greatly pleased with it, he ordered several more of Herr Silbermann. In all these instruments, those who, like myself, had seen one of the two earlier ones, were especially able to see how industriously Herr Silbermann must have worked at improving them. Herr Silbermann had also the praiseworthy ambition to show one of these new instruments to the late Herr Kapellmeister Bach, and to get him to try it, and he was warmly praised for it.[195]

Silbermann's continued efforts to overcome Bach's objections were the result of pride in his own craftsmanship and a desire to uphold the high standards for which the Silbermann family, producers of organs, clavichords, harpsichords, and pianofortes, had become known all over Europe. Eventually his pianofortes became highly refined. They never clicked or made other noises, no matter how much they were used; they seldom needed tuning; their actions were flexible and trouble-free, permitting a wide range of dynamics in playing, with a minimum of unwanted resonance.[196]

Bach remained faithful to the harpsichord and clavichord, however, and his son Emanuel was never very enthusiastic about the pianoforte. Frederick, on the other hand, bought seven of Silbermann's improved instruments at once for the price of seven hundred thalers each,[197] and later purchased a few more.[198] Frederick's delight over the new instruments and his support of Silbermann was, then, an important factor in the history of the piano. Within a remarkably short time the piano had begun to supplant the harpsichord and clavichord, and the number of piano makers grew. This trend was illustrated by

[195] Cited by Albert Schweitzer, *J. S. Bach*, trans. by Ernest Newman, I, 202.
[196] Kothe, *Friedrich der Grosse*, 54.
[197] Ernest Closson, *History of the Piano*, trans. by Delano Ames, 78–84.
[198] Kothe, *Friedrich der Grosse*, 32.

Mozart, who definitely gave up the harpsichord when he discovered the pianos of Stein in 1777.[199] This is not to say that Frederick's influence was decisive, but it is probable that he hastened the general acceptance of the piano in Germany by several years.

[199] Closson, *History of the Piano*, 85.

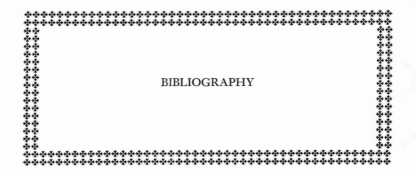

BIBLIOGRAPHY

BOOKS AND PAMPHLETS

Abert, Anna Amalie. *Die Oper von den Anfängen bis zum Beginn des 19. Jahrhunderts.* Köln, Arno Volk-Verlag 192—.

Adlung, Jakob. *Musica Mechanica Organoedi, herausgegeben von* Christard Mahrenholz. Kassel, Bärenreiter-Verlag, 1931.

Bach, C. P. E. *Essay on the True Art of Playing Keyboard Instruments,* translated by W. J. Mitchell. New York, W. W. Norton and Company, 1949.

——. *Kleine Stücke für Klavier, herausgegeben von* Otto Vrieslander. Leipzig, Verlag Adolph Nagel, 1940.

——. *Preussischen Sonaten,* Nr. 1–3, *herausgegeben von* Rudolf Steglich. Kassel, Verlag Adolph Nagel, 1927.

——. *Preussischen Sonaten,* Nr. 4–6, *herausgegeben von* Rudolf Steglich. Hanover, Verlag Adolph Nagel, 1937.

——. *Sinfonie Nr. 3, herausgegeben von* Dr. Ernst Fritz Schmid. Hanover, Verlag Adolph Nagel, 1931.

Benda, Franz. *Sonata in A Major for Violin and Piano,* edited by Alfred Moffatt. Berlin, N. Simrock, *c.*1899.

Benda, Georg. *Ariadne auf Naxos,* edited by Alfred Einstein. Leipzig, C. F. W. Siegel, 1920.

Bitter, K. H. *Carl Philipp Emanuel und Wilhelm Friedemann Bach und deren Brüder.* 2 vols. Berlin, W. Müller, 1868.

Bobillier, Marie. *Histoire de la symphonie à orchestre, depuis ses origines jusqu'à Beethoven inclusivement,* par Michel Brenet [pseudonym]. Paris, Gauthier-Villars, 1882.

Borris, Siegfried. *Kirnbergers Leben und Werk.* Kassel, Bärenreiter-Verlag, 1933.

Brachvogel, A. E. *Geschichte des Königlichen Theaters zu Berlin.* 2 vols. Berlin, O. Janke, 1877–1878.

Bratuschek, Ernst. *Die Erziehung Friedrichs des Grossen.* Berlin, Georg Reimer, 1885.

Brinsmead, Edgar. *The History of the Pianoforte.* London, Petter and Galpin, 1868.

Brode, Reinhold. *Friedrich der Grosse und der Konflikt mit seinem Vater.* Leipzig, S. Hirzel, 1904.

Bruun, Geoffrey. *The Enlightened Despots.* New York, H. Holt and Company, 1929.

Bukofzer, M. F. *Music in the Baroque Era.* New York, W. W. Norton and Company, 1947.

Burchardt, Friedrich (ed.). *Friedrich II. Eigenhändige Briefe an seinen geheimen Kämmerer Fredersdorff.* Leipzig, Friedrich Fleischer, 1834.

Burney, Charles. *A General History of Music from the Earliest Ages to the Present Period,* with critical and historical notes by Frank Mercer. 2 vols. New York, Harcourt, Brace, and Company, 1935.

———. *The Present State of Music in Germany.* 2 vols. London, T. Becket, 1775.

Burrell, Mary. *Thoughts for Enthusiasts at Bayreuth.* London, Pickering and Chatto, 1891.

Carlyle, Thomas. *History of Frederick II of Prussia.* 8 vols. London, Chapman and Hall, 1858–1865.

Carse, Adam von Ahn. *Eighteenth-Century Symphonies.* London, Augener, 1951.

———. *The Orchestra in the Eighteenth Century.* London, W. Heffer and Sons, Ltd., 1940.

De Catt, Henri. *Frederick the Great, the Memoirs of His Reader, Henri de Catt,* translated by F. S. Flint. London, Constable and Company, 1916.

Closson, Ernest. *History of the Piano,* translated by Delano Ames. London, P. Elek, 1947.

Delizie dell'Opere, Le. 10 vols. London, n.p., 1776.

Fasch, K. F. C. *Ariette avec variations, herausgegeben von* Ludwig Landshoff. Hanover, Verlag Adolph Nagel, 1929.

Fitzgibbon, Henry Macaulay. *The Story of the Flute* (2nd ed.). New York, C. Scribner's Sons, 1928.

Flade, Ernst. *Gottfried Silbermann.* Leipzig, Breitkopf und Härtel, 1953.

Floessner, Franz. *Reichardt, der Hallische Komponist der Goethezeit.* Halle, Gebauer-Schwetschker, 1929.

Forkel, Johann N. *Johann Sebastian Bach,* with notes and appendices by Charles Sanford Terry. London, Constable and Company, 1920.

Förster, Friedrich. *Friedrichs des Grossen Jugendjahre.* Berlin, Louis Quien, 1823.

Forstner, Kurt Freiherr von. *Friedrich der Grosse, Künstler und König.* Berlin, Max Hess, 1932.

Frederick the Great. *Friedrichs des Grossens Musik Werke.* 3 vols. edited by Philipp Spitta. Leipzig, Breitkopf und Härtel, 1889.

———. *Oeuvres de Frédéric le Grand,* edited by Johann D. E. Preuss. 30 vols. Berlin. Imprimerie Royale, 1846–1857.

Friedländer, Max. *Das Deutsche Lied im 18. Jahrhundert.* 2 vols. Berlin, J. G. Cotta, 1902.

Gaxotte, Pierre. *Frederick the Great,* translated by R. A. Bell. New Haven, Yale University Press, 1942.

Gebhardt, Bruno. *Handbuch der Deutschen Geschichte,* edited by Robert Holtzmann. 2 vols. Genf, des Weltkomitees der Christlichen Vereine junger Männer, n.d.

Geiringer, Karl. *The Bach Family.* New York, Oxford University Press, 1954.

Gent, Werner. *Die geistige Kultur um Friedrich den Grossen.* Berlin, Junker und Dünnhaupt, 1936.

Georgii, Walter. *Klaviermusik.* 2 vols. Zürich, Atlantis-Verlag, 1950.

Goldschmidt, Hugo. *Die italienische Gesangsmethode des XVII. Jahrhunderts und ihre Bedeutung für die Gegenwart.* Breslau, S. Schottlaender, 1890.

Goldsmith, Margaret. *Frederick the Great.* New York, Charles Boni, 1929.

Graun, K. H. *Montezuma,* edited by A. Mayer-Reinach. Leipzig, Breitkopf und Härtel, 1904.

Graun, K. H. *Der Tod Jesu.* Berlin, E. H. G. Christiani, n.d.

Grout, Donald J. *A Short History of Opera.* New York, Columbia University Press, 1947.

Hamilton, Andrew. *Rheinsberg: Memorials of Frederick the Great and Prince Henry of Prussia.* 2 vols. London, J. Murray, 1880.

Hermann, Kurt (ed.). *Lehrmeister und Schüler Joh. Seb. Bachs.* 2 vols. Leipzig, Gebrüder Hug, 1935.

Hinrichs, Carl. *Der Kronprinzenprozess, Friedrich und Katte.* Hamburg, Hanseatische Verlagsanstalt, *c.*1936.

Jahn, Otto. *Mozart.* 2 vols. Leipzig, Breitkopf und Härtel, 1919.

Kahl, Willi (ed.). *Selbstbiographien deutscher Musiker.* Köln, n.p., 1948.

Kothe, Wilhelm. *Friedrich der Grosse als Musiker, sowie als Freund und Förderer der Musikalischen Kunst.* Braunsberg, E. Peter, 1869.

Lang, P. H. *Music in Western Civilization.* New York, W. W. Norton and Company, 1941.

Lange, Carl. *Johann Friedrich Reichardt.* Halle, Literarischemusikalischen Vereinigung, 1902.

Lenzewski, Gustav. *Die Hohenzollern in der Musikgeschichte des 18. Jahrhunderts.* Berlin, C. F. Vieweg, 1926.

Loewenberg, Alfred. *Annals of Opera.* New York, Broude Brothers, 1943.

Macaulay, Thomas Babington. *Critical and Historical Essays.* 2 vols. London, J. M. Dent and Company, 1907.

McHose, Allen I. *The Contrapuntal Harmonic Technique of the Eighteenth Century.* New York, Appleton-Century-Crofts, Inc., 1947.

Marpurg, F. W. *Historisch-Kritische Beyträge zur Aufnahme der Musik.* 5 vols. Berlin, G. A. Lange, 1754–1778.

Mattheson, Johann. *Beyträgen zur critischen Historie der deutschen Sprache, Poesie und Beredsamkeit,* Leipzig, in Verlegung des Verfassers, 1741.

———. *Grundlage einer ehren-pforte.* Hamburg, in Verlegung des Verfassers, 1740.

Mennicke, Carl H. *Hasse und die Brüder Graun als Symphoniker.* Leipzig, Breitkopf und Härtel, 1906.

Mersmann, Hans. *Die Kammermusik XVII. Jahrhunderts bis Beethoven.* Leipzig, Breitkopf und Härtel, 1933.

Moser, Andreas. *Geschichte des Violinspiels.* Berlin, M. Hesse, 1923.

Moser, H. J. *Geschichte der Deutschen Musik.* 2 vols. Stuttgart, J. G. Cotta, 1923.

Müller, Georg. *Friedrich der Grosse, seine Flöten und sein Flötenspiel.* Berlin, A. Parryhysius, 1932. (Pamphlet.)

Nettl, Paul. *The Book of Musical Documents.* New York, Philosophical Library, 1948.

Nichelmann, Christoph. *Concerto for Continuo and Strings,* edited by Carl Bittner. Hanover, Verlag Adolph Nagel, 1938.

Nicolai, C. F. *Beschreibung der königlichen Residenzstäte Berlin und Potsdam.* Berlin, C. F. Nicolai, 1769.

———. *Beschreibung einer Reise durch Deutschland und die Schweiz, im Jahre 1781.* Berlin, C. F. Nicolai, 1783–96.

Nissel, Elfriede. *Die Violintechnik Franz Bendas und seiner Schule.* Kassel, Bärenreiter-Verlag, 1930.

Noack, Friedrich. *Sinfonie und Suite.* Leipzig, Breitkopf und Härtel, 1932.

Pincherle, Marc. *Vivaldi, Genius of the Baroque.* New York, W. W. Norton and Company, 1957.

Quantz, J. J. *Concerto for Flute, Strings, and Basso Continuo,* edited by Walter Upmeyer. Kassel, Bärenreiter-Verlag, 1951.

———. *Sonate für drei Flöten, herausgegeben von* Erich Doflein. Celle, Verlag Adolph Nagel, n.d.

———. *Versuch einer Anweisung die Flöte traversière zu spielen, herausgegeben von* Arnold Schering. Leipzig, Kahnt, 1926. *Facsimile-Ausgabe herausgegeben von* H. P. Schmitz. Kassel, Bärenreiter-Verlag, 1953.

Reddaway, W. F. *Frederick the Great and the Rise of Prussia.* London, Putnam and Company, Ltd., 1935.

Riehl, W. H. *Musikalische Charakterköpfe.* 2 vols. Stuttgart, J. G. Cotta, 1899.

Riemann, Hugo. *Alte Kammermusik.* 4 vols. London, Augener, Ltd., n.d.

———. (ed.) *Collegium Musicum.* 59 vols. Leipzig, Breitkopf und Härtel, n.d.

———. *Geschichte der Musiktheorie im IX–XIX Jahrhundert.* Leipzig, Max Hesse, 1898.

Robinson, J. H. *Readings in European History.* 2 vols. Boston, Ginn and Company, 1904–1906.

Robinson, J. H., and C. A. Beard. *Outlines of European History.* 2 vols. Boston, Ginn and Company, 1918.

Rolland, Romain. *A Musical Tour through the Land of the Past,* translated by Bernard Miall. New York, H. Holt and Company, 1922.

Rowen, Ruth. *Early Chamber Music.* New York, Columbia University Press, 1949.

Sachs, Curt. *Musik und Oper am kurbrandenburgischen Hofe.* Berlin, J. Bard, 1910.

Schiedermair, Ludwig. *Bayreuther Festspiel in Zeitalter des Absolutismus.* Leipzig, C. F. Kahnt, 1908.

———. *Die deutsche Oper.* Berlin, Dümmlers Verlag, 1940.

Schletterer, H. M. *Das Deutsche Singspiel.* Augsburg, J. A. Schlosser, 1863.

Schneider, Louis. *Geschichte der Oper und des Königlichen Opernhauses in Berlin.* Berlin, Düncker und Humblot, 1852. Also in a de luxe edition (*Pracht-Ausgabe*).

Schünemann, Georg. *Carl Friedrich Zelter, der Begrunder der Preussischen Musikpflege.* Berlin, M. Hesse, 1932.

Schweitzer, Albert. *J. S. Bach,* translated by Ernest Newman. 2 vols. London, A. and C. Black, 1938.

Shirlaw, Matthew. *The Theory of Harmony.* DeKalb, Illinois, Birchard Coar, 1955.

Spitta, Philipp. *Johann Sebastian Bach,* translated by Clara Bell and J. A. Fuller-Maitland. 3 vols. London, Novello and Company, Ltd., 1899.

———. *Zur Ausgabe der Compositionen Friedrichs des Grossen.* Leipzig, Breitkopf und Härtel, 1890.

Terry, C. S. *Bach.* London, Oxford University Press, 1928.

Thayer, A. W. *The Life of Ludwig van Beethoven,* translated by H. E. Krehbiel. 3 vols. New York, the Beethoven Association, 1921.

Thouret, Georg. *Friedrich der Grosse als Musikfreund und Musiker.* Leipzig, Breitkopf und Härtel, 1898.

Treitschke, Heinrich Gotthard von. *The Confessions of Frederick the Great,* translated and edited by Douglas Sladen. New York Knickerbocker Press, 1915.

Le Trésor des Pianistes. 12 vols. Leipzig, Breitkopf und Härtel, 1866.

Ulrich, Homer. *Chamber Music.* New York, Columbia University Press, 1948.

———. *Symphonic Music, its Evolution Since the Renaissance.* New York, Columbia University Press, 1952.

Yorke-Long, Alan. *Music at Court.* London. Weidenfeld and Nicholson, 1954.

Young, Norwood. *The Life of Frederick the Great.* London, Constable and Company, 1919.

Zeller, E. *Friedrich der Grosse als Philosoph.* Berlin, Weidmann, 1886.

Zelter, C. F. *Karl Friedrich Christian Fasch.* Berlin, J. F. Unger, 1801.

ARTICLES

D'Alcona, A. *"Frederico il Grande e gli Italiani,"* *Nuova antologia: rivista di lettere, scienze ed arti,* Vol. XCVI (November 16–December 16, 1901), 195–648.

Altmann, Wilhelm. *"Zur Geschichte der Königlichen Preussischen Hofkapelle,"* *Die Musik,* Vol. III (July, September, 1903), 1–227.

Batka, R. *"Friedrich II als Musiker,"* *Der Kunstwart,* Vol. XXV (January 24, 1912), 131–34.

Becker, Otto. *"Musik und Musiker Am Hofe Friedrichs des Grossen,"* *Die Musikwoche,* Vol. XXIV (1939), 366–67.

Benda, Franz, *"Auto-Biographie von Franz Benda,"* edited by C. Freiherr von Ledebur, *Neue Berliner Musikzeitung,* Vol. X (August 6–August 27, 1856), 251–76.

Bernhardt, R. *"Van Swieten und seine Judas Maccabäus-Bearbeitung,"* *Zeitschrift für Musikwissenschaft,* Vol. XVII (December, 1935), 514.

Biellinger, Karl. *"Die Kunstpolitik Friedrichs des Grossen,"* *Musik,* Vol. XXXII (June, 1940), 297–99.

Bourke, John. "Frederick the Great as Music-Lover and Musician," *Music and Letters,* Vol. XXVII (January, 1947), 63.

Brückner, Fritz. *"Georg Benda und das deutsche Singspiel,"* *Sammelbände der Internationalen Musikgesellschaft,* Vol. V (1903–1904), 571–73.

Conrat, Hugo. *"Friedrich der Grosse und die Mara,"* *Neue Musikzeitung,* Vol. XXIV (February 19, 1903), 86–87.

Dubinski, M. *"Beiträge zum Musikgeschichte Berlins während des Siebenjährigen Krieges,"* *Die Musik,* Vol. XI, (1911), 137–42.

Fitzgibbon, H. M. "Of Flutes and Soft Recorders,'' *Musical Quarterly,* Vol. XX (April, 1934), 219–29.

Frensdorff, E. *"Die Sängerin E. Mara am Hofe Friedrichs des*

Grossens," *Mitteilungen des Vereins für die Geschichte Berlins*, Vol. XXIV (January 12, 1907), 27–30.

Koegler, Horst. "Berlin Controversy," *Opera News*, Vol. XIX (February 7, 1955), 31.

———. "New Life for the Berlin Opera," *Opera News*, Vol. XIX (April 11, 1955), 21, 31.

Kohut, Adolph. "Johann Friedrich Reichardt," *Neue Musik-zeitung*, Vol. XXIV (November 27, 1903–January 8, 1904), 5–47.

Mara, Gertrud Elisabeth (Schmeling). "*Eine Selbstbiographie der Sängerin Gertrud Elisabeth Mara*," edited by O. von Riesemann, *Allgemeine Musikalische Zeitung*, Vol. X (August 11–September 29, 1875), 497–613.

Martens, H. "*Friedrich der Grosse und Quantz*," *Zeitschrift für Musikwissenschaft*, Vol. XIV (1932), 26.

Mayer-Reinach, A. "*C. H. Graun als Opernkomponist*," *Sammelbände der Internationalen Musikgesellschaft*, Vol. I (April–June, 1900), 446–529.

Mennicke, Carl H. "*Zur Biographie der Brüder Graun*," *Neue Zeitschrift für Musik*, Vol. VIII (1904), 129–31.

Mersmann, Hans. "*Beiträge zur Aufführungspraxis der vorklassischen Kammermusik in Deutschland*," *Archiv für Musikwissenschaft*, Vol. II (1920), 99–143.

Müller, F. "*Friedrich der Grosse und J. S. Bach*," *Zeitschrift für Musik*, Vol. CIII (August, 1936), 931–36.

Müller-Blatteau, Joseph K. F. "*Karl Friedrich Zelters Rede auf Friedrich den Grossen*," *Deutsche Musikkultur*, Vol. I (August–September, 1936), 170–74.

Münnich, Richard. "*Friedrich der Grosse und die Musik*," *Zeitschrift für Musik*, Vol. CIII (August, 1936), 913–16.

Osthoff, H. "*Friederizianische Heeresmusik*," *Die Musik*, Vol. XXX (December, 1937), 152–58.

———. "*Friedrich der Grosse als Komponist*," *Zeitschrift für Musik*, Vol. CIII (August, 1936), 917–30.

Pulver, Jeffrey. "Music at the Court of Frederick the Great," *Musical Times*, Vol. LIII (September 1, 1912), 599–601.

Reichardt, J. F. *"Autobiographie,"* Berlinische Musikalische Zeitung, Vol. I (1805), 215–354.

——. *"Autobiographie"* (additions), Allgemeine Musikalische Zeitung, Vol. XVI (January 12, 1814), 46–78.

——. *"Musikalische Anekdoten von Friedrich dem Grossen,"* Musikalisches Kunstmagazin, Vol. II (1791), 40.

Schering, Arnold. *"Kirnberger als Herausgeber Bachser Choräle,"* Bach-Jahrbuch, Vol. XV (1918), 141–50.

Schwarz-Reiflingen, Erwin. *"Friedrich der Grosse als Flötist,"* Allgemeine Musikzeitung, Vol. LXVI (1939), 478–79.

Simon, Ernst. *Friedrich der Grosse und die Mechanischen Musikinstrumente,"* Zeitschrift für Instrumentenbau, Vol. XXXII (April 11, 1912), 743–46.

Steglich, Rudolf. *"Karl Philipp Emanuel Bach und der Dresdener Kreuzkantor Gottfried August Homilus im Musikleben ihrer Zeit,"* Bach-Jahrbuch, Vol. XII (1915), 39–145.

Wasielewski, W. J. von. *"Musikalischen Fürsten vom Mittelalter bis zum Beginne des 19. Jahrhunderts,"* Sammlung Musiker Vorträge, Vol. 1 (1879), 323–46.

Wechsberg, Joseph. "Behind the Golden Curtain," Horizon, Vol. I (November, 1958), 23–27, 133.

Witt, Berta. *"Der königliche Musikus,"* Allgemeine Musikzeitung, Vol. LXIII (August 21, 1936), 34.

ENCYCLOPEDIA ARTICLES

Becker, Heinz. "Friedrich II," *Die Musik in Geschichte und Gegenwart,* Vol. IV. Kassel, Bärenreiter-Verlag, 1955.

"Berlin School," *Harvard Dictionary of Music,* edited by Willi Apel. Cambridge, Massachusetts, Harvard University Press, 1950.

Blume, Friedrich. "Agricola, Joh. Friedrich," *Die Musik in Geschichte und Gegenwart,* Vol. I. Kassel, Bärenreiter-Verlag, 1949.

"Frédéric II," *Biographie Universelle des Musiciens,* 2nd ed. by François J. Fétis, Vol. III. Paris, Firmin-Didot Frères, 1874.

"Frederick II," *Oxford Companion to Music*, 2nd ed., by Percy A. Scholes. London, Oxford University Press, 1955.

"Friedrich II," *Quellen-Lexicon der Musiker und Musikgelehrten*, by Robert Eitner, Vol. IV. New York, Musurgia, 1898.

Gehring, Franz. "Agricola, Johann Friedrich," *Grove's Dictionary of Music and Musicians*, 5th ed., Vol. I. New York, Macmillan and Company, 1954.

———, "Kirnberger, Johann Philipp," *Grove's Dictionary of Music and Musicians*, 5th ed., Vol. IV. New York, Macmillan and Company, 1954.

———. "Marpurg, Friedrich Wilhelm," *Grove's Dictionary of Music and Musicians*, 5th ed., Vol. V. New York, Macmillan and Company, 1954.

Gehring, Franz, and Alfred Loewenberg. "Frederick II," *Grove's Dictionary of Music and Musicians*, 5th ed., Vol. III. New York, Macmillan and Company, 1954.

"Kirnberger, Johann Philipp," *Baker's Biographical Dictionary of Musicians*, 4th ed. New York, G. Schirmer, Inc., 1940.

"Kirnberger, Jean-Philippe," *Biographie Universelle des Musiciens*, 2nd ed., by François J. Fétis, Vol. V. Paris, Firmin-Didot Frères, 1874.

Loewenberg, Alfred. "Hasse, Johann Adolph," *Grove's Dictionary of Music and Musicians*, 5th ed., Vol. IV. New York, Macmillan and Company, 1954.

Maczewsky, A. and Alfred Loewenberg. "Graun, Karl Heinrich," *Grove's Dictionary of Music and Musicians*, 5th ed., Vol. III. New York, Macmillan and Company, 1954.

Mizler, Lorenz. *Lorenz Mizlers Neu eröffnete musikalische Bibliothek*, 4 volumes (not arranged according to definite headings). Leipzig, im Mizlerischen Bücherverlag, 1743.

"Nichelmann, Christophe," *Biographie Universelle des Musiciens*, 2nd ed., by François J. Fétis, Vol. VI. Paris, Firmin-Didot Frères, 1874.

"Opera," *Musikalisches Lexicon*, by Johann Gottfried Walther,

Facsimile-Nachdruck herausgegeben von Richard Schall. Kassel, Bärenreiter-Verlag, 1953.

"Orchestre," *Dictionnaire de musique,* by Jean-Jacques Rousseau. Paris, Garnery Librarie, 1823.

"Quantz, Johann Joachim," *Baker's Biographical Dictionary of Musicians,* 4th ed. New York, G. Schirmer, Inc., 1940.

"Reichardt, Johann Friedrich," *Baker's Biographical Dictionary of Musicians,* 4th ed. New York, G. Schirmer, Inc., 1940.

Sime, J., and Anonymous. "Frederick II," *Encyclopaedia Britannica,* Vol. IX. Chicago, Encyclopaedia Britannica, Inc., 1955.

Straeten, Edward van der. "Agricola, Benedetta Emilia," *Grove's Dictionary of Music and Musicians,* 5th ed., Vol. I. New York, Macmillan and Company, 1954.

Terry, C. S. "Bach, Carl Philipp Emanuel," *Grove's Dictionary of Music and Musicians,* 5th ed., Vol. I. New York, Macmillan and Company, 1954.

———. "Bach, Johann Sebastian," *Grove's Dictionary of Music and Musicians,* 5th ed., Vol. I. New York, Macmillan and Company, 1954.

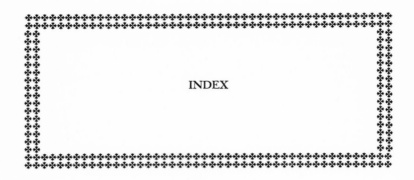

INDEX

Frederick II, the Great (1712–
1786), king of Prussia: *see* specific
topics
Frederick William I (1688–1740),
king of Prussia: 3–15, 20 f., 82 ff.,
90, 143
Frederick William II (1744–1797),
king of Prussia: 25, 221 f.
Frederick William IV (1795–1861),
king of Prussia: 40
Fredersdorff, Michael Gabriel: 8,
13, 87 f., 119, 163
Furstenbund: 25
Fux, Johann Joseph: 157

Galanter Stil: 177, 183
Galatea ed Acide (K. H. Graun):
42
Gasparini, Giovanna: 92, 94, 109,
128 n., 157, 169
Geminiani, Francesco: 194
George II, king of Great Britain and
Ireland: 11 f.
German Democratic Republic:
100 n.
Gerstenberg, Heinrich Wilhelm
von: 178, 185
Glein, Johann: 23
Gluck, Christoph Willibald: 69, 71
Goering, Hermann: 100 n.
Goethe: 77, 129, 180, 219, 222,
223 f.
Graun, Johann Gottlieb: xv, 72,
87 f., 108, 108 n., 141, 141 n., 191,
197–205, 231
Graun, Karl Heinrich: xv, 16, 21,
41 f., 48 f., 66 f., 69, 71 ff., 76, 78 ff.,
87 ff., 120 ff., 141 n., 141–56, 175,
191, 197 ff., 200, 202, 206 f., 218 f.,
231, 241 f.
Gravesande, Guillaume-Jacob: 16
I Greci in Tauride (Agricola):
124, 126, 208
Grenser flute: 163
Grundke, Johann Caspar: 17 n., 88,
108
Il Guidizio di Paride (K. H.
Graun): 42

Hamburg: 83, 92, 176 f., 188, 215,
221, 229, 239
*Hamburger unpartheiischer Cor-
respondent:* 180
Handel: 49, 61, 72, 79, 89, 111, 156,
165
Handel Festival: 220
Hapsburgs: 22, 24
Hasse, Johann Adolph: xv, 9, 42,
49, 68 f., 71 ff., 76, 80, 88 f., 102 f.,
111, 123 ff., 141, 144 ff., 157 f.,
218 f., 238–43
Haydn: 71, 179, 181, 220
Heinichen, Johann David: 179
Hénault, Charles Jean François: 16
Heyne, Gottlieb: 5, 47, 49
Hiller, Johann Adam: 129
Hock, Anton: 88, 108
Hohenzollerns: 3
Horzizky, Joseph Ignatius: 88, 108
Hotteterre, Jacques: 164
Hubertushof, Peace of: 24

Ifigenia in Aulide (K. H. Graun):
66, 103, 123, 127, 147, 150 f., 153
Infantry music: 63
Instrumental recitative: 52 f., 184
Intermezzo: 72, 104 f., 107, 109, 121,
206
Italy: 90, 92, 95, 115, 120, 138

Janitsch, Johann Gottlieb: 88, 107 f.
Jomelli, Nicola: 156
Jordan (Prussian minister): 114
Joseph II, Holy Roman emperor 25

Kapelle: see Orchestra
Kassel: 222
Katte, Lieutenant: 10, 12
Kieth, Lieutenant: 12, 21
Kirnberger, Johann Philipp: xv,
141, 160, 212, 224, 231, 233–40
Kleiber, Erich: 100 n.
Knobelsdorf, Georg Wenzeslaus
von: 21, 90 f., 93, 95, 97 ff., 245
Kothe, Wilhelm: 39

Lancret, Nicolas: 16

94, 101, 104, 107 ff., 112 f., 119 ff.,
130 f., 143, 149, 186, 190 ff., 199,
230, 233, 242
Orfeo (K. H. Graun): 103, 111,
123 ff., 135, 139, 149, 153
Overture: 40 n., 61, 94, 106, 144 n.,
145 f.; French, 74, 144 f., 200;
Italian, 144 f.; *see also Sinfonie*

Panthée (Reichardt): 221
Paradisi, Pietro Domenico: 128
Paris: 90, 95, 162, 164, 220 f., 225,
247
Passione di Gesu (Reichardt): 220
Pasticcio: 42, 61, 104
Pastorale: 42, 105
Paulino (Paolo Bedeschi): 110
Pergolesi: 79, 105, 156
Peter III, czar of Russia: 24
Petrovitch, Paul, grand duke of
Russia: 124, 132, 135 ff.
Pinetti, Gaetano: 91, 94
Pisendel, Johann Georg: 9, 198
Poitier (ballet master): 96, 114 f.
Poland: 19, 25, 233
Pöllnitz, Karl Ludwig: 127
Porpora, Nicola Antonio: 241
Porporino (Antonio Uberi): 109 ff.,
128, 134, 136 f.
Prague: 22, 122, 189, 199, 215
Prelleur, Peter: 165
Preussischen Sonaten (C. P. E.
Bach): 181 ff.
Prussian Academy: 27
Prussian Sonatas: *see Preussischen
Sonaten*
Prussianism: 25

Quantz, Johann Joachim: xv, 9 f.,
16, 32 ff., 43 ff., 47 ff., 55, 57, 71 f.,
76 ff., 88 f., 104, 108, 120, 128 f.,
141, 156–73, 175, 178, 189, 195,
206, 211, 223, 229, 231
Quinault, Philippe: 67, 103, 132

Racine: 16, 52, 103
Rameau, Jean-Philippe: 225, 227,
237

Ramler, Karl Wilhelm: 153
Reichardt, Johann Friedrich: 29 f.,
32, 39, 40, 48, 72, 77, 124 f., 131 ff.,
136 f., 139, 141, 154, 160, 186 f.,
193–94, 208, 215–24
Rellstab, Johann Karl Friedrich: 47
Rhadamiste et Zenobie (Crébillon):
96
Rheinsberg: 16–20, 21, 29, 34, 44, 49,
86 ff., 94, 114, 142, 161, 174, 191
La ricamatrice divenuta dama
(Agricola): 206
Rodelinda (K. H. Graun): 94, 102,
125
Rollin, Charles: 16
Romani, Antonio: 109, 119, 207
Rome: 91 f., 95
Rossbach, Battle of: 24
Rousseau, Jean-Jacques: 88
Ruppin: 15–17, 20, 86 ff., 89, 89 n.,
142, 161, 189 ff., 199
Russia: 24 f., 122, 132 f., 135 ff.

Sacred music: 71, 75, 122, 154, 156,
188, 207
Salaries of performers: 122 f.
Salimbeni, Felice: 110 ff.
Sancio und Sinilde (K. H. Graun):
142
Sans Souci: 15 f., 23, 33, 35, 104, 129
Santarelli, Giuseppe: 91, 94
Saxony: 24, 36, 121
Scarlatti, Alessandro: 144 n., 157,
158, 241
Schäferspiel: 40 n., 72, 105
Schaffrath, Christoph: 17 n., 88
Schale, Christian Friedrich: 109
Schauspiel: 73, 132
Schmeling, Elizabeth: *see* Mara,
Elizabeth (Schmeling)
Schmid, Balthasar: 40
Schneider, Louis: 82–83
Scholes, Percy: 48
Schulz, Johann Abraham Peter: 222
Schwerts, Baron von: 113 f., 119
Semiramide (K. H. Graun): 69,
104, 124

Semiramis (Voltaire): 207
Serenata: 40 n., 41, 41 n., 61, 104–105,
    123 f.
La serva padrona (Pergolesi): 105
Seven Years' War: 24, 37, 44, 46 f.,
    47, 76, 81, 102, 110 f., 113, 121–22,
    156, 172, 176, 211, 231
Siècle de Louis XIV (Voltaire): 23
Silbermann, Gottfried: xv, xv n.,
    141, 244, 247–49
Silesia: 22, 24, 36, 93, 93 n., 95, 118
Sinfonie: 40 n., 41 ff., 49, 88, 144 n.,
    194, 213
Singakademie: 131, 215, 222
Singers: see Opera: singers
Singspiel: 72, 131, 139, 219, 222
Sonata: 34, 41, 44 ff., 50–55, 72, 120,
    164, 167, 172 f., 194, 200, 204, 208 f.,
    213, 230
Sonata form: 178, 180 ff., 200 ff.
Song: 71 f., 188, 208 f., 222, 231, 238;
    see also Berlin School, Lied
Sophie Charlotte, consort of Fred-
    erick I: 84
Sophie Dorothea, consort of Fred-
    erick William I: 11, 59, 61, 85,
    100, 121
Spandau: 12, 137
Spary, Pierino: 95
Lo specchio della fedeltà (K. H.
    Graun): 142
Spener'sche Zeitung: 114
Spitta, Philipp: 39 ff., 44 ff., 50,
    51 n., 245
Stamitz, Johann: 119
Stefanino (castrato): 110
Steffani, Hans Jürgen: 109
Stuart-Mackenzie, James: 115 ff.
Sturm und Drang: 177 f.
Sulla (K. H. Graun): 66 f., 103 f.,
    125, 219
Symphony: 72, 145, 186 ff., 200 ff.

Tagliazucchi (librettist): 66, 103 f.,
    152
Tamerlan (Reichardt): 221
Tartini, Giuseppi: 50
Te Deum (K. H. Graun): 122, 154

Telemann, Georg Philipp: 89, 157,
    176, 194, 229
Il tempio d'amore (Agricola): 66
Teschen, Treaty of: 25
Tessier (ballerina): 114
Thouret, Georg: xiv n., 39, 64, 70,
    77, 99, 153
Der Tod Jesu (K. H. Graun):
    153 ff., 206
Il trionfo della fedeltà (K. H.
    Graun): 42
Triulzi, Giovanni: 91, 94

Uberi, Antonio: see Porporino

Vanloo, Charles André: 117
Venice: 91 f., 92, 95, 115 f., 241
Versuch einer Anweisung die
    Flöte traversière zu spielen
    (Quantz): 51 n., 165–67, 194–95
Versuch über die wahre Art das
    Clavier zu spielen (C. P. E. Bach):
    178–80, 194–95
Vienna: 69, 116, 128, 138, 157, 215,
    220, 222, 239
Villati (librettist): 40 n., 66 f., 103,
    132, 152 f.
Vinci, Leonardo: 73, 78 f., 155
Vivaldi, Antonio: 50, 55, 57, 78, 157,
    189, 199
Voltaire: xiv-n., 10, 16 f., 19, 23, 69,
    71, 90, 104, 144, 207

Walther, Johann Gottfried: 157
Watteau, Jean Antonio: 16
Weimar: 174
Weiss, Silvius: 9
Wilhelm I, emperor of Germany:
    41
Wilhelmina, margravine of Bay-
    reuth, sister of Frederick II: 5, 9,
    11, 14, 42 ff., 68, 74, 89, 158, 190
William, prince of Orange: 72
Wolff, Christian: 10, 16, 21

Zelter, Karl Friedrich: 47, 214, 223
Zeno, Apostolo: 102, 123, 152
Ziegler flute: 163
Zierotin-Litgenau, Count: 128 f.